T5-AXN-096

Managing the Embedded Multinational

Managing the Embedded Multinational

A Business Network View

Mats Forsgren

Ulf Holm

Jan Johanson

Department of Business Studies, Uppsala University, Sweden

Edward Elgar

Cheltenham, UK • Northampton, MA, USA

658.049
F73m

ℋ

© Mats Forsgren, Ulf Holm and Jan Johanson 2005

All rights reserved. No part of this publication may be reproduced, stored in a retrieval system or transmitted in any form or by any means, electronic, mechanical or photocopying, recording, or otherwise without the prior permission of the publisher.

Published by
Edward Elgar Publishing Limited
Glensanda House
Montpellier Parade
Cheltenham
Glos GL50 1UA
UK

Edward Elgar Publishing, Inc.
136 West Street
Suite 202
Northampton
Massachusetts 01060
USA

A catalogue record for this book
is available from the British Library

ISBN 1 84542 615 0

Printed and bound in Great Britain by MPG Books Ltd, Bodmin, Cornwall

Contents

v   University Libraries
Carnegie Mellon University
Pittsburgh, PA 15213-3890

Figures

Tables

Preface

This book has emerged from a research program, known as Managing International Networks, or the MIN program, that has been conducted between 1990–2005 at the Department of Business Studies, Uppsala University. A short time after we initiated the program two of us published an edited book entitled *Managing Networks in International Business* (Forsgren and Johanson 1992). The book, which consists of a number of papers written together with other members of our department at Uppsala University, explores research problems and possibilities associated with networks in international business. In the preface to the book we quoted Sune Carlson's pioneering empirical study 'Executive Behavior':

> Before we made the study, I always thought of a chief executive as the conductor of an orchestra, standing aloof on his platform. Now I am in some respects inclined to see him as the puppet in a puppet show with hundreds of people pulling the strings and forcing him to act in one way or another. (Carlson 1951, p.51)

The puppet-on-a-string metaphor has also been a source of inspiration to the MIN program and to the present book. It captures important characteristics of business reality that are absent from the mainstream literature of the multinational corporation. The multinational corporation operates not in an environment of anonymous forces but in a business context comprising distinct actors, such as customer firms, supplier firms and subsidiaries in foreign markets. These actors 'pull the strings' in different and sometimes conflicting directions, reflecting their own interests, resources and contexts.

An overarching purpose of the MIN program has thus been to learn more about these processes in the type of organization known as the multinational corporation, or MNC. The main focus has been on the role of individual subsidiaries and on how their relationships with corporate headquarters are shaped by the different business contexts in which they are embedded. The research program has focused in particular on issues such as the control of subsidiaries by headquarters, the sources of power for individual subsidiaries, and the development and transfer of knowledge between subsidiaries.

By definition the MNC is an organization with subsidiaries operating in different, distinctive markets, and can itself be characterized to some extent as a 'quasi-market'. In order to understand the organizational processes in the

MNC we thus need better tools for analysing the markets in which the MNC subsidiaries are embedded, externally or internally, and the way these markets affect the position of the individual subsidiaries in the MNC. Business network theory offers such tools. Consequently the MIN program draws heavily on research about the market as a business network that has been a lively and fruitful element in our department over the last twenty years or so.

The overall purpose of our book is to analyse managerial issues in the MNC. Our main intention has been to promote a more nuanced understanding of these issues than has previously been possible by making explicit use of a 'business network view'. To help the reader to grasp the fundamental building blocks of this approach and how it can be applied in an international setting, the business network theory is presented in some detail in the first part of the book. In the second and third parts the theory is applied to analysing specific managerial issues in the MNC.

Acknowledgements

Up to now the MIN program has published, apart from four doctoral theses, 24 articles and book chapters, as listed in Appendix II. The present book can be seen as an attempt to summarize and synthesize the different findings that have emerged from the program. We are therefore greatly indebted to our colleagues on the MIN program, Ulf Andersson, Cecilia Pahlberg and Peter Thilenius, who have all contributed to the task of collecting data from all the participating corporations, and, in a very substantial way, to ideas and line of thought presented below. Special thanks go also to the many managers who have contributed valuable insights and data to the study.

We would also like to acknowledge Davide Pisano for his excellent assistance in preparing the data for our empirical analysis in Chapter 8, and Nancy Adler for checking our English.

Finally we would like to thank the Handelsbanken Research Foundation and Centre for Innovation and Industrial Dynamics (CIND) for their financial support.

Mats Forsgren
Ulf Holm
Jan Johanson

Uppsala

1. The multinational corporation from a business network angle

The multinational corporation (MNC) is one of the most significant institutions of modern societies. The MNCs control resources all over the world and conduct business activities in most countries and between almost all countries. It is generally recognized that they are efficient, that they generate huge profits and are among the most powerful actors in the world. The general view of the MNC is that its corporate management possesses superior information about world markets, formulates clear strategies for the development of the corporation, allocates resources in accordance with these strategies to the most promising markets and that it controls operations wherever they are performed. But MNCs are complex organizations operating in a complex world. Anybody who has been in close contact with any part of an MNC knows that reality is not as perfect as the general view would have it. Strategic plans are frequently thrown over, resource allocations are affected by power relations between different parts of the company, control systems cannot capture all the important aspects of operations, and corporate management often has only vague ideas about business in most of the countries concerned.

When Edith Penrose, the author of the influential book *The Theory of the Growth of the Firm* (1959), turned to the study of large firms in the international petroleum industry she reported that 'the role of the very large privately-owned companies in a modern economy is still ill-defined and controversial, and also subject to great confusion of thought because the "models" of the "firm" … are inadequate, even for analytical purposes' (Penrose 1971, p.266).

This statement has remained as relevant as ever, as the globalization of economies has given rise to many new forms of internationalization and ways of organizing economic activities. In the 1960s and 1970s the dominant factors in the analysis of internationalization were still export and foreign direct investment. Today many more forms have appeared, including joint ventures, strategic alliances, managing contracts, and so on. In addition, the focus has shifted from exploiting competitive advantage to developing competitive advantage that requires closer relations with the environment. And knowledge management too has become a central issue. These developments have made the management of MNCs more complex. It has become increasingly difficult to grasp how the roles of different managers are related to each other and to the company as a whole. Managers at all levels of the MNC organization need a better understanding of their own roles in the corporations. At the same time the large MNCs with resources and operations dispersed over many countries and product markets have become relatively even more dominant. To understand the logic underpinning these firms is becoming an increasingly challenging task for scholars in the field of international business, and one that must clearly be just as pertinent for managers of the MNCs themselves. How is it possible for them to grasp what is going on in the organization as a whole and to have any control over its strategic behavior?

Although the picture has become much more complicated over the years, there are nonetheless two fundamental themes that run through the history of research in international business: the MNC's environment and the MNC as an organization.

The first theme addresses the question of what is outside the firm and what is inside it, and how what is outside should be conceptualized. This theme is as old as the open-systems view of the organization, but it becomes even more critical and complicated in the case of the MNC, with its multiplicity of markets and products. For instance, is it appropriate to characterize the pertinent markets of the MNC and its different units in general conceptual terms such as degree of complexity, dynamism, competition, etc? Or should we identify important actors in the sub-units' surroundings in terms of customers, suppliers, competitors and so on, in an attempt to understand what the environment is, and what role it plays?

The second issue concerns the conceptualization of the MNC as an organization. For instance, what part do the different sub-units located in different markets actually play in the overall strategy process vis-à-vis corporate management? Is the organization of the MNC above all a deliberately designed instrument for implementing a corporate strategy, or is the coalition model (Cyert and March 1963; Hatch 1997), with conflicting interests among sub-units, a more appropriate image of the MNC?

The two themes are of course related, because the open systems view implies an interaction between the organization and its environment. However, there is a striking difference among scholars as to how this interaction is defined and treated. Scholars who are inclined to treat the environment in more general terms, for instance, also tend to adopt a more instrumental view of the MNC. This view often leads to the assumption that the MNC is capable not only of analysing the environment correctly, but also of matching the organization to this analysis, thus optimizing overall performance.

Scholars who adopt the coalition model are less optimistic about this ability, arguing instead that the environment is fragmented and context-specific and, for those not directly involved in interaction with specific environmental actors, difficult to understand. The impact of the environment on the organization is reflected, rather, in the interests that the different sub-units choose to pursue and in the resources they can use in the bargaining process.

The first approach has been fairly dominant ever since Fouraker and Stopford (1968) and Stopford and Wells (1972) published their work on the causal link between the environmentally oriented strategies of the MNC and its formal structure. The geographical spread and product diversification were related to structural archetypes such as the mother–daughter structure, the international division structure, the global division structure and the matrix structure. Subsequent research on the organizational design of the MNC adopted the same basic logic of a causal relationship between the environment, the strategy and the organization. Egelhoff (1988), for instance, based his contingency model on the information-processing view advocated by Lawrence and Lorch (1967) and Galbraith (1973). At the center of his analysis lies the quality of the fit between the information-processing requirement imposed on the MNC by its choice of strategy/environment, and the information-processing capacity of the organization. Although this approach emphasizes the fit itself rather than the forces that have created it (Egelhoff, p.28), it is above all, like Stopford and Wells's model, a functionalist, top management driven perspective (Doz and Prahalad 1993). It is assumed that top management evaluates the environment of the MNC, designs its strategy and chooses the appropriate organizational structure and control systems.

Some of the recent influential work on the management of MNCs has adopted essentially the same perspective. A typical example is the research conducted by Ghoshal and Nohria (1997). In their conceptualization of the MNC as a 'differentiated network' these scholars state explicitly that their overarching theoretical perspective is contingency theory (ibid. p.6). Unlike the studies referred to above, though, they emphasize that an MNC consists of diverse subsidiaries operating in unique national environments, which cannot be adequately addressed by a uniform organization-wide structure. The decisive point of the analysis is the premise that the structure of the MNC can be regarded as a differentiated network of linkages: between the headquarters (HQ) and subsidiaries and between the different subsidiaries, as well as the 'local' linkages of the individual subsidiaries.

Compared to other work in the contingency theory tradition, Ghoshal and Nohria emphasize particularly that their focus is on the differences *within* the MNC rather than *between* MNCs. The logic of their model is thus 'internal differentiation'. Subsidiaries differ from one another in terms of their environmental complexity and their access to local resources, which require that the control mechanisms used by HQ have to be adapted to the needs of each subsidiary individually. Differentiated fit, rather than overall fit, is the bottom line for management.

In addition to the usual mechanisms applied by earlier researchers in this tradition, such as formalization, centralization and so on, Ghoshal and Nohria introduce normative integration through shared value creation as a distinctive control mechanism. The basic idea here concerns not so much a differentiated fit between the environment/strategy and management systems, but rather the use of shared values as a countervailing force against internal diversity. The problem of subsidiaries differing from each other is addressed at HQ by the creation of common norms intended to legitimize actions at the subsidiary level in line with the interests of the overall organization.

Although this conceptualization of the MNC differs from that in earlier work in the contingency theory tradition, due mainly to the introduction of the MNC as an internal network and the explicit use of normative integration, surprisingly little has changed in Ghoshal and Nohria's analysis relative to the earlier attempts by Stopford and Wells (1972) and others. For instance, the top-management-driven perspective is as explicit as ever. It is still HQ that is supposed to create the necessary fit between environment, strategy and structure. Top management's ability to implement organizational changes based on an evaluation of the environment and the necessary strategies is barely discussed. It could be claimed that this ability becomes even more of a critical issue in Ghoshal and Nohria's model, because it requires funda-mental knowledge at the top management level of *several* environments and *several* local resources. In Ghoshal and Nohria's version the demand on top management's information-processing capacity has increased tremendously since the model was introduced by Galbraith (1973), as has the difficulty of implementing organizational changes in a highly differentiated MNC.

Another striking feature is that, although the multiplicity of the environment of the MNC is stressed, it is defined in the same broad categories that earlier researchers had used. Thus, when Ghoshal and Nohria link subsidiary environment to the design variables centralization and formalization, the complexity of the subsidiary environment is still analysed in terms of the degree of local competition and technological dynamism in different countries, both of which are assessed by respondents at the corporate-level (on a scale from 1 to 5). A similar approach is adopted for measuring resources at the subsidiary level. The main difference compared to earlier research is that the measure is taken at the country (subsidiary) level. However, the concepts used to define the characteristics of the MNC's environment are as unspecified as they were in earlier research. The approach still begs the question as to how much information is really contained in general statements about competition and dynamism in national markets, when neither the subsidiary's products nor its business counterparts in the market are defined. The environment is still rather 'faceless'.

Under the MNC as a 'differentiated network' approach, the network is first and foremost defined and treated as a *communication* network, in which information flows vertically between HQ and subsidiaries and horizontally between the subsidiaries. This type of network is a result of the dispersal of resources and roles and responsibilities among the sub-units of the MNC, which calls for effective communication among the subsidiaries (Ghoshal and Nohria 1997). However, there is no doubt that HQ represents the strategic apex of the MNC with ultimate responsibility for designing this network (ibid., p.135).

A BUSINESS NETWORK MODEL OF THE MNC

Against this model of the MNC we posit a network model that takes the firm's relations to the environment as its point of departure. We mentioned at the outset that over recent years interest has been growing in other forms of international operations apart from export and foreign direct investments. A common feature of these alternative forms is their focus on resources and capabilities outside the traditional boundaries of the firm. Another closely related shift in interest has appeared in the literature of MNC strategy, away from ways of *exploiting* MNC competitive advantage through international expansion (Hymer 1976; Caves 1982; Dunning 1988) and towards ways of *gaining* such advantage through international expansion (Cantwell 1991; Madhok 1997). The two interests are obviously interrelated, but the shift in interest clearly signifies that relations with the environment have been assigned a more significant role. Sources of competitive advantage no longer reside exclusively within the boundaries of the firm.

A second shift in interest consists in the importance that has been assigned to cooperation between firms in the international business literature – and in the business practice – since the mid-1980s (Contractor and Lorange 1988; Beamish and Killings 1997). Cooperative inter-firm arrangements, such as strategic alliances, joint ventures, partnerships, distribution and franchising agreements, now play an important part in international business strategies both among firms and in the academic literature. While the international business literature on cooperation has been dominated by the above-mentioned arrangements, which are explicitly characterized as formal cooperation, this may be only the tip of an iceberg. After all, most cooperation occurs between firms that do business with each other as suppliers and customers without anyone explicitly regarding it as a case of formal cooperation. But it can be found in most firms that have working exchange relationships with suppliers and customers.

A third development concerns the growing interest in knowledge and knowledge development. Firms that used to be described in terms of their physical resources and products are now analysed with reference to their knowledge about the utilization of resources and the building, development and accumulation of knowledge. Correspondingly, relations with the markets used to be considered mainly in terms of demand and supply curves. Interaction with competent and demanding customers and suppliers is now seen as critical to the accumulation and development of a firm's knowledge base. In fact, the firm's knowledge base is no longer seen just as a matter of internal knowledge. It embraces knowledge residing in a network of important suppliers and customers and other business partners (Kogut 2000), an altogether wider knowledge base that the firm can access through its exchange relationships with these network partners.

In light of these developments there seems every reason to consider a conceptualization of the MNC that explicitly emphasizes the exchange relationships between a firm and its most important business partners. We thus propose a model of MNC that focuses on market exchange and exchange relationships as distinctive elements.

Hence we regard the MNC as a unit primarily engaged in exchange activities and not necessarily as an entity engaged in international production. When we say that exchange is the basic element of competitive advantage in international business or in the internationalization of the firm we are not referring to single, sporadic market exchanges in international or foreign markets, but to exchange of a more continuous kind. We have in mind exchange relationships in which the partners are committed to future exchange and relationships that comprise important elements of knowledge development. The critical role of such exchange relationships is not to consider immediate gains; its role consists in forming the platform for future business. In our present context, exchange is important because it has long-term consequences for the firm as a whole as well as for the individual sub-units. Thus, since we see these relationships as critical to the business activities of the firm, we call them 'business relationships'. Similarly, we call the networks of business relationships 'business networks'. Consequently, our model of the MNC is a 'business network model'. In this book we have chosen to label this model the 'Embedded Multinational'.

The Embedded Multinational has a set of subsidiaries, each and every one embedded in a *unique* network of business relationships. Although embeddedness in itself is a trait common to all subsidiaries, the degree of embeddedness can vary with the closeness of the relationships with customers, suppliers and other business counterparts. The degree of embeddedness at the subsidiary level, therefore, is an important but hitherto rather neglected element in MNC research. Our book demonstrates how the notion of subsidiary network embeddedness can help us to understand the different roles in an MNC, the reasons why certain subsidiaries are more influential or less 'controllable' than others, and the conditions for knowledge transfer within MNCs. It also demonstrates the relevance of conceptualizing the MNC as a 'federative' or 'loose-coupled' organization, in which control from corporate HQ is more circumscribed than is usually assumed.

The Embedded Multinational deviates from Ghoshal and Nohria's Differentiated Network on two important counts. First, the relationships in the network are above all business relationships associated with resource interdependencies. Different units exchange resources with each other because they are linked to each other through the business activities in which they engage. These activities have evolved over time, they are relatively stable, and the corresponding exchanges include a broad range of resources and capabilities. An important aspect is that the power structure in an MNC is dependent on this network of resource interdependencies. Power flows to units and people who control resources and capabilities, irrespective of their hierarchical position (Doz and Prahalad 1993). This implies that decisive influence on strategic behavior is not limited to HQ; it can also reside in different subsidiaries. Sometimes the tail is wagging the dog. It also implies that the critical resources used by different units with a view to exerting influence are embedded in these business relationships.

Second, in contrast to Ghoshal and Nohria's model our business network does not stop at the border of the MNC. Relationships within the MNC cannot be understood without an explicit analysis of the relationships enjoyed by different organizational units with external customers, suppliers, competitors, etc. The network model that we advocate encompasses both internal and external business counterparts. From the point of view of the individual subsidiary there is no dramatic difference between corporate units and external units in terms of the interdependencies experienced by that subsidiary. Furthermore, the individual subsidiary may use its relationships with important local actors with a view to limiting the influence that HQ may exert over its operations (Doz and Prahalad 1993, p.50).

The Embedded Multinational model in this book is in line with basic ideas behind the coalition model of the firm (Cyert and March 1963), and the resource-dependence perspective (Pfeffer and Salancik 1978; Pfeffer 1981), where conflicting interests based on local rationality among the different unit are a dominating feature. Similar lines of thoughts have been applied in a variety of ways in the analysis of the MNC over the years (see, for example, Negandhi and Balige 1980; Doz and Prahalad 1981; Forsgren 1989; Ghoshal and Bartlett 1990; Forsgren et al. 1995). One important conclusion to emerge from this approach concerns the dual role of every subsidiary: the business network role and the corporate role. The business network role is shaped by the subsidiary's interaction with its business partners, inside or outside the MNC. The corporate role is the one assigned to the subsidiary by HQ, in line with the corporate strategy. There is nothing that tells us a priori that these two roles coincide, because they are rooted in different local rationalities. Important questions, though, concerns the way these two roles affect each other, and how the conflicts between them are solved.

Our approach is also specifically indebted to the research on markets as business networks that has been evolving since the 1980s, much of which has been conducted at the Department of Business Studies, Uppsala University (see, for example, Håkansson 1982; Johanson and Mattson 1987; Håkansson 1989; Axelsson and Easton 1992; Snehota 1990; Håkansson and Snehota 1995; Ford 1997; Håkansson and Johanson 2001). Although this market-as-network model has been used in an MNC context before (see, for example, Forsgren 1989; Forsgren and Johanson 1992; Björkman and Forsgren 1997; Holm and Pedersen 2000; Havila et al. 2002), we make a more comprehensive attempt in the present book to apply the model to the MNC. Economists have also pointed out the need for such an approach to the analysis of MNCs (Dunning 1995; Kogut 2000).

THE CONTENTS OF THE BOOK

Fundamental to our analysis of MNC embeddedness is the concept of *business*, in the sense of exchange activities carried out by actors under market conditions in order to achieve long-term profits. In the first chapters, therefore, we develop our view of the *business firm*, that is to say an actor involved in exchange activities with other actors in a market. Relationships and networks are the basic instruments in identifying the business context of such an actor. In subsequent chapters about the MNC the focus is on *the subsidiary as a business firm,* embedded in a business network of a similar type as any other market actor. Our view consequently implies that an MNC consists of *several* business firms rather than being conceived of as *one* business firm. In terms of embeddedness the objective of the first part of the book is to give the reader a rich understanding of the relevance of business embeddeness to the analysis of the MNC.

More precisely, Part I, 'The business firm in an international context', consists of Chapters 2–5. Chapter 2, 'The business firm in international business networks', explains what we mean by a business firm. Our fundamental messages are first that a business firm is an exchange rather than a production entity, and second that the business firm through commitment to continued exchange with other actors is embedded in networks of business relationships. The chapter focuses on the nature and importance of the relationships between business firms.

In order to illustrate the theoretical discussion in Chapter 2, an extensive case regarding the development of the business relationships of a specific business firm, nationally and internationally, is presented in Chapter 3, 'Development of business relationships – the case of Danke', and in Chapter 4, 'Development of a business network – the case of Danke'. The Danke case illustrates the presence of continuous changes in a business firm's relationships and shows how these relationships impinge on each other in a never-ending process. It also demonstrates that in the shift from operating as a domestic to operating as an international business firm, the process of moving away from arm's-length exchange to close business relationships, and the connections between these relationships all play a crucial role.

In Chapter 5, 'Internationalization of the business firm', the discussion about the business firm's foreign market expansion is further developed by comparing the traditional view of foreign market entry with the business-network view adopted here. While surmounting institutional and economic country barriers is an important factor in the first view, establishing relationships with specific customers and suppliers is the crucial factor in the second. The resulting network embeddedness has a strong influence on the pace and direction of subsequent foreign market expansion. Thus, Chapter 5 contributes to an understanding of the dynamics of embeddedness.

Part II, 'Introducing the Embedded Multinational', consists of the three chapters 6–8. While Chapter 5 deals with the internationalization process, Chapter 6, 'Three dimensions of MNC internationalization', introduces the concept of the MNC and discusses different ways of defining the degree of internationalization of an MNC's operations.

In Chapter 7, 'The Embedded Multinational', we specify our model more precisely and introduce the dual role of the subsidiary: the business network role and the corporate role. Chapter 8, The Embedded Multinational – an empirical illustration' continues the discussion about the dual role of subsidiaries by applying the concept of network embeddedness to a sample of 98 subsidiaries belonging to Swedish multinationals. Embeddedness is specified, defined and operationalized. It is demonstrated that the degree of embeddedness varies quite a lot at the relationship level as well as at the subsidiary level. It is also shown that the degree of embeddedness varies as much between subsidiaries *within* one and the same MNC division as within the total sample of subsidiaries. A major conclusion in the chapter is that the traditional picture of the MNC as being highly integrated internally while having a more or less anonymous group of customers and suppliers externally, is not supported. On the contrary, at the subsidiary level the degree of external embeddedness dominates over the internal (corporate) embeddedness.

Part III, 'Management of the Embedded Multinational', consists of five chapters. Starting from the discussion in the preceding chapters, Chapter 9, 'Control and influence in the Embedded Multinational' offers a model of HQ's control. It is posited that the influence of HQ over a subsidiary's behavior is largely dependent on the character of the subsidiary's business network as well as on the HQ's own knowledge of the subsidiary's network. The relevance of such a model is demonstrated empirically in an analysis of data from the 98 subsidiaries described in Chapters 8–9.

Chapter 10, 'Subsidiary power in the Embeddded Multinational', turns the spotlight on to the subsidiary side. The chapter discusses the factors that are important to the influence wielded by the subsidiary over strategic decisions in the MNC. In line with the argument in the preceding chapter it is argued that the subsidiary's own business network and the MNC's dependence on the subsidiary both represent important sources of power bases when it comes to exerting such an influence. Data from the 98 subsidiaries is used again in this chapter to underpin the arguments.

A factor that has clearly attracted the interest of many scholars is the concept of shared values (sometimes referred to as normative integration), not least in relation to MNC management. In the conceptualization of the MNC as a Differentiated Network this concept is crucial, since shared values between the HQ and the different subsidiaries are supposed to act as the 'glue' that coordinates and holds the MNC together, along with what can be achieved through the formal organization (Ghoshal and Nohria 1997). However in Chapter 9 we had already raised some doubt about the impact of shared values. We argued that the possibility of achieving shared values in an MNC is probably much less than the Differentiated Network model assumes. In Chapter 11, 'Transfer of knowledge in the Embedded Multinational – the role of shared values and business networks', we discuss the relative importance of shared values as a mechanism for knowledge transfer in a business network context. On a basis of data from the 98 subsidiaries it is concluded that the participation of a subsidiary in knowledge transfer in an MNC is better explained in terms of its embeddedness in business networks, of the corporate HQ's knowledge about these networks and of the subsidiary dependence on HQ, than in terms of shared values between HQ and the subsidiary.

In Chapter 12, 'Learning in the Embedded Multinational', we analyse the relationship between embeddedness and how knowledge is developed and transferred in the MNC. We claim that there is a fundamental difference between relationships that exist in order to coordinate *complementary* activities and relationships that link *similar* activities to each other. This difference, in its turn, points at different types of learning processes and different managerial issues related to knowledge management in the Embedded Multinational.

In Chapter 13, 'The Embedded Multinational – an epilogue', we conclude by elaborating on some of the major characteristics of our model of the MNC. Thus we highlight the differences between our approach and two alternative approaches that have been used to analyse the interplay between the MNC and its environment and the role of HQ, namely institutional theory and contingency theory. One of the main messages of this epilogue is that even though globalization has caused an increasing interest in cultural and institutional differences between countries, we recommend students and managers to bring business back into the center of the analysis of management in MNCs.

PART I

The business firm in an international context

2. The business firm in international business networks

In the previous chapter we presented some basic features of the embedded MNC, which is regarded as a network of interconnected exchange relationships. This network not only comprises the relationships between units within the MNC, but also includes the MNC's direct and indirect relationships with external parties. In particular, we stressed the role of relationships with other firms. Against this background, Chapter 2 focuses on the nature of exchange relationships between firms. We will refer to important exchange relationships between firms doing business with one another as 'business relationships'. The first section of the chapter deals with the nature of such business relationships, the second discusses the way the business relationships affect the firm while the third addresses the nature of the firm's markets. Through the business relationships the business firm is embedded in a network of relationships.

BUSINESS RELATIONSHIPS

Every experienced business person knows that doing business is not only a matter of selling or purchasing; it also means establishing and developing business relationships with important customers or intermediaries, and suppliers. These relationships, the business people recognize, are the framework within which future exchanges will take place. Every business person also knows that it takes time and effort to build a working relationship and, once such a relationship has been established, that it is an important asset on which the firm can base its future business. Obviously, not all the sales and purchases of firms occur within business relationships, but for most firms, relationships with a limited number of counterparts are of special importance with regard to the volume of their business and to their competence development. In such cases exchange takes place not in anonymous markets but between specific market actors with well-known identities. Although every business relationship is unique, we have reason to examine and discuss the general nature of business relationships in some detail.

The experience of business people is reflected in a growing academic interest in cooperative relationships (Alter and Hage 1993; Beamish and Killings 1997; Grabher 1993; Nohria and Eccles 1992; Ring and Van de Ven 1994) and, in particular, in vertical cooperative relationships between firms in business markets (Anderson and Narus 1984; Eccles 1981; Johnston and Lawrence 1988). One important strand of research in this field, on which we lean heavily, consists of studies conducted within the European IMP (industrial marketing and purchasing) tradition (Ford 1997; Håkansson 1982; Håkansson and Snehota 1995; Turnbull and Valla 1986).

Business Relationship Development

Business relationship development is a process whereby two firms, as a result of their interaction, gradually increase their commitment to doing business with each other (Anderson and Weitz 1992). One of the firms, it could be the supplier or the customer, takes the initiative to embark on exchange and, to the extent that the counterpart responds and both firms are satisfied with the outcome of the exchange and build up some trust in each other, a relationship is gradually developed and a mutual commitment is created (Blankenburg Holm et al. 1999). The mutual commitment is the basic characteristic of business relationships. In the relationship-development process the firms learn about each other's capabilities, needs and strategies and form routines for handling transactions (Håkansson and Johanson 2001). From their recurrent business exchange the two parties discover possibilities for reducing the cost of exchange and raise their joint productivity by adapting to each other (Zajac and Olsen 1993).

In the early phase of such relationship development the interdependence between the two firms is weak, as in ordinary arm's-length market exchange. But as the process develops, this state is gradually transformed into the strong interdependence of a business relationship in which the two parties are mutually tied to each other (Heide and John 1988). In the following discussion we refer to the firms engaged in business relationships as *business partners*. The business relationship between two actors is illustrated in Figure 2.1. It shows the mutuality between the partners in terms of trust, commitment, dependence and knowledge. It also shows the dynamic aspect in terms of exchange of products, money and information.

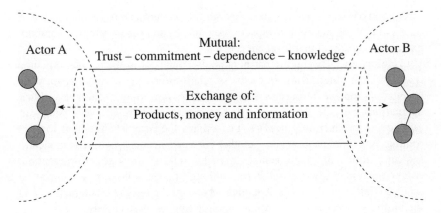

Figure 2.1   The business relationship

Coordination between Relationship Partners

Although we have stressed that selling and purchasing are the distinctive features of business activity, it should also be emphasized that exchange is not *just* a matter of selling and buying. An important aspect of the exchange is the exchange of information. In a business relationship, managers in the two firms develop and maintain extensive contacts with each other. Marketing and purchasing managers are not the only ones involved in such contacts, which can also include production, R&D, quality and logistic managers on several levels, all of whom learn about each other's needs and capabilities and ways of dealing with different problems (Cannon and Perreault Jr 1999; Cunningham and Homse 1986; Hallén 1986). Information exchange is thus a matter of coordinating activities and resources between the two firms. As a consequence of this coordination, activities and resources are adapted and modified in such a way so that joint productivity is improved. In this way business relationships enable the firms involved to create a value that is absent from arm's-length market exchange.

Coordination between supplier and customer firms may be general, encompassing the overall activities of the firms, or it may be limited to the integration of specific activities only. An instance of specific coordination that has attracted much attention during the 1990s is the just-in-time relationship, whereby the two firms closely coordinate deliveries in order to speed up the flows of components and to reduce stocks (Frazier et al. 1988). Another example of specific coordination that requires intimate relationships between firms is total quality management, in which quality controls and standards are closely integrated (Westphal et al. 1997). Correspondingly, on-line ordering systems are based on close relations between the partners. As our earlier discussion has suggested the specific coordination arrangements may be based on existing working relationships, or they may be steps in developing yet more extensive coordination between the firms.

Coordination between the partners is also manifest in the adaptations they make to each other. Thus, in business relationships the partners adapt their products, processes, routines and administration to one another's. Such adaptations may be extensive and encompassing considerable changes in products or production processes. Or perhaps the firms change their logistic routines and systems to match the other partner's needs. Frequently, however, the adaptations are incremental, growing out of the current interaction. Adaptations may also be unilateral, although on the whole they seem to be mutual (Hallén et al. 1991). Adaptations are thus often made interactively as the partners successively coordinate their activities more closely.

Knowledge Transfer through Business Relationships

With their recurrent interactions, business relationships offer both partners good opportunities for passing knowledge on to each other. Thus a supplier can let a regular customer know more about its own capabilities than if they were involved with different counterparts at every deal. Similarly, a customer can let the supplier know more about its needs during an ongoing relationship than during a one-off transaction. A relationship allows for repetition with some variation – a combination that is conducive to effective knowledge transfer.

Knowledge Development in Business Relationships

We have pointed out above that exchange in business relationships goes beyond the simple exchange of products associated with selling and purchasing. It also includes an important element of knowledge development. This does not simply mean that information exchange occurs and is intertwined with product exchange in business relationships. It also means that as a consequence of the recurrent interaction between producer knowledge and user knowledge in a business relationship, unique new knowledge is created (Dahlqvist 1998). Obviously, much of this knowledge is of a tacit nature and cannot be transferred to others. The knowledge is embedded in the joint system created by the two partners. It is important to note that this knowledge development does not occur in isolation, separated from product exchange. Rather, it should be considered as one aspect of that exchange.

Business relationships are crucial to the development of competence, as well as to the development of new products and processes and the modification of old ones (von Hippel 1988; Håkansson 1989; Lundvall 1985). There are many examples of new products and processes that have been developed in close relationships between supplier and customer firms. Further, relevant information about technical and business issues is also mediated primarily via business relationships. In addition, when a firm develops a product or a process together with a relationship partner, it has reason to expect that at least the partner firm will be committed to taking up the new product or process concerned. In fact, it could be contended that new knowledge and competence is developed primarily in interaction between business relationship partners rather than as a result of in-house R&D activities. In other words, capability development is an outcome of the exchange structure of the firm.

Long-term Consequences of Business Relationships

A working business relationship is the result of earlier investments associated with exchange activities with a business partner. It may take years of costly activities before partners have sufficiently demonstrated their willingness and ability to each other to be able to reap the benefits of the relationship in question. The relationship becomes an important asset: as a platform for future business transactions and knowledge development, and as the generator of knowledge and competence that may be of wider significance for the firm's competitive ability.

Certain important aspects of business relationships call for particular comments. First, although business relationships are lasting and can be viewed as structural constraints, they are by no means stable in the sense that they are 'given' once and for all. They are the outcome of interaction between two partners, and they last so long as both sides consider it worthwhile to continue doing business with one another. In fact they exist only because the partners think it is advantageous that they continue to do so, that is, so long as each partner thinks the other one has something to offer that is better than anything that a switch to a different counterpart might yield. This, in turn, depends on each one's belief in the other's willingness and ability to maintain the exchange in the future.

Obviously, there is a great difference between this kind of structural constraint and the kind of structural constraint associated with a production unit. The relationship we have been discussing is fundamentally dependent on the partner; it represents a more fluid phenomenon than the production unit; it is a social construction and, in quite a different way, it is a matter of interpretation. It cannot be created as a result of a unilateral decision. It is created and developed by way of interaction between two parties. Nonetheless, some business relationships are more important to a firm as strategic assets, and in considering the competitiveness of a firm there is good reason to pay attention to relationships of this kind.

The Invisibility of Business Relationships

As noted above, business relationships are multifarious in their nature. They differ as regard the interdependencies – technical, social, cognitive, legal, administrative, etc. – between the partners. Further, they are based on trust and mutual knowledge, and they comprise intentions, expectations and interpretations. Consequently they cannot be understood by those who are not personally involved, and still less can they be controlled from outside.

Business relationships are difficult if not impossible for outsiders to understand. Moreover, such relationships arise only because resources have been invested in their very existence. Together these two characteristics can be problematic. Only the insider can tell whether or not the efforts spent on a particular business relationship represent a sufficient investment to increase its future value. Thus, insiders can invest in a relationship or divest themselves of it, without outsiders being able to tell which they have done.

Inter-firm Control through Relationships

Since the partners are interdependent, power relation also arises between them. They can exercise some, albeit limited, control over each other. Naturally, this control is not restricted to the direct exchange between the partners. It may equally well concern either partner's strategies or relations with others. This inter-firm control implies that each firm may have to adapt to developments in the products or processes of the other one. Thus, the partner firms are not sovereign units. They are tied directly to each other as well as being indirectly tied to, and embedded in, a wider network of business relationships.

Business Relationships with Non-business Actors

Although our discussion so far has focused on relationships between business firms, there is good reason to consider relationships with public and semi-public agencies as well (Hadjikhani and Ghauri 2001; Welch and Wilkinson 2004). Thus, a firm may need to develop an exchange relationship with a regulating government agency. Such an arrangement resembles a business relationship except that it is not a question of business exchange between the parties. It calls for the development of an exchange relationship in which the parties exchange information about the nature of certain products and the application of specific regulations. For this purpose the firm also has to demonstrate its commitment to abiding by the regulations and show that it has the required knowledge and resources. Just like business relationships, such public-agency relationships take time and effort to create and develop.

Summary

Business relationships are important sources of capability. They are developed in interaction between business partners. They provide a means for coordinating the activities of the partners. They represent structural constraints that have to be recognized, since they have long-term consequences for the partners. They have to be maintained and developed if they are to remain valuable. They cannot be understood by those who are not involved, and they expose the firm to partial control on the part of another firm. Through the relationships the relationship partners become embedded in a wider network of relationships.

THE BUSINESS FIRM

The above discussion has suggested that due to their importance in terms of product and knowledge exchange, business relationships are a critical source of capability for the business firm.

The Different Roles of Business Relationships

Market exchange is clearly a necessary attribute of the business firm. However, given the importance of the market exchange relations that develop into business relationships, we claim that capability is a fruit of business relationships. Exchange relations transformed into business relationships provide the platform on which the firm can base its future.

Obviously, all the relationships that a firm enjoys are not valuable for the same reasons. The value of supplier relationships is associated with the access to resources that they provide, while customer relationships are valuable as outlets for the firm's products. More precisely, different supplier relationships give access to a variety of resources that complement one another. Different customer relationships may also be valuable for different reasons. One customer may be particularly interesting because it provides the firm with important knowledge about the use of the firm's products, while another might provide a bridgehead to new markets, and yet another can enhance the firm's reputation as a competent supplier.

Coordination across Business Relationships

The specific capability of a business firm emerges from the particular way in which its business relationships are connected. By 'connected' we mean that exchange in one relationship is contingent on exchange in another (Cook and Emerson 1984). More specifically, capability depends on how activities and resources are coordinated across business relationships. Changes in the way business activities are carried out in the relationship with a particularly important customer may require that business activities in relation to other customers be adjusted or that business with suppliers be modified. Product development activities conducted together with a certain customer may mean that development activities have to be conducted together with suppliers and may make it possible to offer the new product to other customers.

In discussing relationship development above we stressed that this is a matter of increasing the coordination between the business partners, that it involves adaptations, modifications and calibrations of their activities in relation to one another. The firm can choose to keep any individual relationship isolated from or connected with its other relationships. By connecting two relationships it may be possible to raise productivity. Activities relating to an important customer may thus be coordinated with activities relating to a supplier, in order speed up the flow of resources between the two. But there is a risk that problems in one of the relationships will damage the other one. Delivery problems on the part of the supplier may endanger the relationship with the customer. Thus, the coordination across business relationships that involves the adaptation, modification and calibration of the partner firms' activities, may also be extended to embrace several relationship partners.

This means that connections are not given once and for all. They are created, developed, modified and broken by those who manage them, as and when it is considered for various reasons that this would be a good thing to do. The connections may evolve when ordinary arm's-length transactions are transformed into business relationships and the partners get to know about each other's specific needs and capabilities. A firm may discover that the needs and capabilities of a new partner link up usefully with their own needs and capabilities, which in turn are based on their business relationships with other business partners. In this way the partner firms coordinate the activities in their evolving relationship with their existing relationships.

Further, a business relationship may be connected with relationships that involve regulatory government agencies. Coordination across such relationships is of the same nature in principle, as coordination across business relationships.

Coordination across relationships is a subtle affair, implying that intentions, interpretations and expectations in one business relationship are interrelated with those in others. It is not only a matter of coordinating present activities in relation to two or more relationship partners; it is also a question of aligning any effort at coordinating future activities in these relationships. The competitive strength of a firm may be a result of this subtle ability to coordinate connected business relationships.

Knowledge Creation in the Business Firm

Every business firm is based on a unique connected set of business relationships. With regard to knowledge, we contend that although every business relationship is unique and provides unique tacit knowledge, the combination of knowledge from a set of business relationships is what gives the business firm its specific competitive ability. Through its market exchange in a set of interrelated business relationships, the business firm creates new knowledge. But it is worth observing that this knowledge-creating process is not set apart from ordinary business activities: it is embedded in them. It is also worth noting that the process is not exclusively a question of the firm's own activities. It is as much a question of the activities of the exchange partners. The knowledge-creating processes of the partners are coordinated through their working business relationships, and this coordination may well extend far beyond the horizon of a specific focal firm. In this way, long-term business relevance is secured. The business firm develops knowledge that is relevant in terms of the needs and capabilities of its most important business partners.

In addition, the business firm possesses knowledge about its partners – their needs, their capabilities, their strategies, and their other relations. This knowledge is obviously comparatively superficial. A firm's business relationship partners are also its main source of information about more distant parts of the relevant markets.

Shared Control and Values in the Business Context of the Firm

A business relationship implies that the two relationship partners are dependent on each other. Consequently, they have some control over each other and, correspondingly, lose some of their autonomy. A business firm that is engaged in a set of business relationships has some control over its business partners but it has also given the partners some control over its own activities and resources.

The close exchange relations between the partners imply that, to some extent, they also share values and expectations. The business firm is thus embedded in a network of business relationships implying some mutual control among the firms, as well as a certain amount of mutual knowledge and shared values and expectations regarding the future. All this is a consequence of being tied to each other and of sharing the future.

The partners with which a business firm shares control and values as a result of its business relationships, constitute its business context. The business context then provides a framework for evaluating business activities.

The Business Firm and Production

A business firm is an entity engaged in business activity. Business is a question of selling and buying. The distinctive feature of the business firm is exchange rather than production. The importance of production in the business firm is derived from exchange. What does this mean? It means that, while according to received economic theory the firm is an entity defined without reference to other firms, the business firm is an entity that is defined on the basis of its exchange relations with others. In fact, in the extreme case, the firm of economic theory exists irrespective of whether or not it is engaged in market exchange, and the business firm exists even if it is not engaged in production. However, the definition by no means excludes the possibility that the business firm is engaged in production. Production activities may well be extensive, but they are performed in order to make exchange possible and profitable.

Production activities, that is to say the transformation of resources into products, can also be seen as an arena for connecting business relationships. Here, supplier relationships are connected with customer relationships, supplier relationships are connected with one another if they are complementary interrelated, and customer relationships can be connected with one another if they are interrelated with production activities. Obviously, there are also further relationship connections due to the structure of logistic activities. In all these cases the connections may be very specific, in that the activities in two particular relationships are closely coordinated, or they may be more general, in that the only links between the different relationships are contingent on production. This line of argument can also be applied to R&D activities.

Summary

The business firm is directly or indirectly engaged in business relationships with a limited set of customers, suppliers and other business partners. This set is the business context of the focal firm, and it provides the framework for evaluating future activities (Snehota 1990). The boundaries of the set are formed by their relevance to the firm. Together they constitute its extended resource base, including knowledge resources. Through the focal firm they are bound to each other and share control over each other.

BUSINESS NETWORKS

As noted above, business firms are engaged in sets of connected relationships. And the partners are involved in turn in relationships with yet other partners, thus generating business networks of connected business relationships. Business networks extend without limit across markets, industries and national boundaries. In fact, business networks are unbounded. Every business firm and every business relationship is embedded in an unbounded network structure.

The unbounded nature of business networks is one of their most interesting features. Nevertheless, every firm is its own center in the business network structure and envisages its own specific boundaries. Clearly, several firms may perceive almost the same boundaries, while others see completely different ones. Two relationship partners will to a large extent see the same network boundaries. In addition, any firm can change the relevant boundaries by creating new relationships. In fact, one important way of strengthening the firm's competitive ability is to develop relationships outside those markets, industries or countries that the competing firms are committed to.

Since all relationships change in a number of ways as a result of interaction between exchange partners, the network structure – although remaining stable – is continuously changing in the sense that some relationships are terminated, others are established and almost all change with regard to their business activities.

Nor do business relationships only concern business activities. They also involve the expectations, intentions and interpretations surrounding these activities. As pointed out above, these expectations, intentions and interpretations are obviously fairly clear to those directly involved, but the distant network structure becomes increasingly difficult to comprehend. But this fluid, ambiguous and complex network structure is still the world in which the firms are embedded and in which they operate.

Although the business network as such is unbounded, an observer can draw boundaries on the basis of such things as product markets, declaring that a certain market has a network structure with specific network characteristics. In this way we can speak of a product market network, for example the printing-paper market network. Correspondingly, we can draw a boundary – also a somewhat arbitrary one – around a certain technology and then analyse the characteristics of this technology network. Thus the characteristics of the biotechnology network may help us understand the dynamics of change in that particular field. From our chosen perspective there is good reason to turn our attention to the network boundaries indicated by countries. Given this identification of boundaries, international business can be viewed as a question of engagement on the part of firms in different country networks.

All markets are populated by firms engaged in more or less connected network structures. Every firm has its specific network context comprising a limited number of important specialized partners, whose needs, capabilities and strategies they know quite well. In some cases they also know about some of the main partners of their partners. In addition, they have some vague idea about yet other business firms engaged in their own line of business and about their relations to each other. All this lies within the network horizon of the firm. Beyond the network horizon they know in a general and vague way that there are a number of firms that are related to each other in various ways. They also know in this general and vague way that there are a number of business firms with specific needs and capabilities that, although engaged in their own specific network contexts, are looking for additional exchange opportunities for possible exploitation. There are some firms searching for new customers and others looking for new suppliers. The incompleteness of the knowledge among all these actors about each other and about the associated business opportunities is a critical problem in the business world.

THE BUSINESS FIRM IN ITS INTERNATIONAL CONTEXT

This is the world in which international business firms operate, and we have good reason to consider the consequences for the firms in question. Our focus is international business, and we need to examine the business firm in its international business context. To what extent, then, is the business firm's context 'international', in the sense that it comprises relationships across country borders and partners in different countries? For instance, it would be helpful to distinguish between international business firms operating in an international context and national business firms engaged in domestic relationships only. The international context gives the firm access to resources and information in international markets. The firm operating in an international context can presumably utilize this context as a bridgehead to international markets. In some cases it may be possible for a firm to accompany its international partners when extending its own international operations (Majkgård and Sharma 1998). In some cases the firm may even be forced by a partner to go abroad. A firm's international partners can also be exploited as information channels to foreign markets and may even be useful in interpreting foreign market information. This suggests that the internationalization of a business firm is a development whereby the firm's business context also becomes increasingly more international. Clearly, a firm also becomes internationalized as a consequence of its partner's internationalization.

Looking at it in another way, we can also say that the network setting of the firm is more, or less, internationalized. In making this distinction we are going beyond the context of the firm and are considering the wider network structure in the relevant field. This setting may comprise firms that are highly internationalized in that they have international contexts, or it may encompass only firms that have domestic business partners. In an internationalized network setting, it can be expected that firms will be internationally oriented and will tend to take international initiatives in a way that firms in a non-internationalized network setting do not. It can also be expected that firms in an international setting will be more prepared to respond to international actions. The internationalization of a firm's network setting increases when other firms in the setting internationalize their contexts.

In line with what has been described above, we can discern the four situations illustrated in Figure 2.2 (Johanson and Mattsson 1988). The upper left quadrant contains the business firm with a domestic context and operating in a non-internationalized setting. There is nothing international in this situation. The upper right quadrant represents a situation in which the business firm operates in an international network setting but has a domestic context. This firm is handicapped by its limited access to international resources and information in a setting where others are well-endowed with such resources and information. The lower left quadrant shows a situation in which an internationalized business firm is operating in a network setting where most other firms are domestic. This firm presumably has a competitive advantage in having access to international resources and information that are not

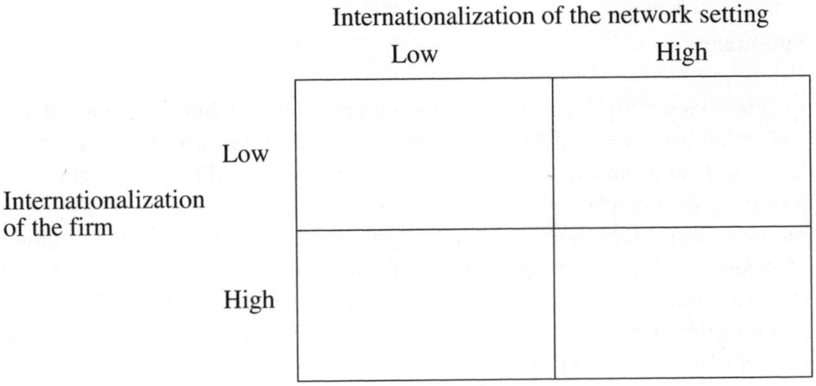

Internationalization of the network setting

Low   High

Internationalization
of the firm

Low

High

Figure 2.2   Internationalization of the firm and the network setting

available to other network actors. Finally, the firm in the lower right quadrant is highly internationalized and operates in an internationalized setting.

Internationalization of the Business Firm

In our discussion we have focused on the business firm's commitment to business relationships. This implies that internationalization is a matter of developing business relationships with partner firms in other countries. As a number of studies and actual business practice have shown, internationalization is an interplay between knowledge development and commitment to foreign market. In a world dominated by business relationships we should expect internationalization to be a question of the development of mutual knowledge together with business partners in other countries and of mutual commitment by these partners.

We also expect internationalization to be driven by a search for new business opportunities. We assume further that internationalization is based on the business context of the firm, that is to say its major business relationships. We claim that this context provides the firm with most of the information that management considers relevant and the knowledge base on which it can evaluate business opportunities. Thus a firm's learning is driven by its business exchange within its business context. In its search for business opportunities a firm's learning from existing business relationships will (1) lead it to explore the possibility of developing those relationships, (2) encourage it to try to coordinate activities across business relationships and thus to create additional value, and (3) try to generalize the experience from its value-creating relationships to its other relationships. The internationalization of the business firm will be further elaborated in Chapter 5.

Summary

In this chapter we have laid the foundations for our later analysis of the embedded multinational firm. In doing so we have developed a view of the business firm as an exchange entity. This approach has directed our attention towards business relationships, which are assumed to play a critical role in the business firm's exchange with other actors. We have also discussed the nature of business relationships in some detail, and have identified certain critical characteristics of the business firm associated with the nature of business relationships. Thus, as a result of its engagement in business relationships, the business firm is also embedded in a wider business network structure. Finally, we have indicated some central characteristics of business networks, that is to say, the structure of connected business relationships.

3. Development of business relationships – the case of Danke

In Chapter 1 we presented our view of the embedded MNC and emphasized the distinctive characteristic role of the business relationships of the MNC units. In Chapter 2 we described at some length the nature of these business relationships, how they come to comprise the business network of a firm, building networks that extend beyond markets, technologies, industries and countries. In the present chapter we present a case to illustrate some important features of business relationships, how they develop over time and the different roles that they may have in the firm.

The case is based on a study of Danke, a firm in the paperboard packaging industry, that was carried out between the years 1991 and 1998. The information about this firm was gathered through successive interviews with managing directors, and sales and purchasing managers. This firm is recognized as possessing a high level of technological competence; it is also unusually international for a firm in its field of business. The case shows how Danke and some of its suppliers and customers successively developed cooperative relationships, and how this in turn affected the firm's competence in developing products, production and business exchange procedures. The focus here is on the development of a set of dyadic relationships. In the following chapter the dynamic connections between these relationships will be analysed.

BUSINESS RELATIONSHIPS – A RECAPITULATION

As business relationships are the fundamental building blocks of the theory of the embedded MNC outlined in this book, there is good reason to consider the important business relationships of firms. Let us therefore recapitulate some of the basic features involved. Most basic of all is that business relationships are about doing business, and they are developed through doing business. They represent a commitment to continue business with another firm. These commitments are frequently mutual. It takes time and effort to build viable relationships, but, once established, they have major consequences for the firms in question. In particular, they offer great potential for developing knowledge. A limited set of business relationships often constitutes the main knowledge base of a firm. Although relationships are often among a firm's most important investments, it is difficult or even impossible for anyone other than those directly involved to understand the usefulness and the value of the investments. This is a matter of interpretation, intention, and expectations. Moreover, by tying the firms to one another, relationships allow the firms a certain possibility of controlling one another. No one firm is free to act without considering the consequences for its relationship partners. Finally, every relationship is unique: it has its own history, its own specific ties, and its own specific role in the development of the firms involved.

A FEW WORDS ON THE PACKAGING BUSINESS

A large part of the packaging business today is associated with products developed in the forest industry. These products, boxes of various kinds made of corrugated paper-board, serve as protection in the storage or transport of customers' goods. The customers' goods and needs vary tremendously, which means that the boxes must also vary to suit each customer's particular use. The handling of vegetables or fruit, for instance, requires relatively simple 'brown boxes' that, at most, have to be water-resistant and carry a printed brand name.[1] Other customers may use their boxes for transporting refrigerators, stoves or furniture, which calls for a much more robust quality. Another example could be small boxes used as packaging for presents, such as perfume or children's toys. They are often printed in several colors and have a smooth surface.

Generally speaking, the paper packaging industry consists of two kinds of producer: those who produce large volumes of relatively uncomplicated brown boxes aiming at high efficiency and low cost, and those who combine this with the production of specialized quality boxes. The majority of the customers, such as the growers and distributors of vegetables and fruit, are often satisfied with relatively simple brown boxes, since all they want is to transport their products safely. But for producers of perfume or children's toys, the function of the box is quite different. For them, packaging is not only a question of storage and transport: through its design it is also an important element in the marketing of the product. Packaging specialists must develop high-level skills in product design and production technology if they are to secure producers of this kind as their customers, since the manufacturing of specialized boxes with color printing is a more complex procedure.

Another feature of this industry is that the box manufacturers' business activities have a predominantly local orientation. Transportation costs and the need for delivery on a more or less daily basis generally impose geographical limits of about 200 kilometers. Thus, to reach a lot of local customers and to secure a large business volume, producers tend to develop a high level of product diversity. Thus, customers demand products of different qualities and a firm with a diversified set of products will often have as many as 1000 customers. The result is that, individually, the vast majority of the customers only account for a small fraction of the business.

Despite the geographical constraints, however, expansion into foreign markets, i.e., export or foreign direct investments, may still occur. Limited export may arise, for instance, if foreign customers are unable to find a suitable local producer. International purchasing, on the other hand, is more common, as local producers may buy more of their input material from foreign suppliers. There are primarily two kinds of input materials that are purchased, apart from ink and glue. These two, namely a lining paperboard called kraftliner (or testliner, a lower quality sometimes used as an alternative) and the (corrugated) paper called fluting, constitute the basis for corrugated boxes.[2] Economic fluctuations, an integral part of international purchasing, affect the access to – and consequently the price of – kraftliner and fluting. As a result, box producers alternate between local and foreign suppliers. There has also been a tendency since the 1970s for local producers to be acquired and vertically integrated into large foreign corporations in the forest industry. This means that these producers are expected to buy at least part of their input material from foreign suppliers.

To sum up, it can be said that the technology and the associated quality differs considerably among different paperboard packaging products, and that the production technology differs accordingly among producers. We can also say that international business activities usually remain limited. Further, there is a general understanding in the forest industry that the big producers of kraftliner are the ones that drive product development, while the corrugated board and box producers need to be flexible in production and in the development of products demanded by customers. But despite the possession of certain general features, every firm has its own unique history based on its particular business relationships and networks (as discussed in Chapter 2 above). In the following sections we look more closely at various features of Danke, a producer of corrugated board and boxes, and discuss the development of relationships in the firm's business network. The focus is on business-related events and commitments in the relationships between Danke and its counterparts, and the development of competence relating to products, production and business procedures.

THE CASE OF DANKE

Danke – a Technological Leader and International Explorer

With its 1100 employees Danke is regarded today as a big producer of corrugated board and various types of boxes for packaging in its domestic market. Its customers amount to 1500, of which the three largest account for 10, 5 and 4 percent of the volume respectively. The national market share is 30 percent, while the rest of the market is divided between three competitors only, since the market as a whole is limited in size. But although box manufacturers are relatively few, competition is recognized as being unusually strong. Danke's sales are mainly local, as are its competitors', but the company also exports to six other countries. In 1996, 13 percent of the total production was exported, accounting for 20 percent of the total turnover. The Danke organization comprises 13 operative sub-units and, although there is a central department for development, as many as 10 of the 13 sub-units conduct their own product development, manufacturing and sales. Three sub-units are located abroad, and all three are engaged in developing their own products for their particular local market needs.

Among managers working in the European-based forest industry, Danke is recognized as fairly outstanding when it comes to the development of new products and the ability to create customized solutions. This applies not only to variations of their corrugated board and ordinary brown boxes, but also to the high-quality boxes that require complex printing techniques. Further, business people have described Danke as an international explorer and have pointed out that its foreign expansion encompasses an unusually high level of export and investments abroad in terms of sales, production and development units. This is in clear contrast to the prevailing local orientation in this industry. As an experienced manager of a large corporation in the packaging industry puts it: 'They are true entrepreneurs, the managers in Danke, especially their top executive'.

Danke's strategic business relationships

Although their customers and suppliers are numerous, Danke representatives maintain that a limited number of relationships have been of strategic importance to the development of their business. Thus, certain specific business relationships have served as a basis for business expansion, for the development of new products and for entry into foreign markets. As can be

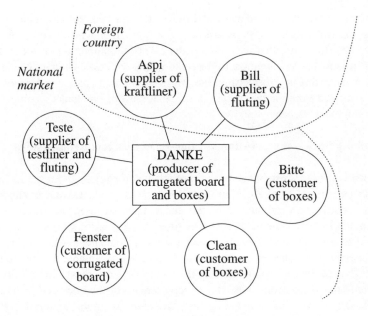

Figure 3.1 Danke in its strategic business network

seen in Figure 3.1, this amounts to a business network of three suppliers and three customers. The national supplier is Teste, which supplies testliner for Danke's production of corrugated board and brown-boxes. The other two particularly important suppliers are located in the same foreign country. One is Aspi, which supplies high-quality kraftliner, and the other is Bill, a supplier of high-quality fluting. The three customers included in this network are all located in the domestic market. The first is Fenster, which buys customized corrugated board for the protection of construction parts, that is to say window frames, during delivery. The other two customers, Bitte and Clean, buy boxes with complex printing for the packaging of toys and washing powder respectively. The suppliers account together for about 40 percent of the total purchasing cost of input material and the customers account for 19 percent of the sales volume.

In the following section we examine the historical development of these relationships with Danke, and the role they have played in Danke's business. Although the business activities occuring within the relationships overlap to some extent in time, we introduce each relationship in chronological order and describe how it relates to the others.

We first describe the creation and the importance of Danke's relationship with its oldest supplier, Teste, which supplies testliner and fluting; and then we examine the way this relates to Danke's relationship with its customer

Fenster. Next, we introduce and briefly describe the development of the relationship with the foreign supplier, Aspi, together with the other foreign supplier, Bill. After that we examine the role of the important customer Bitte and, finally, the development of the relationship with the customer, Clean. We summarize this by discussing the most prominent characteristics of this network and examine the impact of the relationships on Danke's competence development over the years.

Looking Back – the Creation of Long-term Business Relationships

When Danke was established as a joint-stock company in 1952, the intention at that time was to produce and sell one type of product, what is known as solid-board. This product was the main material used in small boxes, particularly boxes for butter. At that time, Danke was only operating in its national market, and the main technological challenges were to achieve efficiency in production and to create a solid-board suitable for its intended use. Behind the decision to start up this business was a local supplier (Teste), which after discussions with Danke representatives, had decided to produce and sell a type of paper that was suitable as input material for the manufacturing of solid-board. Once the right paper quality had been achieved after many experiments, Teste began production and Danke became a relatively big customer.

A few years later, in 1958, when the two parties had developed a fairly close business relationship, Teste undertook heavy investments in new machinery and started producing testliner and fluting. As noted above, these represent two of the main materials used in the production of corrugated board. Then, once Teste was ready to deliver, Danke in turn invested in machinery for the production of corrugated board, partly as input for its own production of brown boxes and partly for selling to the market (other box producers). Thus, Danke was now becoming thoroughly established as a company in the packaging business. Many new contacts were made with a variety of customers, and deliveries from Teste consequently increased. Moving on from a couple of hundred customers, Danke now had more than 500 customers for corrugated board and different kinds of brown boxes.

During this period Teste was very important to the build-up of Danke's new business – something that became less marked over the years. But although the relationship with Teste no longer accounts for the introduction of many new customers to Danke, the other firm's great flexibility in producing testliner of different qualities and its flexible production capacity still boosts Danke's ability to serve customers demanding specially designed boxes or suddenly requiring an increase in volume. Hence Danke still regards this supplier as relatively important to the maintenance of its own business with its existing customers. In the domestic market there are as many as ten alternative suppliers, but Danke does not consider replacing Teste. Rather, their relationship has proved its strength in that Danke and Teste still do business together, although they have been acquired by two large competing corporations in the forest industry.[3] Their belonging to competing corporations has not meant the total eradication of their mutual business, although its relative volume has declined over the years: Teste used to account for about 40 percent of Danke's total costs for input material, whereas the figure today is 12 percent.

But Danke's purchasing relationship with Teste has not been an isolated affair. As Danke's business developed, this relationship became closely connected with one of Danke's customers, namely Fenster.

Fenster – the first critical customer

Fenster is a local window-frame manufacturer. At the time when it first went into business with Danke in 1956, Fenster was in need of a packaging board (that is, brown corrugated board in reels rather than stiff board for boxes) for the protection of its window-frames. Danke was then constructing corrugated board of this kind, but before embarking on business with Fenster it contacted Teste to secure the input of testliner and fluting.

At first the volume of business was average, but a few years later, Fenster made some big investments and expanded in its market. Danke was then able to increase its production and sales of this packaging paper, and its purchases from Teste also increased accordingly.

In 1976, after another 15 years or so of business exchange, a major technological change occurred. Fenster started inserting the glass into the frame before delivery. This called for a totally new kind of packaging board, since the glass needed extra protection. Color-printing was also required on the packaging board. Danke could no longer rely on a single supplier of testliner, because the quality of some of the corrugated boards would not be sufficiently good. To ensure solid and reliable quality, Danke made enquiries at Aspi, a foreign supplier with whom it had been doing business for ten years, and this company was able to deliver kraftliner as input material.

This new branch of activity had several implications. First, Danke had to create a new packaging product, calling for a new design and different quality. Second, for its business with Fenster, which was now increasing, Danke had to rely on large deliveries from a foreign supplier. It was thus essential that Aspi could deliver on time. Third, the machinery at the production plants had to be adapted to suit Aspi's kraftliner quality, which in some ways differed from that of the usual testliner. Technical adjustments also had to be made because printing was now to be included in the production process. Even so, although the business with Fenster called for new investments and higher costs, this did not bother Danke, since there were good prospects of an increase in business volume. Likewise, for Fenster, there was 'no other conceivable supplier'.

Shortly afterwards Fenster expanded even more and started exporting to several foreign customers, which meant that its business with Danke increased further. Today, Fenster accounts for 10 percent of Danke's turnover, which is 50–100 times more than for the average customer. As a supplier, Danke provides more than 80 percent of Fenster's packaging board needs.

One effect of the expansion of business with Fenster was that the role of the alternative supplier, Aspi, became more central to Danke's business. This had two further effects: one was that it affected Teste's business with Danke negatively, and the other that it had a positive impact on Danke's business with Fenster. Since Teste used to be and still is extremely important to Danke, we will examine Aspi's (and Bill's) supplier roles more closely and compare them to the rather competitive role of Teste, before looking further at Danke's other customer relationships.

Aspi – securing high quality delivery and creating new business

Although the business relationship with the Teste was good, Danke needed an alternative supplier (Aspi) at an early stage in its business development. The reason was twofold: first, as noted above, Aspi supplied kraftliner, the quality of which is more suitable than testliner for some packaging products. Second, as business expanded, and when supply was insecure in periods of a rising economic trend, it was necessary to secure the flows of alternative input material.

Consequently, in 1966, Aspi became a supplier. At that time the company was producing standard brown kraftliner, which as we have seen was used later for Danke's production of corrugated board (for example, for Fenster). To begin with, deliveries from Aspi were small and it was not until 1976 that volumes assumed any great size. But this expansion was not due solely to Aspi's involvement as a supplier in Danke's increasing sales to Fenster. An acquisition had made Danke part of the same international corporation as Aspi, whereupon the new corporate headquarters expected a greater volume of brown kraftliner to be bought from Aspi. In responding to this instruction, Danke introduced kraftliner from Aspi into some products that had previously been made with testliner from Teste.[4] All this together meant a sudden acceleration in the business exchange between Danke and Aspi, which suited them both. Thus, for reasons of quality, Danke needed to replace Teste as a supplier for some of its products and, to secure the sales flow, a parallel supplier was needed in case Teste was unable to deliver. Aspi was also known as a highly competent producer of paper products.

Today Aspi accounts for 39 percent of Danke's purchases of input material, which makes it the company's largest supplier.

The introduction of 'white-top' quality
An important step in Danke's development in connection with its business with Aspi was the introduction of what are known as 'white-top' quality corrugated board boxes. In the early 1980s Danke thus started to use small volumes of what was to them a new kind of kraftliner, 'white top'. This was a major change that made a significant impact on Danke's production technology, as it then became possible to print directly on the reels of board. It also meant that boards were preprinted before being used in the manufacture of boxes. The result of this innovation was that Danke opened a new plant well adapted to the production of boxes using this technology. Initially Danke bought white-top kraftliner on the international market, but in 1985 Aspi took note of this development and started producing this kraftliner quality as well, whereupon Danke immediately began to buy the new quality from Aspi for its white-top boxes. But the task of using the white-top kraftliner and incorporating it into the production set-up was not a simple one. Technicians from Aspi had to visit Danke's white-top box factory several times to test the board in the machines before deciding on the appropriate quality. Even so, to make it work, the Danke technicians had to adjust their plant to match the new paper-board.

Corrugated board and boxes from this plant have a special design; they are white and often printed with text and pictures in various colors. Danke's interest in using white top had been triggered by some market research conducted by a large corporation in the forest industry. The aim was to test customers' reactions to the color of boxes containing products (apples) for sale, by placing the same product in three boxes of different kraftliner quality: one made of brown kraftliner, another of white mottled (oyster shade) kraftliner and the third in the white-top variety. The result suggested that the products in the white-top box were preferred by customers, since the contents of that box disappeared much sooner than the others.

However, white top accounts for only 5 percent of kraftliner production in the European market as a whole – which according to a former Aspi manager is surprising, since the profitability of white-top boxes is higher than that of ordinary brown boxes. But in Danke, white-top products account for as much as 20 percent of its total production, due to the relatively large proportion of sales to 'quality customers'. Nowadays, whenever Aspi develops a new paper quality, the Danke white-top plant is used to test it, with the result that the Danke managers still refer to this plant as one of their 'competence units'. Danke is thus interested in learning about new qualities of input materials, while Aspi needs to test new materials under real market conditions.

An interesting development during the late 1990s has halted the business expansion of Aspi's high-quality paper-board and affected its business with Danke. The environmental movement has made an impact on the production of kraftliner (and fluting), such that Aspi has started to mix the pulp with 20 percent recycled paper. As a result the difference in quality between testliner and kraftliner has decreased in recent years, and Danke representatives have said that … 'it is not impossible that we will start buying more from Teste again'.

Bill – a supplier of fluting recommended by Aspi

The increased production of kraftliner-based boxes and corrugated board also meant that Danke had to use a high quality of fluting. In 1976 Aspi recommended Danke to make contact with Bill, a foreign company with a long tradition in the forest industry. Bill produced fluting from birch, which according to Aspi would yield an end product that was more solid and relatively resistant to water.[5] Aspi's recommendation to import fluting from Bill was based on its knowledge of Bill through the complementary roles that the two firms had played as supplementary suppliers to packaging companies on several markets. Thus, Aspi knew Bill and acted as an intermediary in bringing the firm to Danke's attention.

The introduction of Bill replaced the relationship with Teste as a supplier of fluting to Danke, in the same way that Aspi's supply of kraftliner had partly replaced Teste's supplies of testliner. Over the next 15 years purchases from Bill reached a high level, but in 1994 the international corporation (Aspa) to which Danke belonged, wanted to replace Bill by a recently acquired corporate producer of fluting. Danke responded to this suggestion but only in part, since the quality of Bill's fluting was higher than that of the new subsidiary and a total change would have meant reducing the quality of some of Danke's corrugated boards and boxes. Today, Bill accounts for 20 percent of the total costs of input material and 50 percent of the fluting costs.

Thus, it can be seen that Aspi, and to some extent Bill, have had a considerable impact on the development of Danke's business with Fenster. But as suppliers of high-quality input material, they were also associated with the business development of a completely different kind of customer, namely Bitte.

Bitte – a demanding customer

Bitte is not Danke's largest customer in terms of volume, but it is the one that Danke now considers to have been the most important on grounds of strategy. The first contact occurred in 1966 when Bitte bought ordinary brown boxes from Danke for storing and transporting children's toys. At that time, sales to Bitte were thus closely related to Danke's business with its supplier, Teste, even though a few of the box qualities needed kraftliner from Aspi. Between the late 1960s and the mid-1970s, two things happened: Bitte's business expanded rapidly and their products were marketed and sold to an increasing extent by supermarkets. This meant that Danke had to handle a large and continuing increase in production volume, in combination with delivery several times a week. Another result was that Bitte wanted a more customized type of box that would advertise the toys inside. Thus, the box had to be attractive (colorful) and easy to open, i.e., suitable for children.

The development activities with Bitte coincided with Danke's increasing contact with Aspi and Bill. As they both produced high-quality kraftliner and fluting, they were chosen as suppliers and became associated with Danke's business with Bitte. Teste was thus not considered in the development of the new box quality. However, all these changes called for an increase in foreign input material, which happened to coincide with a period of upward economic trend. Consequently, in the late 1970s Danke's foreign suppliers had difficulty in delivering on time, which in turn affected Danke's own ability to deliver. This caused particular trouble in the relationship with Bitte, whose purchasing department became increasingly frustrated with the effect on their production.

In 1980 Bitte's purchasing manager broke off the business relationship with Danke in favor of alternative suppliers, because it no longer trusted Danke to meet its delivery requirements. Nonetheless, relations were still good between the two companies' development departments. So, despite not selling to Bitte, Danke's technicians continued to cooperate in improving the quality of its boxes to make them suitable for Bitte's products. Then when the white-top plant was established in 1985, Danke acquired the means for producing the right qualities at a volume that could attract Bitte, with the result that business exchange started up again between Danke and Bitte over the following years (the former purchasing manager having retired by then). After this change Danke was more advanced than its competitors, who were replaced in favor of Danke.

Bitte and Danke put a lot of effort into their cooperation and altogether about twenty people from the two companies were involved. One thing that still worried Bitte, was the weight of the corrugated board, a question that Danke passed on to Aspi and Bill. The task was to make a lighter corrugated board without significantly reducing the quality. In due course this was accomplished, but the result demanded a relatively large investment on Danke's part, since new machinery had to be bought for the white-top plant. Another subject of interest was the further improvement of the current technique for printing directly on the paper reels, as Bitte wanted several colors in the correct shades. Together with Bitte and the suppliers of paint, a printing technique was developed that includes six different colors.

The creation of 'lightweight' colorful boxes not only meant that the volume of Danke's sales to Bitte grew; it also led to the export of preprinted corrugated boards to other sister units within the international corporation (Aspa), which in turn produced similar boxes for customers with similar demands on their local markets. Further, when Bitte established a subsidiary in the USA, Danke became an exporting supplier in the absence of any locally available alternative of this quality.

A development with somewhat intricate effects during the 1990s, initiated by the environmental movement, was the move away from bleaching or using white paper to attract customers. This has gradually resulted in deliberately giving some of the boxes delivered to Bitte a brown and more environmentally friendly finish. Another development during the early 1990s has been a growing need to develop less heavy paper and boxes, and thus producing smaller boxes, because customers have become more sensitive about using more packaging (i.e. forest) material, than absolutely necessary. Consequently, to avoid earning a negative reputation among its customers, Bitte required Danke to construct boxes exactly the size of the specific toys they are to hold.

Clean – from development partner to customer to development partner

The first contact with Clean, producer of a variety of healthcare products, detergents and washing powders, was made in 1967. Like Bitte, Clean was increasingly marketing its products in supermarkets, but the company used other kinds of packaging material, not paper or board products. In 1975, realizing the great potential for business, Danke started to cooperate with Clean in a project for creating a suitable box for washing powder. The box was to be used in laundry-rooms, etc. and had to be resistant to water. Color printing was also wanted. The development, which embraced Aspi and Bill as suppliers, resulted in a box that was ready for production in 1979. The first sales to Clean were made the same year.

During the 1980s, the volume of business gradually became relatively substantial, accounting for 4 percent of Danke's total volume. But there was heavy competition in Clean's market, which put pressure on the advertising of the washing powder as well. The result was that the technical departments at Danke and Clean continued to work on improving the packaging box. This occured just when Danke was engaged in intensive cooperation with its customer, the toy producer Bitte. The requirements stipulated by Clean were similar to those put out by Bitte, and the light-weight corrugated board that had been developed as a result of the relationship with Bitte was also suitable for the development of the Clean box. Coincidentally, a further important driving force here was again the environmental movement, which was calling for optimal sizes for paper-packaging products. Finally, in 1990, when it was possible to print with several colors, manufacturing started on a lighter and slightly smaller box for washing powder.

Business increased and appeared to be stable since this box fulfilled all the technical and market requirements. However, in 1993, a major competitor that specializes in this business established itself in a neighboring country, marketing a box with similar qualities but at a price that was 30 percent lower. Danke, who did not enjoy the same economies of scale, was unable to match this price and despite its close relationship with Clean, Danke was replaced, and the sales to Clean were practically wiped out. Even so, the development departments and business managers of the two organizations still maintained extensive contact. As a result, and because Clean is a large company involved in several kinds of business, a new project for developing a special kind of box started shortly after the former business exchange had been wound up.

The Impact of Relationships over Time

To summarize, let us start with Teste. This firm, with its local roots, has a close contact and a history of mutual product development in common with Danke. Although Teste once had considerable impact on Danke's product development, this supplier is now more important to Danke's current business exchange with local customers. Due to its great flexibility in providing testliner qualities and quantities, Teste has underpinned Danke's capability for constructing customized product solutions and for responding to any increases in demand. This relationship is, or at least used to be, closely associated with the sales to Fenster.

This last relationship with Fenster has played an important part in Danke's development, since it lay behind the initiation of business with high-quality products. The product development conducted together with Fenster thus enhanced Danke's capability for engaging in a new type of business with larger volumes. At the same time, compared with the kind of products that Danke was later to develop and sell to other customers, such as Bitte and Clean, the technical demands of the packaging paper for Fenster's window-frames were modest.

The relationships with the foreign suppliers Aspi and Bill have primarily had quality-securing roles. At first, Aspi's role was much concerned with the development and production of new paper qualities. This improved not only the general quality of Danke's products – corrugated board and boxes – but also of its production technology, since investment had to be made in new machinery. It should be noted that Aspi's role in securing Danke's deliveries failed during one critical period with regard to the business with Bitte. But Aspi was still important when it comes to the restoration of that business. Further, Bill's role increased over the years and proved to be important. It was mainly through the influence of Danke's foreign mother company that a partial replacement for Bill occurred.

Perhaps most important has been Danke's relationship with its customer Bitte, which has driven much of the company's market-related quality development. The demands of Bitte's market were a powerful impetus behind the cooperation with Danke on product development, and it was because of Bitte that Danke also had to improve its capacity for production and delivery. This was achieved partly through investments in the new white-top plant.

The relationship between Danke and its customer, Clean, is interesting because the qualities and the character of the technology used were similar to those needed in the relationship with Bitte. As in the case of Bitte, Danke has continued to cooperate on technical issues with Clean even after their business exchange ceased, albeit not as intensively.

Figure 3.2 summarizes the main impact of Danke's business relationships on the company's development of technology and business.

Concluding Remarks – Development of Business Relationships

Perhaps the most obvious development within the set of Danke's six relationships is the change in balance and character between two sub-systems.

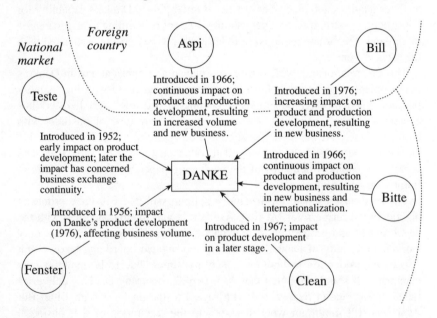

Figure 3.2   Main impact of Danke's strategic business relationships

The first is the system consisting of Danke, Teste and Fenster, which was dominant at first but whose significance began to decline after a few years due to Fenster's change in its packaging technology, which in turn meant that Aspi came to play a more prominent role. The second relational subsystem consists of Danke's interaction with Bitte, Aspi, and Clean, which spurred the company to develop its products and to make large investments in production, thus strengthening its technological and business competence and generating new business opportunities. The last point manifested itself in Danke's exports to its subsidiary in the USA and to sister companies in the multinational corporation to which Danke belonged.

Turning to relationship development, we also see that changes in technology and business in Danke are closely related to the company's commitment to its business relationships. Danke has been engaged in constant intensive interactions that have produced a series of challenges resulting in the development of new knowledge. In this way the adoption of new technical solutions has been followed by an improved capability to take on new tasks, sometimes in direct cooperation with suppliers and customers.

We will now look at four important aspects of business relationship development that have been highlighted in the case of Danke.

Long-term development
First, it appears that the development of business and technology is closely associated with a succession of interactive cooperative ventures and requirements over a long period of time. All the relationships studied here were developed over a period of 20–50 years. The development and perpetuation of a business relationship seems to be related to the degree of a mutually rather than a one-sidedly driven commitment. A change by one actor induces a reaction on the part of the relationship partner that may be followed in turn by further development, thus successively creating mutual commitment on a long-term basis. In the relationship between Danke and Bitte, for example, the two parties shared a profound long-term expectation that their intensive efforts would result in a new product quality with positive effects on profits for both parties. Even during the period when Danke was unable to ensure delivery they still cooperated on developing a new product.

Stability and change
Second, long-term development is closely related to the question of stability and change. New technology and solutions related to business procedures appear to require a certain level of stability, implying an interconnection between stability and change. It is obvious that Danke's relationships are stable, since they have existed over a long period of time, and that within those relationships changes occur. It also appears that when two actors make certain

mutual investments, they create a certain degree of interdependence. This in turn reinforces the stability of the relationship, in that quitting it becomes more difficult or less attractive. Danke's business and technological development have called for big efforts and investments of various kinds on the part of individuals on both sides of the relationships. Of the relationships investigated, only in the case of Clean was the mutual commitment ultimately not strong enough and the business exchange ceased. Even in this case, however, there is still an active contact between the technical departments of the two companies.

Specific and generalized development
A third point here has been that the development of the relationship has been very specific, in that the history of each relationship, and the development within it, was unique. Development issues were thus based on specific interactive problem-solving procedures within each relationship. However, the knowledge generated by these processes was partly for specific use and partly open to generalization. In other words, all the development processes involving Danke were unique and specific to each relationship. At the same time solutions to technological or business procedures lent themselves to use in exchanges with more than one partner. One example of specific development and generalized usage is provided by Danke's white-top paper and new color-printing technique, which were developed in connection with Bitte and Aspi and then adapted to the development of the light-weight box quality in the company's relationship with Clean.

Connectedness
The development of Danke's relationships with its various counterparts was not primarily a matter of dyadic evolution in isolation. Rather, it was conditioned by interrelationship connectedness. In the set of business relationships analysed here, the effect of the connectedness was both positive and negative, inducing increases and decreases in the business exchange between Danke and some of its relationship partners. For instance, the change in product quality in Danke's exchange with Fenster, had a negative impact on the volume of business with Teste, whereas business with Aspi was affected positively. Further, in several cases there was also a connection between a change in a product or production technology in certain relationships, which then induced changes in others. An example of this was the continuous interconnectedness between Danke's relationships with its customer Bitte and its suppliers Aspi and Bill that resulted in the input of new paper qualities and new production technology.

A complex picture thus emerges of how change in one relationship affects change in others, suggesting that over time, relationships will be connected in different ways and to varying degrees. Danke can be said to have played the role of coordinator, handling the connections between its business relationships. The ability to coordinate relationship connections is closely associated with the degree of interdependence between the relationships concerned, which function in turn as a driver when it comes to adapting to changes induced by another partner in a relationship. When connections between relationships are strong, this will condition changes undertaken in a certain relationship. The case of Danke clearly demonstrates that when investments are being handled in a specific relationship, it is necessary to consider the consequences of these for other relationships.

In the next chapter we analyse the connections between Danke's relationships with a view to enriching our understanding of business development in a dynamic and interconnected business network.

NOTES

1. The expression 'brown boxes' will refer here to boxes where quality is a matter of resistance to water and bumping, and the extent to which they can be printed in various colors. Further, the expression 'customized boxes' is associated with the capability for making more specialized solutions for brown boxes and other boxes of higher quality.
2. When manufacturing corrugated board, fluting is inserted between two boards of kraftliner or testliner. Corrugated board then serves as the input material for the production of different kinds of boxes.
3. In 1976 Danke was incorporated into a larger MNC called Aspa. For more information about this, see Chapter 6.
4. In some cases Aspi's kraftliner could easily replace testliner as the input material.
5. It should be mentioned that Bill has not been involved as a supplier in the development of 'white-top boxes'.

4. Development of a business network – the case of Danke

In the previous chapter we described the development of relationships in which Danke was engaged during periods of business exchange lasting anything from 20 to 50 years. We observed that Danke's business had developed within an essentially stable network, although certain aspects of its long-term relationships changed over the years. It was clear that every relationship with a customer or a supplier affected Danke's business behavior, both its volume and its technological competence, albeit to a varying degree and at different times.

In this chapter we illustrate the evolution of relationships from the arm's-length stage to the close and more profoundly cooperative level. We then relate this development to the connectedness of relationships, and describe the way that two of Danke's most important relationships – with Aspi and Bitte – have influenced the company's exchange in its other business relationships. The chapter closes with some comments on certain important characteristics of connectedness and some of the issues facing management.

THE DEVELOPMENT OF A BUSINESS NETWORK

The more immediate part of Danke's network consists today of a mix of local and foreign business relationships with suppliers and customers. As we saw in Chapter 3, as a result of direct cooperation and the requirements thus generated, these relationships have driven Danke to acquire a special competence in the development, manufacture and sale of new product qualities. The creation of new solutions has made the business relationship with Danke more significant to its customers; its competitive strength is no longer limited to the local market but encourages expansion to foreign markets as well. Looking back at these events, we describe below how various features

of the relevant network structure have successively evolved to produce
Danke's current capability (see Figures 4.1–4.3).

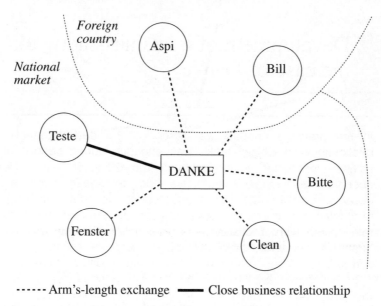

----- Arm's-length exchange ▬▬▬ Close business relationship

Figure 4.1   Danke's business network before 1976

Before 1976 (see Figure 4.1), Danke was primarily a domestic company,
since its relations with Aspi and Bill were of an arm's-length kind. Thus,
although Danke had been doing business with Aspi, its foreign supplier, since
the middle of the 1960s, this could still best be described as an arm's-length
exchange relation. The only really close relationship in which Danke was
involved was the one with Teste, a supplier who delivered testliner and fluting
for Dante's production of corrugated paper and board. But this was a local
affair and was not much affected by the development of Danke's other
relationships.

Next, between 1976 and 1980 Danke developed its relationships with Aspi
and Fenster, and its business exchange with these firms was closely
coordinated (see Figure 4.2). The closer relation with Aspi emerged in 1976
when Fenster began to incorporate glass in their window-frame deliveries, and
closer business exchange with these two partners was developed in order to
meet the new technical requirements. This connection meant an increase in
business volume for all three parties. Although business with Aspi had already
begun to expand as a result of the exchange with Teste, the relationship with
Teste was still close and involved large volumes.

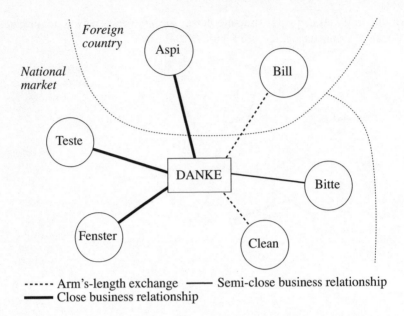

Figure 4.2   Danke's business network between 1976 and 1980

Although cooperation with Bitte on product development had started during this period, the relationship was only semi-close, since the business exchange had been terminated because of delivery failure due to problems in the flow of the paper input from Aspi. In fact, at that point there was a negative connection between the Bitte and Aspi relationships.

After 1980 Danke developed close relationships with the domestic actors Bitte and Fenster and semi-close relationships with Teste and Clean. Thus, although still relatively important, the two latter relationships were not as close as they had been. The relationship with Teste was close as regards existing delivery capability, and less close in terms of cooperation regarding new technology. With Clean it was close as regards cooperation between technicians, while business exchange was not close – at least not at the end of the period when it was in fact terminated.

Compared with the earlier situation illustrated in Figure 4.1, the network relationships in Figure 4.3 have generally become closer. The creation of more intensive relationships started mainly with domestic relationships such as those with Teste and Fenster. But relationships with actors in other countries have also become successively closer, beginning with Aspi and Bill on the input side. But Danke's relationships with foreign actors on the output side had also started by that time. One concerned the creation of an arm's-length export relation with Bitte's American subsidiary. Another was the creation of

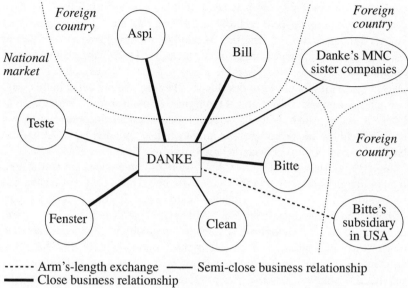

----- Arm's-length exchange ——— Semi-close business relationship
——— Close business relationship

Figure 4.3   Danke's business network after 1980

foreign customer relationships with other corporate units. These last can be described as semi-close, as they involved fewer cooperative activities than those with Danke's external market partners. Nonetheless, they have been of some importance to Danke, since they led to the sharing of knowledge about similar market problems.

Figures 4.1–4.3 have illustrated the development of Danke's business network. Two points emerge. First is the unique competence that Danke developed by way of a long-term process of exchange and problem-solving, transforming its initial arm's-length relations into close business relationships. However, it has to be noted that the creation of these more intensive relationships reflects neither a final nor a static situation, as there are also clear indications of relationships changing back from close to the semi-close kind. The case indicates that both the creation and dissolution of close relationships are affected by developments in other network relationships. Thus, the second point is that the process involves a number of historic connections over time, between customer relationships, between supplier relationships and between customer and supplier relationships.

The capability that Danke developed to produce unique products and its ability to coordinate connections between suppliers and customers enabled this company to establish a competitive position, even on the international stage. Looking at the last few years, we see that this capability was closely connected with the interplay between Danke's relationships with Bitte, Aspi and Bill. But looking back a little further, we can similarly conclude that Fenster's incorporation of glass into its window-frames played a major part in the structural evolution of Danke's network, as it led to a change in the content of Danke's purchases from Aspi. It seems reasonable to ask ourselves how Danke's activities would have developed if Fenster had not acted in this way.

Figure 4.4 opposite illustrates the progress of major actions undertaken in Danke's relationships with its suppliers and customers. The company's development can be traced back not only to actions in individual relationship, but also to connections between relationships over time.

In 1976, as shown in Figure 4.4, Fenster instituted a change and started integrating glass directly into its window-frames. This meant that Danke had to develop a new quality of corrugated board, which led in turn to the import of higher paper qualities from Aspi. At a later stage Danke and Bitte began cooperating on the development of a white-top quality box, which meant new deliveries from Aspi and investments by Danke in new production facilities. Ultimately, the long period of cooperation with Bitte, Aspi and Bill greatly improved Danke's capability in printing techniques and led to a new lightweight paper-board. Danke was therefore chosen as a foreign supplier for Bitte's American subsidiary and as a corporate supplier of paper-board for its own foreign sister companies in the larger MNC.

In the next section we will look further at the question of connections between relationships and the part they play in business development. We provide a short introduction to some important aspects of connectedness and then offer an empirical description of the main effects that Danke's relationships with Aspi and Bitte have on its other relationships.

CONNECTIONS BETWEEN RELATIONSHIPS

Empirical studies have shown that the character of the exchange between two firms in a specific business relationship can be connected to – or influenced by – events and activities in other relationships (Blankenburg and Johanson 1992). As noted in Chapter 2, managers of business firms engage in coordination across a number of business relationships. The way the business exchange evolves in a particular relationship can thus be better understood if the ongoing impacts between relationships are included in the analysis. For example, although a specific business relationship may be important to the development of new technical solutions during one period, its influence may fade or alter in later periods. An underlying reason for this may have to do with changes in other interrelationships' influences. Some connections may thus dwindle over time or assume other characteristics, or be altered by other

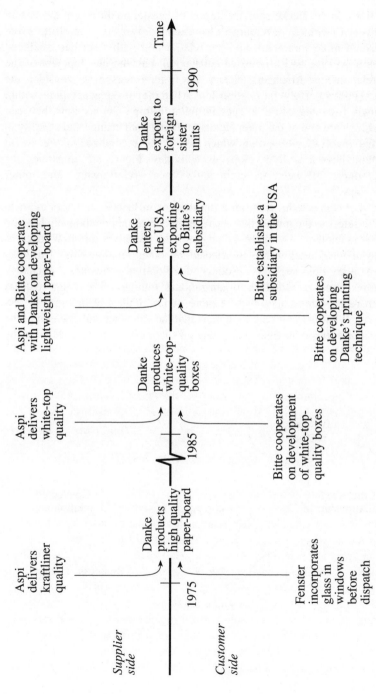

Figure 4.4 Main actions in the development of Danke's international expansion

connections. In the Danke case, the impact of Fenster on the rest of the system as a driver of technical development has declined over the years. Bitte's role has become more important, and the relationship with Aspi has oscillated between a positive and a negative connection with the development of the Bitte relationship. Managers clearly have good reason to consider the historical context of several relationships when they make adaptations within their own firm regarding a specific relationship. Connections between relationships are one of the main factors affecting both change and stability in the firms involved, something which has to be recognized if we are to understand how a firm develops its activities. Figure 4.5 illustrates the connectedness between a company's focal relationship and other relationships.

Note that connectedness is not a question of influence on actors as such. Rather, it refers to the impact that activities in one certain relationship have on activities in another. As Figure 4.5 suggests, an important question concerns the way a focal relationship is affected by other relationships. This may concern activities such as product development, business exchange procedures, manufacturing or organizational routines. The connectedness between relationships may also be more or less unilateral or more or less reciprocal. What is important, though, is that the character and strength of the connections varies over time, depending on successive actions undertaken by

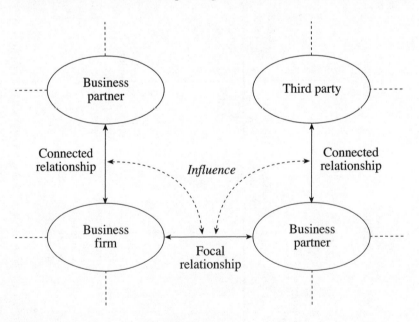

Figure 4.5   Connected relationships

the interacting parties. Above all, connectedness is thus a process rather than a structure, compounding the sequence of impacts on a firm's behavior in relation to its relationship partners. The structural change, that is to say the creation of new activities, the change in behavior and the emergence of new business relationships, is what signifies such a process.

In the case of Danke it was fairly clear that the development could be explained to a great extent by connections between the various business relationships in which Danke operated as the link. Hence, not only did Danke have to manage its relationships with each one of its partners; there also had to be some awareness of the way activities in one relationship affected or are affected by other relationships.

We will now discuss the relationships with Aspi and Bitte, which – as the case description in Chapter 3 has shown – have had an impact on other relationships in Danke's focal network.

The Impact of the Danke–Aspi Relationship

Figure 4.6 illustrates the impact of the Danke–Aspi relationship on the other relationships in Danke's focal network. At the beginning Dankes's two relationships with Teste and Fenster had a positive impact on one another. Later, however, when Fenster made changes in its product, Aspi's role

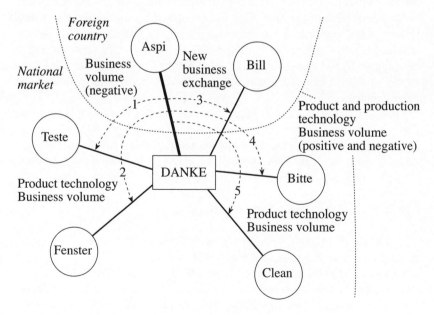

Figure 4.6   The influence of the relationship between Danke and Aspi

increased to the detriment of Teste's, because Teste lost business to Aspi. Thus as Figure 4.6 shows, a negative connection (1) emerged between the two suppliers, Aspi and Teste.

However, between Aspi and Fenster the connection was positive (2). To begin with the impact of Aspi had a technological basis, since the business with Fenster depended on the development of a more solid packaging paper, which involved Aspi. The technological impact of Aspi's relationship with Danke consequently made it possible to sustain a large volume of business with Fenster over the years. A contributing factor here had to do with the high degree of mutual commitment between the two parties, which in turn depended on the ability to secure the right kraftliner quality from Aspi.

Aspi introduced Bill (3) as a supplier of so-called 'fluting', which meant that a new foreign supplier relationship was created on the initiative of another supplier. There was a relationship based on previous business experience between the two suppliers. This altered Danke's purchases from Bill in terms of quality, volume and distance, again on account of local purchases from Teste.

Next, the Aspi relationship had a strong impact on several aspects of Danke's business with its customer Bitte (4). The great dependence of these two relationships on one another was revealed when Bitte was unable to continue its production because of a delay in deliveries from Aspi to Danke. But the impact of Aspi had technological aspects too, as the company was able to construct a lighter kraftliner (and Bill constructed a special fluting), which boosted Bitte's volume of business with the help of Danke's production of a new box quality. This was demonstrated by Bitte's American subsidiary deciding to import this box quality from Danke, and Danke launching the export of lightweight and preprinted paper-board to its sister companies in other countries.

Finally, Clean also used to be a customer, but this firm's dependence on Danke's relationship with Aspi (5) was never as strong as Bitte's, since its business exchange with Danke could be terminated relatively easily when prices became too high. Even so, Aspi did play a minor part at the time when Clean's washing-powder box was being developed.

The Impact of the Danke–Bitte Relationship

The impact of Danke's relationship with Bitte on its other relationships provides a further example, as illustrated in Figure 4.7.

Compared with the situation in Figure 4.6, we can see immediately that the connection between Danke's relationships with Aspi and Bitte was reciprocal (1). The most significant manifestation of this appears in Aspi's contribution to Bitte's increased purchase from Danke, and Bitte's contribution to Aspi's

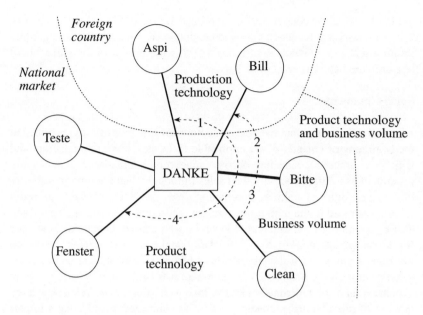

Figure 4.7   The influence of the relationship between Danke and Bitte

launching of its production and delivery of white-top kraftliner. It should be noted, however, that the customer relationship with Bitte accounted for a limited volume only. Nor was it the only reason why Aspi started producing this kraftliner quality. Having said that, it was certainly one motivating factor, since the Danke–Bitte relationship operated in entrepreneurial mode, to some extent opening up a new field of business for Aspi.

Bitte's influence on Danke's relationship with Bill (2) was more limited than Aspi's, since Bill was not involved in the development of the white-top paper. Even so, the relationship with Bitte did influence the relationship with Bill when Bitte wanted a new and lighter board. When Bill managed to produce the fluting used in this board, the volume of business between Danke and Bitte increased, which in turn had a positive impact on Danke's purchases from Bill.

There were close connections between the Bitte–Danke–Clean relationships (3). Danke was in fact able to benefit from the quality development in the Bitte relationship and to use it in the specific development with Clean. This connection was evident to all, and when the development stage was over it resulted in big sales volumes from Danke to Clean. However, Clean's dependence on Danke and its connections with Bitte (and Aspi) were not sufficiently strong: their business exchange was broken off when an alternative supplier appeared who was able to offer a lower price.

Finally, a subtle connection has emerged between Bitte and Fenster (4). This was based on the general knowledge that Danke had developed regarding printing technique, which in turn has affected the design of the paper-board box delivered to Fenster.

Some Comments

All in all, we can say that the general features of this industry, as described at the beginning of Chapter 3, are applicable to Danke. First, through Aspi and Bill, the purchasing side has become relatively international and is more prominent as a foreign activity than sales (although Danke's foreign sales are unusually high). Danke's purchasing was in fact already partially internationalized in the mid-1960s through the import of kraftliner from Aspi. These foreign purchases increased when Fenster started demanding kraftliner for some packaging boards, and when Danke started buying white-top kraftliner from Aspi for the production of boxes for its customer, Bitte. Thus, a contributory force behind this development was Bitte's and Fenster's market expansion and their demand for new box technology. The relatively large amount of international purchasing was also connected with Danke's import of fluting from Bill.

The emerging internationalization of Danke's sales is closely related to its relationship with Bitte. It seems probable that the usual 200-kilometer limit was dissolved because the box quality was specifically developed for Bitte's products. Contacts with Bitte in Danke's domestic market led to the exports to Bitte's subsidiary in the USA. The packaging board for this box is also exported, but this has more to do with the preference of Aspa sister subsidiaries – the MNC to which they all belonged – for doing business with Danke instead of buying from the external market.[1] The percentage of purchases or sales is thus only one aspect of internationalization. For instance, it can be claimed that Danke's network on the input side has become more international over the years, since its relationships with Aspi and Bill developed into a fruitful cooperation with a further bearing on other relationships in its network.

The level of Danke's local sales is high, but the company can still be regarded as an international firm on account of its foreign supplier and sales relationships. It should be noted, though, that Danke has connected relationships across borders in a variety of aspects, which serves to strengthen its international structure.

The quality of Danke's packaging board and boxes is closely linked to the development of paper qualities among its suppliers. However, the evidence of its various relationships reveals that Danke's customers drive the development of complex quality boxes at least as much as its suppliers do. Whether or not it has been entirely deliberate, Danke's strategy appears to have been to engage in close cooperation with certain customers who might prove important in the long term, and to combine this with selling corrugated board and boxes of lower quality to a fairly large number of small customers. Danke's managers have made successive commitments to specific relationships, triggered by changes and demands associated with other relationships. Here there seems to have been an awareness of existing connections.

However, this does not mean that Danke has always been able to act upon these connections, or has been able to exert exclusive control over the way they have developed. For instance, the temporary termination of business exchange with Bitte was connected with the delivery problems in the exchange relationship with Aspi, which Danke's managers recognized but were unable to affect. In the case of Clean, the adoption of solutions linked to developments in Danke's exchange with Aspi and Bitte, has not yet helped Danke to get Clean to increase its own commitment.

CONCLUDING REMARKS

Three comments in particular arise from the case of Danke. First, the company's focal network is in constant change. Second, the development of one relationship impinges on other relationships in a never-ending process. Third, the shift away from a domestic-firm identity and towards that of an international firm also, crucially, means moving from arm's-length exchange to close business relationships. And this process is powerfully driven by connections between relationships.

Even though important aspects of Danke's technological development and strategic direction can be explained by the selection of a particular network, it should be noted that the present study is based on only six of the company's various relationships with its customers and suppliers. However, according to Danke managers, these relationships do go a long way towards explaining the way their company has evolved; in fact, there are not many close cooperative partners beyond this group.

The managing of a firm's long-term development is conditioned by connections between business relationships that involve a number of exchange aspects and a variety of actor interests. The strategic intentions of managers and their decisions to make certain commitments do not exist in a vacuum. Rather, they are dependent on commitments that others are making, which means taking account of the way every individual relationship also belongs to a broader structure of other direct and indirect relationships. Thus, handling expansion into new markets, or making changes in product qualities and production technology or business routines, are not a purely intra-firm matter; nor are they part of a process that can be fully controlled. In the most extreme case, such activities may be almost fully determined by a variety of connected relationships, which means that the way a firm develops is to some extent unpredictable and 'externally' controlled. It is not therefore surprising that it takes some time for a relationship between a firm and any one of its specific partners to become reliable enough to induce major adaptations, which in turn implies that specific investments (and divestments) are implemented gradually and with some caution.

The connectedness that thus exists between relationships presupposes an infinite number of business-related factors that may be affected by other business relationships between two firms. In a management perspective it is important that relationships should be regarded not as a series of dyadic 'islands', since development frequently concerns issues related to other relationships. Consequently, the impact of connectedness on the development – and the handling of the development – of a firm can sometimes be highly complex. Conversely, the unconnected dyadic types of relationship are likely to be more institutionalized and more predictable, as the absence of connectedness reduces complexity and unpredictability.

In this chapter we have examined the development of a business network. The two main elements in this development were the generation of closeness in cooperative relationships and the connections between relationships. Together these elements define a firm's degree of network embeddedness. While the closeness of the relationships signifies the extent of the interaction and mutual problem-solving between the relationship partners, the connections signify that changes are dependent on the interplay between relationships thus emphasizing the extent to which we are looking at network processes rather than dyadic affairs between two business partners.

NOTE

1.   Danke also has foreign sales in other areas, but this is part of another story not described here.

5. Internationalization of the business firm

The preceding chapters have focused on business relationships, and a number of important features of such relationships have been discussed. In particular we have examined the role of business relationships in the development of the individual firm. The present chapter builds on this material by turning to the role of business relationships in the internationalization of the firm. It will be shown how the firm becomes increasingly embedded in foreign markets. It will also be demonstrated that network embeddedness has a strong impact on the pattern and pace of the internationalization process of the firm. Illustrative examples will be taken from the Danke case discussed above, so readers will again be meeting not only Danke itself but also Aspi, Bitte, Clean and others.

LEARNING AND COMMITMENT IN THE INTERNATIONALIZATION PROCESS OF THE BUSINESS FIRM

Two issues are repeatedly discussed and analysed in the literature on international business strategy, namely foreign market entry and foreign market expansion. The underlying basic assumption is that foreign country markets are distinct entities in which operations are, or are not, conducted. A related assumption is that since they are distinct entities, country markets require specific modes of operation or forms of organization. Consequently, a great deal of the international business literature is devoted to discussing the appropriate entry modes or governance modes in different foreign countries. Although the two issues are often analysed separately it is generally recognized that they are interrelated, and in the literature on the internationalization of the firm they are treated as two different albeit closely interrelated aspects of firm internationalization.

In the second section of the chapter we look at some important findings and implications from the literature of the internationalization process itself, which constitutes one of the main strands of internationalization research. We then return to the network approach outlined in Chapter 4 and discuss some of its consequences in relation to the internationalization process of the business firm. In this perspective we find that the basic assumption of the foreign country market as a distinct entity loses its significance, a viewpoint that in turn has some far-reaching implications.

Studies of the internationalization of the firm suggest that internationalization can be regarded as a process driven by the interplay between learning about international business operations on the one hand, and commitments to international business operations on the other (Johanson and Vahlne 1977; Blomstermo and Sharma 2003). According to this research the main obstacle to internationalization is a lack of knowledge about foreign markets and operations, and such knowledge can be developed primarily through direct experience of operations. Foreign business opportunities are discovered as a result of experience of foreign markets and operations. In addition, experience enables the firm to evaluate business opportunities, thus reducing the uncertainty associated with a commitment to foreign operations. And, since knowledge develops gradually, international expansion evolves by way of incremental commitments to foreign operations.

Viewing internationalization as a process has several implications. One is that internationalization is seen as a gradual development proceeding via a number of small steps. Initially the process view was conceptualized to explain two observations regarding the international development of firms. First, it was noted that, to start with, firms usually move abroad to close and familiar markets and then gradually extend their foreign operations to more distant and unfamiliar countries, which indicates that learning about foreign markets and operations is an important element in the internationalization of a firm. Second, it was observed that operations in specific country markets also develop in a gradual way. Firms seem to start with sporadic exports that are later organized by independent agents or other intermediaries in the market. Later still, sales subsidiaries are established, complemented in some cases by local manufacturing as well. This also suggests that learning about foreign markets is critical to the foreign market expansion of the firm.

THE IMPORTANCE OF EXPERIENCE

A point that has been emphasized repeatedly by businessmen and academics is the importance of experience in the internationalization process (Delios and

Beamish 1999; Luo and Peng 1999). Only by doing business abroad is it possible to learn about the way customers, intermediaries, competitors and public authorities act and react in different situations in a specific country market. Only by doing business in a country is it possible to gain this subtle understanding of the market, an understanding that can never be replaced by general market information or surveys. This means not only that it takes time to develop foreign business skills and knowledge, but also that these skills and this knowledge are associated with the specific situations and contexts in which they have been developed. Hence, it is difficult to transfer this kind of experiential knowledge to other markets. Empirical studies have indicated that a distinction can be made between market-specific experience and operation experience (Eriksson et al. 1997). Market-specific experience is developed by operating in that particular market and can only be transferred to, and utilized in, other markets with considerable difficulty.

Operational experience concerns ways of organizing and developing international business operations, such as the establishment of sales subsidiaries, and can be transferred more easily from one market to another. Operational experience can also be considered in a more general way as internationalization experience, that is to say, experiential knowledge about the use of different modes of operations in the internationalizing of a firm. Overall, it seems that an important implication of the process view of internationalization is that the development, the integration and the transfer of knowledge should be regarded as critical elements in the strategic management of internationalization. For example, in planning engagements in foreign markets, an eye should be kept on any resultant learning or any opportunities for exploiting the new knowledge in the overall international development of the firm.

INCREMENTAL COMMITMENTS AND COMMITMENT DECISIONS

According to the process view, internationalization is a process of incremental commitments to foreign operations. When firms do business abroad, and learn from doing so, they are getting something that is likely to be of value in the future. By doing business the firm builds up market-specific assets, but the value of these assets is to some extent connected with and dependent on specific contexts. A firm doing business internationally will always increase its commitment to international business in general and, in particular, to the country markets where it is already operating. An important element of the internationalization of the business firm, according to this view, consists of successive commitments stemming from its current business activities. These commitments will also be positively affected by demand-driven expansion in foreign markets.

Thus, it appears that the internationalization of the business firm is also associated with distinct steps subsequent to commitment decisions. These decisions may concern direct investments in manufacturing abroad, agreements with new distributors in foreign markets, cooperative arrangements with other firms, the acquisition of firms, etc. They, or rather actions they launch, constitute steps in the increase of the firm's international commitment. According to the process view of internationalization the decisions are influenced to a large extent by the firm's earlier internationalization events, and the consequences of those events are greatly dependent on the subsequent development processes with regard to the development, integration and utilization of knowledge. Such events provide the firm with new experiences and affect the successive commitments that ensue. The process view stresses that internationalization is not only, or even primarily, an outcome of such events: rather it proceeds in the shape of the current activities undertaken within the frame of the preceding and subsequent operation structures.

INVESTMENTS IN CONTEXT-SPECIFIC ASSETS AND MARKET POSITIONS

There is also reason to allow for the fact that by undertaking activities the firm is investing in context-specific assets, that is to say assets whose value is connected with and dependent on the contexts in which they have been created. For instance, Danke's interaction with Fenster, Bitte and Clean (described in Chapter 3) represents a series of investments that are expected to lead to future business. Obviously, the investments are highly dependent on the specific context in which they are made, and insofar as this is so, the resulting assets bind the firm to the contexts concerned. The greater the assets, the more specific they are and the more integrated they are with other firm activities, the greater is the firm's dependence on the contexts in question. All this implies that the firm is establishing foreign market positions that it has powerful reasons to defend, which means in turn that there is very good reason to make commitment decisions that develop its own positions. Thus, there is an interplay between current activity commitments and specific commitment decisions. For example, a firm operating in an expanding market would have reason not only to continue serving the market to the same extent as before, but also to increase its investment in the market to match its own growing dependence on the sales in that market. In this view there is an implicit assumption of embeddedness which, however, does not concern specific business relationships but the particular market.

SURMOUNTING MARKET BARRIERS IN INTERNATIONALIZATION

In Chapter 2 above we outlined a network perspective on business firms and business markets based on the assumption that business firms engage in a set of close business relationships with important customers, suppliers and other business partners, and that business markets are structured as networks of interconnected business relationships. The Danke case illustrates an important section of a firm's business network, comprising a set of interconnected business relationships. This perspective has certain consequences which we must take into account in developing our view on the internationalization of the business firm. Let us first examine the basic assumption in received international business theory, which sees the country market as a specific, bounded entity.

In Figures 5.1 and 5.2 we present two ways of regarding foreign country markets. Figure 5.1 gives the traditional view and Figure 5.2 the network view. The figures show two foreign country markets and the firm's domestic market. In both, the foreign country markets are demarcated by lines denoting the country borders. In Figure 5.1, in addition, the country markets are surrounded by fences corresponding to economic, institutional and cultural barriers to business.

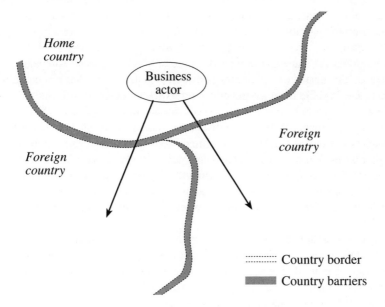

Figure 5.1   Foreign market entry from a traditional view

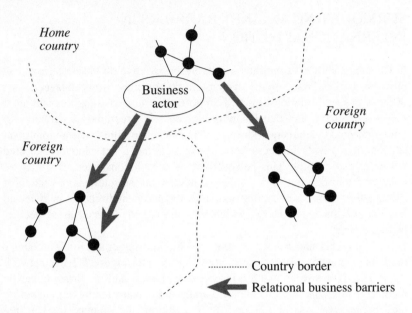

Figure 5.2　Foreign market entry from a business network perspective

Whereas early international trade theory stressed economic barriers, international business literature of the last 20 years or so has paid more attention to institutional and cultural barriers. Thus, in the internationalization literature, these types of barriers are constantly cited as major obstacles to foreign market entry and to the management of multinational companies. The size of the obstacles is usually considered in terms of psychic or cultural distance. Psychic distance generally refers to obstacles to information flows between countries due to differences in business laws, education levels, business language, etc. Cultural distance usually refers to differences between countries in terms of four cultural dimensions (Hofstede 1980). Although the two distances are closely related and are initially conceptualized as inter-country distances, some scholars using the psychic distance concept have also focused on inter-firm distances, and in some cases it has also implied the influence of firms' own operational experience (Hallén and Wiedersheim-Paul 1979).

It is also assumed that within the country borders in Figure 5.1, the market mechanism operates, and specific customers, suppliers and customers are not relevant. The market is faceless. Entering a country market, according to this view, is a matter of surmounting the barriers and thus becoming a market insider. There is a qualitative difference between an insider and an outsider. The managerial problems associated with foreign market entry are thus qualitatively different from those connected with foreign market expansion. This explains the sharp distinction between foreign market entry and foreign market expansion. It is generally assumed that the form of organization used in a foreign country is chosen with a view to overcoming the psychic or cultural distance in an appropriate way. For instance, direct export differs from acquisitions or greenfield investments in this respect.

BARRIERS TO RELATIONSHIP BUILDING

In Figure 5.2 we can still see the country borders, but they are not associated with any institutional or cultural barriers to business. Instead the markets are structured as networks of business relationships, and some of them are also cross-border relationships. Entry problems in this figure are associated not with country markets but with customers or suppliers. Instead of foreign-market entry and foreign-market expansion, we have reason to consider managerial problems associated with the establishment and development of relationships with suppliers and customers. Since each relationship is unique due to the characteristics of the relationship partners and the history of the relationship, the traditional international business issues are irrelevant in the extreme network case.

In the extreme network world, internationalization is no more than a general expansion of the business firm that is in no way affected by country borders. All barriers are associated with the establishment and development of relationships. One reason for this is that all relevant information is channeled through network relationships. There is nothing in between.

RELATIONSHIP COMMITMENT AND LEARNING

Although country borders are no longer relevant, the network model has similar implications for the internationalization process as those discussed above (Johanson and Vahlne 2003). We can still expect an internationalization process that is an outcome of interplay between experiential knowledge development and commitment, although both of these refer not to countries but to potential and existing relationships. Relationships develop successively as firms learn from their interaction with each other and commit themselves more strongly to the relationship.

First, when firms do business in a relationship they learn some things that are customer-specific, such as the customer's way of reacting to certain kinds of action or the roles of different individuals in the customer firm, or the willingness and ability of the customer firm to adapt in various ways

(Håkansson and Johanson 2001; Pahlberg 2001). Thus they learn about each other in a way that enables them to develop the relationship even more. Developing a relationship in this way also implies a further commitment to it. Danke's relationship with Fenster is a typical example of a relationship that has developed over the years in such a way that the partner firms can solve a number of problems together, just because they know each others' needs and capabilities so well. Consider also, for instance, the relationship between Danke and Bitte. After some years of intensive interaction in the relationship, Bitte terminated business between the two partners because Danke could no longer deliver in the way Bitte wanted. Even so, the development departments of the two firms continued to interact, because they were so familiar with each others' capabilities and needs. And they were so successful that some time later Bitte returned as a customer.

Second, two partner firms in a relationship learn certain skills that can be transferred to, and used in, other contexts. They may learn something useful about how to get in touch with new customers or various steps that can be taken to develop other relationships. This sort of thing can be regarded as a relationship-development experience. It is a type of experience likely to be useful when the firm develops relationships with other customers, in particular those who are in some way similar to the earlier ones. For instance, when Danke was developing its relationship with Bitte, it learnt how to develop relationships in a way that enabled it to start interacting with a number of foreign customers. In addition, its development department learnt some product-development skills that helped it to establish a relationship with Clean; a firm with needs similar to those of Bitte.

This relationship-development experience is also likely to be useful when a firm develops relationships with other firms that are connected with certain strategic relationships, that is to say relationships that are regarded as particularly critical. To the focal firm it is important to defend the strategic relationships, perhaps by developing and strengthening other relationships that support and protect them. For customers, such supporting relationships are most likely to be developed with suppliers. Thus, in order to handle the quality demands associated with a product developed for Bitte, Danke had to develop a relationship with another firm, Aspi, who could supply the necessary high-quality paper. In some cases, however, relationships with other customers or with customers associated with the focal customer, may also take on this role. Thus, Danke established a relationship with Bitte's US subsidiary to safeguard its relationship with Bitte.

Hence we can expect internationalization to be an outcome, first, of a firm developing its existing relationships and, second, of it establishing new relationships with customer firms that in some important respects resemble the customers with whom it already has successful relationships. Third, the internationalization of the firm arises from its development of relationships with customer firms linked to others with whom it is already working. There is nothing in the network model as such that says anything about the countries that this involves. The internationalization process of the business firm proceeds in much the same way as posited by the general internationalization process literature, but country markets are no longer meaningful entities (Chen et al. 2004).

Commitments are made to specific business firms whether they are customer firms, supplier firms, intermediary firms or other cooperating firms. It is also primarily a question of a gradual development of relationships in which the focal firm is already engaged. Also as posited in the internationalization process literature, the firms develop close interdependencies vis-à-vis their most important partners and are subsequently prepared to defend these relationships by increasing their commitment to the firms with which they are already doing business. They also tend to develop other relationships that can be expected to support these important relationships. They are thus engaged in building business network structures that surround and support their strategic relationships.

INTERNATIONALIZATION OR INTERNATIONAL NETWORK DEVELOPMENT

The greatest difference between the internationalization process approach and the network model concerns not the nature of the process itself but the empirical observations on which the internationalization process approach was initially based. Since country-specific barriers do not exist in the network world, the network model says nothing about the countries that firms will enter and expand in. And since the organization of operations according to the received view concerns operations in specific countries, we have no reason to expect firms to follow what is known as the establishment chain within specific countries, but all the more reason to expect firms to organize their business primarily in order to develop, support and coordinate relationships (Chen and Chen 1998). We also have reason to expect that the development of the organization proceeds in step with the development of important relationships, for instance to enhance relationship learning or to demonstrate commitment to various relationships. But this type of organizational development is not related to specific country markets. It is more likely to be related to particular strategic relationships and sets of connected network relationships. Danke, which is a foreign subsidiary of an MNC, has internationalized itself a lot by developing relationships with customers in other countries. Danke internationalized itself because its foreign relationships are closely connected with some of its strategic relationships, which are domestic. Although the parent company has a number of foreign subsidiaries that are basically organized around country markets, their operations do not correspond to specific countries.

We can also expect that a firm's commitments may be continuous, as a consequence of current interaction with specific partners, or discontinuous, following upon commitment decisions of various kinds. Acquisitions of other firms may be made, for instance, in order to secure critical relationships when these are threatened by competitors, or even in order to establish relationships with interesting customers or suppliers. Such acquisitions lead to discontinuous changes in the business firm's set of critical relationships, which may result in expansions that diverge from the patterns suggested by the internationalization process literature. Even so, subsequent development is influenced by current activity commitments within the framework of the new relationship structure. By acquiring a company, the firm thus becomes involved in a set of business relationships, and by way of its interaction in these relationships it gradually develops in response to the value generated by these relationships.

EXPERIENCE AND NETWORKS

The network model is simply a model with its own particular simplifying assumptions, just as the received international business view is based on its own specific assumptions. Studies of internationalization have suggested that two kinds of market experience can be distinguished, namely business experience and institutional experience (Eriksson et al. 1997). According to the network view, the firm's business experience consists of experience with which it is doing, or trying to do, business. Thus, this kind of experience is specific to the business network. Institutional experience concerns such things as laws, regulations and public or semi-public authorities that implement laws and regulations. Thus, institutional experience is country-specific, and refers to many of the factors that constitute the psychic distance between countries. The clear distinction between those two kinds of experience means that we can expect them to be developed in different ways and to induce different consequences.

Against this background it appears reasonable to combine the two models, assuming that there is one set of direct business-related managerial problems that are relationship-specific and another set of problems associated with country-specific institutional and cultural barriers. We refer to this combination henceforth as the network approach to internationalization.

Figure 5.3 combines Figures 5.1 and 5.2 in one figure embracing country

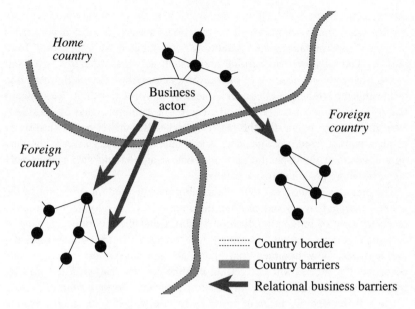

Figure 5.3   Foreign market entry from a combined approach

market barriers and network relationships. It shows two foreign country markets and one domestic country market bounded by institutional and cultural barriers, structured and connected by network relationships. The figure also shows that the focal business firm is engaged in relationships with two firms in one of the foreign countries but only indirectly with one firm in the other.

NETWORK RELATIONSHIP DEVELOPMENT IN INTERNATIONALIZATION

Looking first at foreign market entry we see a picture containing several paths to foreign market entry. In Figure 5.1 foreign market entry is a question of surmounting the barriers; in Figure 5.2 this was not an issue. Here we see patterns of connected network relationships both within country borders and between countries. However, it is important to recognize that no actor can actually 'see' such patterns in the real world. They are theoretical in the sense that the actor, like the observer, can know that they exist but not how the network is structured in the specific case. Each specific relationship is unique and composed of a variety of interdependencies and links that are very much a question of interpretations and intentions that can never be known except to the exchange partners. Thus, they are invisible to those who are not involved. Furthermore, the ways in which the relationships are connected are also a matter of interpretations and intentions and cannot be understood from outside. The only way of learning about such network structures is to start interacting with one or more of the network actors, thus provoking them into disclosing the strength and connectedness of their relationships. This means that foreign country market networks cannot be comprehended by outsiders, even if these are aware that the networks exist. But this is not a question of country market insider or outsider; it is a question of each actor's knowing only about their own specific network context and having vague ideas only about the more distant network patterns.

The picture also shows us that relationships can be used for surmounting the country market barriers and entering the country market. Moreover, while the received view of internationalization assumes that there is only one way of entering a country market – climbing over the barrier to the country market – the network view assumes that there are several points of entry and, consequently, several ways of getting into the country market. The firm may try to establish a relationship with a customer firm in a foreign country market. There will be several different firms to approach, and since each potential counterpart is unique and may require its own specific development process and can also be expected to trigger its own particular consequences, the decision to approach one rather than another is an important and difficult decision.

However, as noted in Chapter 2, the establishment and development of a relationship is never a result of unilateral action but requires bilateral or even multilateral interaction. Thus, the development of a relationship in a foreign market is a complex, uncertain and time-consuming process that may require strong commitment on the part of the entering firm.

But foreign market entry may equally well be the result of initiatives taken by an intermediary, a customer or a supplier in the foreign market, who is interested in developing a relationship with our focal firm. Thus, Bill's entry into the Danke market was a result of an initiative undertaken by Aspi, a complementary supplier of Bill. And Danke's entry into the US market was demanded by Bitte. Evidently, there are differences between firms with respect to their willingness to respond to initiatives taken by other firms, but studies seem to suggest that smaller firms are generally more inclined to be responsive.

Foreign market entries may also come about when a firm's partner requires the firm to accompany them abroad or is otherwise interested in extending their relationship to encompass business in foreign markets as well. This is frequently the case when the firm enjoys close relationships with firms that are in the process of internationalizing themselves. This has been observed particularly in connection with service firms (Majkgård and Sharma 1998). In this case, the foreign market entries are likely to occur in countries where the focal firm's customers are operating, rather than in countries with large markets or countries of a short psychic or cultural distance. Another consequence of such a client, or more often a partner, accompanying the focal firm is that the latter's internationalization may proceed fairly quickly.

While a qualitative difference between foreign market entry and foreign market expansion is assumed in the earlier internationalization models, the network approach to internationalization implies that the two phenomena are related to similar problems. Foreign market expansion is a question first of developing a firm's relationships in the specific market, second, of establishing and developing supporting relationships, and third, of developing relationships that are similar to, or connected with, the focal one. Although all this may be confined to one country market, it may equally well cross country borders and lead to entry into other foreign markets. In order to support a strategic relationship, the firm may be forced to develop a relationship in another country, thereby entering that country's market. Danke entered the US market. In that case the foreign market entry was a secondary issue in relation to foreign market expansion.

FOREIGN SUBSIDIARIES AND NETWORK DEVELOPMENT

Foreign subsidiaries are usually granted a central role in the internationalization of the firm – both in managerial practice and in the international business literature. According to the received view of internationalization, it is assumed that the foreign subsidiaries manage the development of operations in specific country markets. This may entail entry into the market as well as the expansion of operations in the market. In addition, it is frequently assumed that some subsidiaries provide information feedback from their markets to the parent firm.

In a network perspective we have to consider a different view of this role. A foreign subsidiary is engaged in a business network, and its role is rather to manage the development of this network. Thus, the role of the subsidiary is not necessarily confined to a specific country market. Even if its operations are focused initially on a specific country market, it can be expected – as the Danke case demonstrates – that the subsidiary also recognizes a need to develop relationships in other country markets, in particular if such relationships support the relationships that it considers being strategic. In such a case, it is engaged in international development of the kind that has been labeled 'internationalization of the second degree' (Forsgren et al. 1992).

When a subsidiary is created so as to manage – develop and coordinate – a set of business network relations in a specific country, these relations are also to some extent decoupled from those of the rest of the firm. The subsidiary's management is aware of problems in these relations and perceives the opportunities in and around them. Moreover, it gives up some control over its own operations to relationship partners. It becomes embedded in a business network, which may be primarily local but may equally well be technology-based or product-based. It also acquires a position, which is to some extent created in interaction with its relationship partners. Since the nature of the relationships cannot be understood by anyone except those involved they cannot even be understood by other parts of the firm organization.

This means that, in the internationalization process, the firm's various subsidiaries are largely decoupled from one another, and each subsidiary strives for the development of its own business network. Since each subsidiary sees problems and opportunities in its own business network, it will strive either for autonomy in relation to the rest of the company, or for the power to influence the development of other parts of the company in a way that supports the development of its own business network.

When firms develop relationships with each other, they also learn about each other's needs and capabilities. This is one of the powerful reasons for developing close relationships between supplier and customer firms. Such learning is an important element in technological development in general and product and process development specifically. Consequently, according to the network approach it can be expected that the foreign subsidiaries will be more engaged in technological development than they are according to the received view. While their role in the latter case is limited to market information-gathering, in the network view it entails knowledge-development. Moreover, this knowledge-development occurs in interaction with their relationship partners and, consequently, is influenced by their needs and capabilities. We can expect development to be linked to the development of the relationship partners within the business network. Thus, while the subsidiary's business is assumed according to the received view to be controlled by the parent firm, it can be expected according to the network approach to be influenced by partners in its business network.

SUMMARY

This chapter has compared the received theory of the internationalization process with a view of the same process using the network approach. One main difference concerns the role of country borders. In the first approach, the possibility and the difficulty of surmounting country borders in the shape of economic, institutional and cultural barriers, play an important part. In the second approach, barriers to internationalization are associated with the possibility of establishing and developing relationships with unique foreign customers and suppliers. In the extreme network case traditional country barriers are irrelevant.

One common prediction based on the received theory of internationalization is that firms organize themselves over time in a foreign country in accordance with what is known as the establishment chain. In the network approach, instead, firms organize their foreign business primarily in order to support, develop and coordinate business relationships. Whether this means that the firm starts with indirect export to a certain country and ends up with a fully-fledged subsidiary in that country is much more difficult to predict, and is anyway perhaps a less relevant issue. The forms chosen by the firm reflect the development of the specific network in which the firm is embedded rather than the development of its knowledge about the country barriers. This leads to forms that are both more variable and less predictable over time than the received theory suggests. There is also relatively less interest in analysing forms in terms of entry modes, as is a common feature in the international business literature, because the focus is now on development of the focal firm's specific business relationships before and after the entry rather than on the entry as such.

However, we have also noted some basic similarities between the internationalization process model and the network approach with regards to the way firms go abroad. The main similarity is that both models emphasize the interplay between current activities, experiential knowledge and commitments undertaken by the firm. These similarities explain the well-known, empirically based, incremental character of the internationalization process. In this respect the process view of internationalization is the same in both models. What differs is the context in which the firm is supposed to do business. In the first model this context is primarily *countries*. In the second model it is primarily *a network of specific business relationships*, in which geography – in the shape of countries – is of secondary importance.

Adopting a network approach to the internationalization of firms, we will in the remaining chapters focus on one particular manifestation of internationalization: the MNC. In the next chapter we discuss different dimensions of internationalization in relation to the MNC, while Chapter 7 is devoted to the role of the subsidiary in such corporations.

PART II

Introducing the Embedded Multinational

6. Three dimensions of internationalization

The underlying theme of this book is that business relationships and networks of relationships are crucially important to the management and development of the multinational firm. Chapters 3 and 4 thus analysed the development of business relationships and the business network in our case-study firm, Danke. The development of Danke's network even included business relationships across borders. In Chapter 5 we looked at internationalization from our business network perspective. In Chapters 6 and Chapter 7 the focus shifts more specifically to the MNC, which is an organization that includes business firms in at least two countries. In Chapter 6 we discuss three dimensions of internationalization of the MNC: internationalization through extended ownership, external business networks, or corporate networks. These dimensions are illustrated by the development of Danke's parent company Aspa.

THE MULTINATIONAL CORPORATION IN A NETWORK SETTING

In Chapter 2 we defined three concepts: the business firm, business relationships and business networks. With these in mind we further proposed that defining the operations of a business firm as 'international' is a matter of perspective. A business firm may, in itself, be rooted in a particular country. But the important business relationships that constitute its business network may be more or less international, in the sense of cutting across country borders. As the network of a business firm is a subjectively defined phenomenon without distinct limits, it is impossible to draw a definite line between networks that are international and those that are not. Even if a firm's direct relationships are within one country, important connected relationships may well be international. Whether or not a business firm is international is a matter of perspective. But one conclusion is obvious: the more the firm's business network extends to business actors in other countries, the more it regards its operations as 'international'.

In this chapter we focus on the MNC. We view the MNC as an administrative/legal unit that includes several business firms, subsidiaries, located in at least two countries. Thus since each subsidiary is embedded in a specific network of business relationships, more or less distinct from the networks of other subsidiaries, this means that the MNC is related to many different networks at once. It also means that an MNC can be defined as more – or less – international, depending on the dimension of internationalization that we choose to focus on. In this chapter we distinguish three basic dimensions. The first one is traditional and concerns the ownership structure of the MNC. The second refers to the internationalization of the external network at the subsidiary level, while the third concerns the integration of the business network within the MNC across country borders. The last two dimensions are important when it comes to understanding and explaining the problems and possibilities involved in managing and developing the multinational.

INTERNATIONALIZATION THROUGH OWNERSHIP ACROSS COUNTRY BORDERS

An MNC can raise its level of internationalization by shifting its legal boundaries to encompass sub-units in several countries. This can be achieved by making greenfield investments in countries other than the home country, or by acquiring local firms in such countries. The international dimension is primarily a question of the share of operations *located in* foreign countries, rather than the volume of operations that cut *across* country borders. This dimension of internationalization is commonly expressed as the percentage of employment, production or investments abroad. It is illustrated in Figure 6.1. The figure emphasizes the ownership dimension with three bold arrows, while other dimensions of the network are indicated by dotted lines. They will be highlighted subsequently in Figures 6.2 and 6.3.

A fundamental feature of this form of internationalization is that it does not change the basic structure of the business relationships in which the MNC units are embedded. For instance, by acquiring a local company in a foreign country an MNC increases its degree of internationalization overnight, even though the business is as local as before. As the MNC has extended its operations to more countries and has a new sub-unit to manage at a distance, no one would deny that it has increased its degree of internationalization. But if we focus on the actors, resources and activities at the business relationship

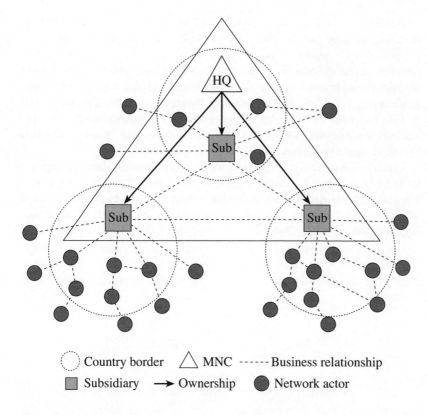

Figure 6.1   *Internationalization through extending ownership across borders*

level nothing has changed. So apparently we can talk about different degrees of internationalization at the corporate level and at the subsidiary level in an MNC, depending on which aspect we look at.

INTERNATIONALIZATION OF THE SUBSIDIARY'S EXTERNAL BUSINESS NETWORK

Apart from extending the geographical range of ownership, a change in the business network in which an MNC subsidiary is embedded can also raise the level of internationalization. This may be a result of the sub-units becoming more international in their external market exchanges, perhaps by exporting to or importing from a third country – a process that has been referred to elsewhere as internationalization of the second degree (Forsgren et al. 1992).

A crucial point of the model described in Chapter 2, though, is that the sub-units' operations can become more international as market exchange is developed with actors in other countries, so that the transactions in the business network acquire a more interdependent, cooperative, socially interactive and trustful character. In other words, the exchange recasts itself in a relationship mold through intensifying the transactions with business actors on the other side of the country border. We call this 'internationalization of the subsidiary's external business network'. This dimension of internationalization is illustrated in Figure 6.2.

The MNC has obviously become more international without changing its ownership structure. A typical path to internationalization among some Swedish companies in the engineering industry has consisted of gradually developing the role of the foreign subsidaries from that of local sales organizations to fully-fledged units with their own production, product

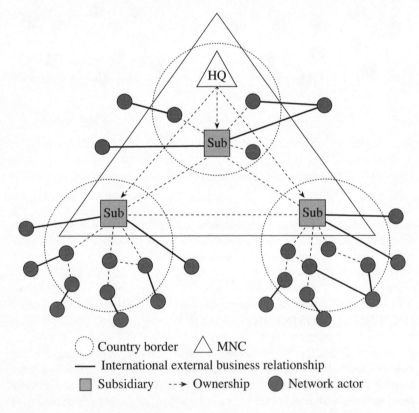

*Figure 6.2   Internationalization of the subsidiary's external business
            network*

development and export. This means that the subsidiaries themselves gradually become more involved in business networks with business actors beyond the local country borders.

It should be noted that this form of internationalization contains both a geographical and a business dimension. By opening up exchange with new partners abroad the internationalization of the subsidiary is reinforced, with visible increases in export or import as a result. However, even if the counterparts remain the same, any transformation of the exchanges into long-lasting relationships with more mutual adaptation of resources, etc, will also imply an increase in internationalization, since the foreign business actors will have become more prominent in the subsidiary's business network. This network can also become more international as a result of new cross-border exchanges among connected business relationships. For instance, if one of the subsidiary's important suppliers establishes a business relationship with a subcontractor in a third country, the subsidiary's own business network has simultaneously become more international. The difference between the subsidiary networks in Figures 6.1 and 6.2 illustrates this point.

INTERNATIONALIZATION THROUGH THE CORPORATE BUSINESS NETWORK

There is also a third path to MNC internationalization. Without any change occurring in the ownership structure or in the subsidiary's external business network, the MNC can raise its level of internationalization by developing the cross-border exchange among its subsidiaries. Or, to put another way, the sister companies become more dominant actors in a subsidiary's business network.

This third type of internationalization is a special aspect of the fact that business networks of the MNC subsidiaries are themselves becoming more international. This time, the extended internationalization of the networks includes sister companies, that is to say there is greater operational integration within the MNC. When the Swedish ball-bearing company, SKF, introduced a production rationalization among its European subsidiaries, the flow of goods and knowledge between the different subsidiaries increased. SKF thus became more international as a result of an increase in business relationships at the subsidiary level across borders but *inside* the MNC. This form of internationalization is illustrated in Figure 6.3.

In some ways this type of internationalization has a certain resemblance with the 'transnational solution' suggested by Bartlett and Ghoshal (1989). However, our conceptualization differs from the transnational solution on two points. First, the latter form is primarily a special form of organization

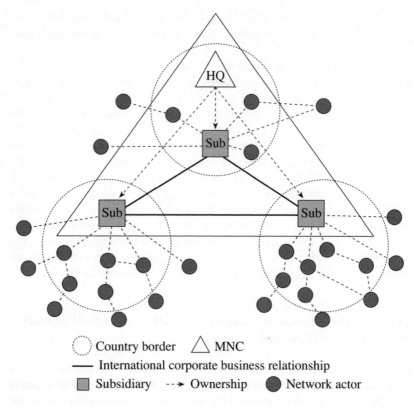

Figure 6.3   Internationalization through the corporate business network

implemented by HQ to solve the conflict between the need for local responsiveness and the need for global integration. Links between the subsidiaries in terms of communication are at the crux of this form. The 'firm as a brain' metaphor has therefore been used in connection with the transnational solution (Hedlund, 1986). In our view, though, important links between subsidiaries exist to the extent that their business networks coincide. The emphasis is on business relationships between subsidiaries, not on their administrative or communication linkages. The more the business relationships between subsidiaries cut across country borders the more internationalized is the MNC.

Second, internationalization 'within' the corporation can also be caused by business links between sister units being developed into longer-lasting and more stable relationships, with more resource adaptations between the sisters, etc. as a result. This is the equivalent of the internationalization through the subsidiaries' external business relationships that was described above.

We will now take the development of Aspa, an MNC in the forest industry, to illustrate the three dimensions of internationalization. We will describe how Aspa became international as a result of its acquisitions of Danke and other subsidiaries in different countries. We then investigate the internationalization of Aspa in terms of the shape of the external business networks and corporate business networks of its subsidiaries.

ASPA'S FOREIGN EXPANSION

Aspa, a Swedish forest company, was founded in 1960. Its business was to manufacture and sell pulp, paper and paper-based products. One such product was kraftliner, which was manufactured in northern Sweden by Aspa's subsidiary Aspi (see Chapter 3). During the 1960s the kraftliner was sold as input to Swedish, European and US manufacturers of corrugated board and boxes. Aspa thus became an international firm based on Aspi's export, which was steadily increasing. But, as the corporation consisted of a few operative units, all of them located in Sweden, it was by no means an MNC.

A prevailing idea in Aspa – and in the forest industry in general – was to create scale economies and to secure the outlets for its home-based production, something that was especially important during business recessions. In the early 1960s, Aspa's top managers therefore studied the behavior of the highly developed American forest companies. They found that many of them practised forward vertical integration, i.e. they had established or acquired foreign companies that bought the kraftliner (or testliner) from which corrugated board and boxes were manufactured. For Aspi's kraftliner production this development would, in particular, promote better long-term scale economies, so the Aspa corporate HQ made a strategic decision, namely to start expanding through the acquisition of national and foreign kraftliner customers.

A complicating factor here was that for some years Swedish and international competitors had been using a similar strategy, which meant that Aspa was competing with other companies that were all looking for vertical forward integration. But in 1967 Aspa finally acquired a Swedish manufacturer of corrugated board and boxes. Although this company was relatively large compared with similar European companies, as a single corporate customer it was quite unable to buy an adequate share of Aspi's kraftliner production. Consequently this was only the first step in Aspa's expansion. Figure 6.4 illustrates Aspa with the two subsidiaries – Aspi, the kraftliner producer, and the Swedish manufaturer of corrugated board and boxes. Apart from their inter-subsidiary business, both these units made further sales to national and foreign customers.

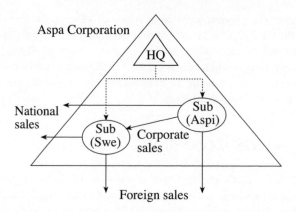

Figure 6.4   The original Aspa corporation

The First Investments Abroad

After the acquisition in Sweden, Aspa started to investigate the possibility of foreign investments. At that time there were basically two factors guiding the Aspa HQ in their search for target companies. One was connected with Sweden's membership of EFTA (European Free Trade Association), which meant that acquisitions in fellow-EFTA countries would give Aspi's kraftliner exports an exemption from duty not enjoyed by its competitors located outside EFTA. Another important factor was that the price level of paper-board and boxes in the target country must be acceptably high, since otherwise the benefits from integrating the customers with the corporate supply of kraftliner would be insufficient. In 1976, taking these considerations into account, Aspa decided to acquire a Swiss customer.

In that same year Aspa also bought Danke (see Chapter 3), which was not located in an EFTA country but which nonetheless had a high average price level for its products due to its oligopolistic situation and its specialization on 'quality boxes'. Danke was also interesting since, by European standards, it was potentially a relatively large customer for kraftliner.

A common feature of the two foreign acquisitions was that they had all been family-owned. The managers of these subsidiaries had long experience of the packaging business and were well-known in their respective markets. Aspa's next two acquisitions (England S and England B) in 1977 and 1979 were in the same situation, but were smaller companies.

In a retrospective analysis a former Aspa manager sees these four acquisitions in the 1970s as successful:

> Since all these companies were profitable and deeply engaged in their markets, we let them continue as independent companies. But we were represented on

their executive committees and ensured that they bought a part of their input from Aspi.

However, it was not always easy to grant autonomy in certain activities such as sales and development, while at the same time trying to ensure that the subsidiaries achieved a certain level of corporate purchasing. In fact, the subsidiaries found it difficult to prioritize the corporate benefits, as they were more interested in sustaining their local business, especially in times of recession when prices fell and kraftliner from Aspi was relatively expensive. This certainly applied to the companies in England (England B and England S).

Further Expansion

Aspa's acquisitions were rather expensive, but the economic prosperity during the second half of the 1970s helped to finance them. However, it took another five years before the next company was bought, in 1984. This one was in Germany (Germany K), and it was followed by a second German company (Germany L) in 1985. Unlike the former acquisitions, these companies had been owned and managed by large US MNCs that were not primarily involved in the forest industry.

As a result of the keen competition and the low prices in the German market, these subsidiaries – especially Germany L – had developed considerable efficiency in the production of brown boxes. This was appreciated by Aspa, but it also involved problems as the focus on producing low-price brown boxes essentially entailed buying testliner from low-price suppliers. Consequently, the integration with the large exports of high-quality kraftliner from Aspi to Germany L had its limitations.

The next acquisition, in 1986, was another company in England, England T. As in the German cases, this company was owned and managed by a large US MNC. England T was large and relatively efficient, and was producing various board and box qualities, but profitability was still a problem. The reason was that most of its box production was delivered as packaging material to other units within the US corporation. This meant low prices, even though prices were relatively high in the external market. Shortly after the acquisition, Aspa HQ realized that it would be difficult to generate substantial economic benefits from integrating with Aspi, unless England T concentrated on the local and more profitable market. This was successively realized, but it was not an easy process; it meant establishing a new market position, which among other things involved developing business relationships with local customers and suppliers. However, England T was interested in integrating with the Aspa corporation, since Aspa was a company with a long tradition in the forest industry and Aspi was regarded as a reliable supplier. Thus England T saw the possibility of a long-term solution to its market problem. This interest, in combination with the substantial size of England T, made Aspa HQ assign to England T a formal responsibility for developing corporate products and a regional responsibility for the business development in England.

As three English subsidiaries were now incorporated, Aspa HQ started trying to get them to cooperate around similar activities on the purchasing, sales and development sides. But a complicating factor here was that these companies had once been competitors and had different business backgrounds and management cultures. Besides, the managers in England B and England S were not as enthusiastic as those in England T about being integrated with Aspa. But as England T was the largest unit, Aspa HQ expected it to assume responsibility for these 'regional' matters and to solve them without too much trouble. This was a 'semi-HQ role' which England T was not enthusiastic about, since it led to friction in their relations with their English sister companies.

With these experiencies in mind, Aspa went on searching for further acquisitions. It was evident that it was difficult to evaluate successful acquisitions in advance and that size, efficiency and market prices were not necessarily the main issues in deciding which companies to buy. It also seemed very important to evaluate the intensity and the character of activities in the companies' business relationships in their local markets. Thus, by no longer relying exclusively on price level and duty-free exports, Aspa deliberately started looking for traditional family-owned companies that enjoyed close contact with local market customers, although this meant a risk of acquiring companies with little interest in being acquired and integrated. On this basis a company in Italy and one in Belgium were acquired in 1989. These companies were not very large but they were profitable and had a good reputation as regards product development, a feature that fitted well with the idea of integration with Aspi. Also, by removing a subsidiary top manager shortly after the acquisitions, Aspa HQ avoided much of the resistance to integration that had faced them in their English acquisitions.

ASPA'S INTERNATIONALIZATION THROUGH EXTENDED OWNERSHIP

Overall, following the initial acquisition of the Swedish box and board company, another nine foreign companies had been acquired in the course of 14 years. Table 6.1 illustrates the internationalization of Aspa from what we can call 'a traditional perspective', i.e. the share of an MNC's business that is conducted by subsidiaries abroad, usually measured in number of employees or sales volume. The figures show that in 1991 the two Swedish-based units accounted for 27.5 percent of Aspa's employees while the nine foreign subsidiaries accounted for 72.5 percent, which according to a traditional view implies a high level of internationalization. It should be noted that among the foreign subsidiaries two enjoyed a certain dominance, namely Danke and England T, which accounted for 20.8 and 22.7 percent of Aspa's employees respectively. The rest accounted for between 2.9 to 5.5 percent each.

Table 6.1   Aspa's internationalization in terms of ownership – foreign subsidiary employees

Year of acquisition/ establishment	ASPA subsidiaries – Sweden and abroad	Employees in 1991	
		(No.)	(%)
	Swedish based units		
	Corporate supplier of kraftliner		
1960	Aspi	820	15.5
	Producer of board and boxes		
1967	Sweden	636	12.0
	Foreign based units		
	Producers of board and boxes		
1976	Switzerland	170	3.2
1976	Danke	1100	20.8
1977	England S	290	5.5
1979	England B	231	4.4
1984	Germany K	152	2.9
1985	Germany L	220	4.2
1986	England T	1200	22.7
1989	Italy	270	5.1
1989	Belgium	200	3.8
	Total	5289	100.0

INTERNATIONALIZATION THROUGH THE SUBSIDIARIES' EXTERNAL BUSINESS AND CORPORATE NETWORKS

As we have seen above, a large share of Aspa's business is located abroad, which means that from the point of view of ownership the company is highly internationalized. But what does the degree of internationalization look like if we consider external business relationships at the subsidiary level?

A first indicator of this form of internationalization is the extent to which the individual subsidiaries are embedded in external business networks that include business actors in countries other than the local country. Table 6.2 (second column) gives every subsidiary's volume of export and import outside the Aspa Corporation thus reflecting the share of internationalization among subsidiaries at the end of the period described above.

Table 6.2   Average internationalization (export and import) for every subsidiary in Aspa

Aspa subsidiaries	External internationalization (%)	Corporate internationalization (%)
Aspi	5	35
Sweden	1	1
Switzerland	9	20
Danke	20	21
England S	10	18
England B	7	20
Germany K	1	0
Germany L	12	16
England T	15	20
Italy	16	10
Belgium	16	15
Average (excl. Aspi)	10.7	14.1
Average (incl. Aspi)	10.2	16.0

The table reveals that the average level of internationalization in terms of external business networks at the subsidiary level varies between 20 per cent (Danke) and 1 per cent (Germany K), with an unweighted average for the group of around 10 percent. Aspa's level of internationalization is thus far lower, when judged by this criterion rather than in terms of ownership internationalization, which suggested a 72.5 percent degree of internationalization. Thus, if we look at external business relationships, Aspa's business appears relatively local, even though a substantial part of its operations are located outside the parent company's home country. It should be pointed out, though, that we are probably underestimating the degree of internationalization since we know that a subsidiary's connected relationships can cut cross borders. Unfortunately we have no data that can help us to adjust for this.

It should also be stressed that the degree of internationalization through external business networks also rises, if business exchange with foreign actors becomes more intensified. This was illustrated by the successive intensification of Danke's relationships with foreign customers and suppliers, as described in Chapter 4.

Table 6.2 also gives the figures for the subsidiaries at the end of the period as regards corporate networking across borders, referred to here as 'corporate internationalization' (third column). As in the case of external business networking the degree of internationalization through the corporate network varies among the subsidiaries – here from 35 percent (Aspi) to 0 percent. The unweighted average is 16 percent (14 percent if Aspi is excluded). Aspa thus appears somewhat more international if its internationalization is defined in terms of the corporate business network than if the subsidiaries' external business network is applied as a criterion.

Perhaps the most striking feature, however, is the considerable variance in terms of internationalization through both external business networks and corporate business networks at the subsidiary level. Figure 6.5 demonstrates the differences in the degree of internationalization among the subsidiaries according to both these dimensions.

As can be seen Danke and England T are far above average in both dimensions (corresponding to 10–20 percent), while Sweden and Germany (K) are in the opposite corner with hardly any export/import at all. Aspi's degree of internationalization depends primarily on its role as a supplier of

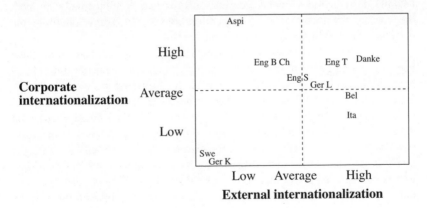

Figure 6.5   *External and corporate internationalization – subsidiary variations*

kraftliner to sister units, while the Italian subsidiary is above all an exporting unit with few business relationships with any sister units.

The figure reveals a high degree of variance in terms of internationalization among Aspa's sub-units. It thus seems somewhat inappropriate to talk about Aspa's degree of internaionalization in general terms, at least if we are viewing it in terms of business relationships. The company includes some units that are completely independent of other country markets and of sister units in other countries. But in other cases about one-fifth of a unit's business cut across country borders. And these are all units in an MNC that has more than 70 percent of its employees abroad!

SUMMARY

This chapter has focused on the concept of internationalization and especially on an MNC's level of internationalization. We have suggested that the application of a business network perspective to the MNC produces a more discerning concept of internationalization. Traditionally, the degree of internationalization is measured as the share of operations to be found abroad, expressed by employment, sales, production or investment. However, if the focus is instead on business networks, a different picture may emerge. First, one important aspect of internationalization concerns the extent to which important business relationships cut across country borders. Second, an MNC consists of sub-units that may differ regarding the level of internationalization expressed in these terms. To define an MNC's degree of internationlization in general terms may therefore be inappropriate. Third, as a firm's business network also includes connected relationships and is subjectively defined, there are no distinct limits, and it is therefore impossible to draw a definite line between contexts in terms of internationalization.

Despite these difficulties, two models of MNC internationalization have been suggested here, in addition to the more traditional concept, referred to here as 'internationalization through extending ownership across borders'. These two models take account of the extent to which the different sub-units' business relationships cut across country borders. The first model focuses on the location of important business actors in the subsidiary's business network, and has been labeled here 'internationalization of the subsidiary's external business network'. The second one is built on a similar logic but considers whether or not the subsidiary has business relationships with sister units in other countries. This model is referred to as 'internationalization through the corporate business network'.

These three ways of conceptualizing an MNC's level of internationalization has been illustrated by the case of Aspa, the parent company of Danke, and eleven other subsidiaries. The data demonstrates that Aspa's level of internationalization differs considerably depending on which conceptualization is used. Further, it shows that if the different business-network-related concepts are used, the degree of internationalization can vary quite a lot at the subsidiary level. To talk about an MNC's degree of interntionalization can therefore be misleading, or at least to be indicating only part of the truth.

Once again, we would like to emphasize that the present chapter's illustration of the different dimensions of internationalization is not only a statistical exercise. Our aim has been to build a platform for a clearer understanding of the problems and possibilities involved in seeking to comprehend and explain the development and management of MNCs.

The subsidiary's business relationships with other *specific* business actors have been an important element in the above analysis. In the subsequent chapters we address the concept of network embeddedness in greater depth. In Chapter 7 we introduce this book's leading actor, the Embedded Multinational. In Chapter 8 we illustrate and measure the level of network embeddedness among 98 subsidiaries in Swedish multinationals.

7.   The Embedded Multinational

In Chapter 6 we introduced the MNC as an organization consisting of several business actors with their own business networks. In Chapter 7 we continue on the same track by introducing and defining the Embedded Multinational. A special feature of the Embedded Multinational is the dual role of the individual subsidiaries, depending on the business network context and the corporate context to which they each simultaneously belong. This feature, in its turn, has a profound impact on the behavior of the MNC. The case-study firm, Danke, once again provides an illustrative example for discussion. It demonstrates how an MNC subsidiary handles the conflict between the two contexts. It shows how the subsidiary strives for influence over a product development process, and in doing so succeeds in modifying both the corporate context and the business network context.

THE HETEROGENEOUS MNC

In Chapters 5 and 6 we laid the foundation for applying a business network view to an MNC. This conceptualization endows the MNC with a somewhat heterogeneous character. First, the different sub-units (subsidiaries) are embedded in unique business networks encompassing other business actors inside and outside the organization. Second, differences in culture, institutional characteristics, language, etc. between the environments of the subsidiaries add to the heterogeneity of the group as a whole. Third, the actual boundaries between the MNC and the environment are diffuse.

Firms are open systems, in that they influence and are influenced by the environment. But implicit in this view, irrespective of how the environment is defined, is that the legal status constitutes the borderline. A unit belongs to an MNC if the latter (through its parent company or a sister company) owns a certain part, often more than 50 percent, of the unit's share capital. It is then a legal part of the firm and consolidated in the group. Thus, when we say that an MNC has twenty-five companies all over the world, we are normally referring to companies in which the corporation, directly or indirectly, owns more than 50 percent.

But what if the corporation owns 40, 30 or even 20 percent of the capital in those companies? It is interesting to note that many MNCs define units like these as associated companies, meaning that they can be viewed as a part of the firm in an operational sense. So, apparently, a unit can be viewed as belonging to and as not belonging to a certain MNC – it all depends on the perspective. On the one hand, the more we stress the operational dependencies between a unit and its corporation the more inclined we are, in business or operational terms, to include it in the same entity as the corporation itself. In principle, there is no lowest level of ownership that disallows such a view. On the other hand, 100 percent ownership does not automatically mean that the unit is integrated with the rest of the MNC in an operational sense.

Therefore, we can conclude that the borderline between what we call the environment and what we call the MNC is both arbitrary and vague, and that it depends on the perspective applied. For practical reasons, though, most definitions of MNCs are based on legal rather than operational attributes. This means that a business firm belongs to an MNC if it is defined as a subsidiary in the corporation's official reports.

THE EMBEDDED MULTINATIONAL

The vague nature of the borderline between the MNC and its environment also becomes apparent if we try to define the environment from a subsidiary's point of view. Essentially the subsidiary has two distinctive environments. The first of these is legal and administrative. The subsidiary is a part of that environment because it is connected with rest of the MNC through ownership and administrative systems. The connections can also include business linkages with other units of the MNC, similar to those between independent firms. This gives the subsidiary its corporate context and reflects the MNC HQ's desire to organize the activities of the subsidiary and its sister units in a specific way. Different groups within the corporation seek to influence the behavior of the subsidiary through its corporate context. It is reasonable to assume that one of the most important actors in this context is the MNC HQ itself, which strives to shape the subsidiary's activities in accordance with an overall strategy.

The subsidiary's second environment is its business network. This network has developed successively, together with the subsidiary's role and position within the network concerned. The different actors are connected with one another through business activities rather than administrative or legal links.

We call this environment the 'business network context'. Unlike the corporate context, it is more difficult this time to distinguish a specific actor seeking to shape the network in accordance with its own interests. However, the subsidiary's behavior influences and is influenced by the interests and activities of other business network actors.

The two subsidiary environments are illustrated in Figures 7.1 and 7.2. which show the MNC is linked to various business network contexts through its subsidiaries in different countries (A and B). The administrative links between the subsidiary and other corporate units within the legal frame of the corporation constitute the corporate context of the subsidiary. But the figures also show how the business network and corporate contexts of a subsidiary overlap to a greater or lesser extent, if other corporate units are actors in the focal subsidiary's network, as in the case of subsidiaries A and B. The extent to which the focal subsidiary's corporate and business network contexts overlap also reflects its position as a unit within the MNC. At one extreme, the subsidiary's business network does not include other units within the MNC, i.e., the contexts overlap only via the focal subsidiary itself. At the other extreme, the overlap is complete, which means that all the actors in the subsidiary's business network are also its sister units.

In view of this dual character of the individual subsidiary's environment, i.e. its corporate and business network contexts – the question as to where we

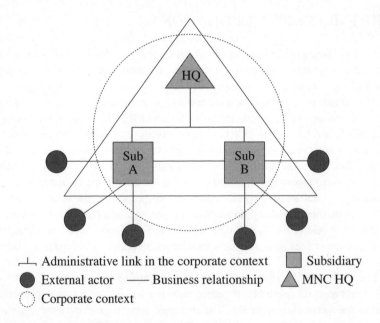

Figure 7.1 The subsidiary corporate context

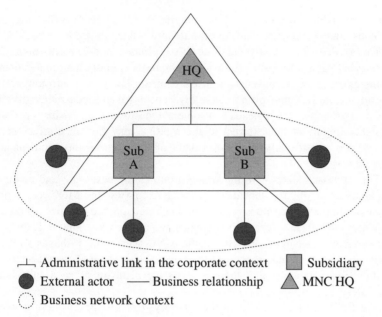

—⊥ Administrative link in the corporate context   ▣ Subsidiary
● External actor   —— Business relationship   ▲ MNC HQ
⚬ Business network context

Figure 7.2   The subsidiary business network context

should start our analysis of a specific subsidiary and its position becomes essentially an empirical one. We can, for instance, start by estimating the character of the business network in which the subsidiaries are *embedded*. Crucial questions then concern the specification of the most important suppliers, customers and other business partners in terms of flows of goods, services and knowledge, and the identification of other relationships in which the subsidiary is involved, for instance with competitors, regulatory agencies or research institutions. These questions focus on the business network context of the subsidiary and its position within that context.

The second step would be to estimate the extent to which the other companies in a subsidiary's business network also belong to the same corporate context, that is to say whether they are sister units of the focal subsidiary. This step will show whether any particular business relationship within the subsidiary's business network is 'reinforced' by an administrative/ legal connection. What we actually do is to lay a pattern of legal and administrative relationships over a pattern of business relationships to see how far the former 'covers' the latter.

In the business network approach to analysing the overall structure of an MNC the point of departure is the business network in which the subsidiary is embedded. The extent to which this pattern also coincides with legal and administrative linkages between the subsidiaries is then explored. An opposite but more traditional way is to start from the MNC as a legal entity, and then to investigate whether the subsidiaries are also related on the business side.

This second way of analysing things is so common that we hardly notice the underlying perspective, namely that the emphasis is on the corporate context at the expense of the business network context. The actors surrounding the subsidiary are selected on administrative and legal grounds rather than on business grounds, which means that some of the subsidiary's business partners – highly important but external to the MNC – may find themselves being treated too superficially, simply as parts of the external environment in a general way.

This approach starts with the whole group as the basic unit and assumes, explicitly or implicitly, that it is constructive to view the MNC as a single strategic unit, albeit composed of several sub-units. Since the focus is on one strategy rather than several sub-strategies, the implicit assumption is that one particular unit – namely the HQ of the MNC – essentially shapes strategic behavior. The issue thus concerns the strategic behavior of General Electric or Philips, for instance, rather than the strategic behavior of each subsidiary, separately.

The first approach above, on the contrary, stresses the business network context of the individual subsidiary. It is the heterogeneous character of the MNC that is emphasized. The subsidiaries are more or less loosely coupled, and are greatly influenced by their business network contexts, irrespective of whether other actors in that network are located inside or outside the MNC. From the individual subsidiary's point of view there is a corporate context, just as there is according to the other approach, but this time it is only part of the picture. More important, perhaps, is the business network context surrounding the individual subsidiary, which has a profound impact on the subsidiary's behavior. This impact may or may not accord with the intentions of the corporate context. This last issue is an important feature of the embedded MNC.

To summarize, this book is based on the assumption that business relationships are essential attributes of the activities of the individual subsidiary and of the MNC as a whole. As illustrated in Chapters 2–5, exchange between business actors often requires investment in relation-specific facilities on both sides. Such investments take time to develop and they evolve as trust gradually builds up between the actors. Such exchanges, therefore, develop into close relationships that differ from arm's-length relations in that they are more difficult to replace, at least in the short term. We call these relationships 'embedded' relationships (Uzzi 1997). Now and then the results of such a development, i.e. new technology or business procedures, are important to exchange in other relationships. We firmly believe that relationship embeddedness and the connectedness between relationships are fundamental attributes of the long-term development of the MNC. Through their role as 'business relationship managers' certain subsidiaries come to occupy a crucial role in this type of development. The concept of the Embedded Multinational thus signifies an MNC whose subsidiaries operate in business networks that, to a notable extent, are characterized by a high level of embeddedness among the relationship actors. The Embedded Multinational is illustrated in Figure 7.3.

The configuration of a business network is specific to each individual subsidiary. First, some subsidiaries may be embedded in relationships that are both external and internal vis-à-vis the MNC, as in the case of subsidiary A, while other subsidiaries like subsidiary B have external business relationships only. Thus we can distinguish between external and corporate embeddedness. Second, individual business relationships can range from arm's-length exchange to a high degree of mutual adaptation of resources and activities, that is to a high degree of embeddedness. A subsidiary may be dominated by

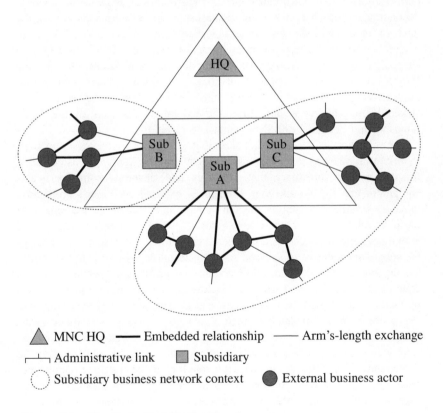

Figure 7.3   The Embedded Multinational

highly embedded relationships – external, internal or both. Other subsidiaries, in contrast, may only have relationships consisting of arm's-length exchanges – external, internal or both. Since every relationship has its own specific characteristics and history, we would expect to find a high degree of variation as regards embeddedness both within the individual subsidiary and between the different subsidiaries in an MNC. Nonetheless, we claim that the overall degree of a subsidiary's embeddedness provides a useful characterization of that subsidiary's business network. But more about this in Chapter 8.

THE DUAL ROLE OF THE SUBSIDIARY IN THE EMBEDDED MNC

At the subsidiary level we can expect to find some tension between the role of the subsidiary as defined by its position in its business network and its role as defined by HQ in the corporate context. The strength of this tension can vary, depending on the character of the relationships in both contexts and on the interests of the various stakeholders. The interests of the actors – be it an external customer, for instance, or an internal supplier or a divisional HQ – are shaped by the immediate context surrounding the actor rather than by the 'larger' context. It is a question of context rationality rather than overall rationality and there is endless bargaining for influence among the different stakeholders. This view underlines the federative character of the MNC (Ghoshal and Bartlett 1990; Birkinshaw and Hood 1998).

The subsidiary is itself a stakeholder that can use its business relationships to influence, among other things, behavior within the MNC. Let us consider, for instance, a subsidiary that produces and develops some particular equipment that is sold and then used in an external customer's production process. Assume, too, that the subsidiary and the customer share a long-term business relationship based on cooperation in technical matters associated with the equipment exchanged between them. Mutual interests in the shape of the subsidiary's desire to sell and generate technological knowledge and by the customer's desire to develop and use efficient and specially adapted equipment, bring the two parties into a close business relationship. They meet frequently and solve mutual problems. But the subsidiary's relationship with the customer is not isolated from its business exchange with other firms. Assume also that the subsidiary constantly interacts with an internal supplier, from whom it buys an important component that it uses in manufacturing the equipment. Hence, changes in product technology in the customer relationship must run together with improvements in the component produced by the supplier. Furthermore, this specific customer is regarded by both the subsidiary and the internal supplier as a large and important buyer. And since the supplier delivers components on a world-wide basis to several other sub-units within the MNC, the improved component quality may be introduced into the customer relationships of other subsidiaries, becoming crucial to the whole firm. This example illustrates how an individual subsidiary can exert influence on other parts of the MNC through its business relationships.

Thus, against the MNC HQ's search for coordination within the group, we can set the subsidiaries' involvement in business activities based on successive and reciprocal adaptations to its various business partners. A subsidiary may desire greater autonomy and influence in order to pursue interests based on the local rationality in its particular business network, although this may not necessarily accord with HQ's interests. Bargaining and conflicts are natural ingredients in the organizational life of the MNC. Changes at the subsidiary business network context and corporate context levels mean that a final consensus on goals and overall strategies between the different subsidiaries and the HQ will hardly ever be reached in an MNC. And the different stakeholders all try to pursue their own interests with the help of the resources under their control. Some of these resources may be acquired due to hierarchical position, to a capacity to tap resources from the environment, or to a position in relevant business networks (Astley and Sachdewa 1984). As implied in Figure 7.3, there may be a tension between the subsidiary corporate role and the business network role. To the extent that the HQ is eager to design a subsidiary role in the corporate context that differs from the requirements of the subsidiary's business network context, the subsidiary will find itself in a never-ending bargaining situation. This may be a very likely case, assuming that the MNC consists of several subsidiaries that are embedded in specific business network contexts. This is problematic in the research context, but it is also what makes the study of MNC behavior so fascinating, as well as complex. However, the tension in the subsidiary's dual role may not always be marked. For instance, if HQ is not too concerned about defining roles and integrating the MNC subsidiaries, any tension arising from high business network embeddedness is likely to have less impact on the development of the subsidiaries' roles. Or again, if the level of business network embeddedness among the subsidiaries is low, HQ's definitions of roles within the MNC are likely to create less tension.

In the next section we illustrate these processes in the Embedded MNC by looking into the Aspa case, familiar to the reader from the previous chapter.

SUBSIDIARY ROLES WITHIN ASPA

The Aspa subsidiaries differ in their business experiences and competencies. In some cases they have a history of being active in product development and special customer applications (e.g. Danke), while in other cases the development of production efficiency for lower product qualities have been more important (e.g. Germany L). Furthermore, some subsidiaries had a strong local business position with close customer and supplier relationships (e.g. Danke, Belgium and Italy), while others have been owned by large MNCs and have been highly dependent on doing business with them (e.g. Germany L and England T). Thus, although all the subsidiaries have been active in the same industry, Aspa's international organization has evolved from experiences from very different business contexts.

Often, though, managers refer to Danke as a 'center of excellence' because of its history of developing high-quality products. As regards product development, Aspa's HQ graded Danke as its most important subsidiary. There were also occasions when Danke's technical solutions and market experiences were adopted by other subsidiaries, although the prevalent character in this industry is that the local product market requires a high degree of local adaptation.

For example, in the late 1980s one of Danke's important customers – CB – needed a new packaging box for cans of beer. The basic problem with this kind of customer group is that customer preferences vary between specific customers and country markets. The prevailing tradition was thus to develop and produce small-scale series of packaging boxes, suited to individual customers. Danke's ambition was to meet the requirements of CB while achieving a higher level of scale economies than was common in the packaging industry. The solution to this problem was to develop a 'flexible' box, easy enough to change so that CB – and other customers – could alter the number of beer cans and bottles in it. This product was not likely to represent the optimal solution from CB's point of view, because some degree of adaptation to CB's special needs had to be sacrificed for the benefit of wider use and larger scale economies.

The cost of developing this new product was much higher than is normal in such cases in the packaging industry. Danke's strategy was thus to share the development costs as much as possible with other subsidiaries in Aspa and to secure a future market for the product that was larger than Danke's local market. Cooperation with other subsidiaries, therefore, was a necessary condition for the project.

To accomplish this, though, was easier said than done. Danke's management knew that such a project would hardly get any support from Aspa's HQ, particularly since Aspa's official strategy – developed and communicated by HQ – was to emphasize local responsiveness to the subsidiaries' business. This strategy was based on the conviction that Aspa's long-term profit and growth would be best accomplished, given the local character of the business, if every subsidiary maximized its adaptation to the demands of specific customers. Behind this view there was also an ambition at HQ to rely on profit-center control as far as possible for the subsidiaries. Consequently an important feature of the corporate strategy was to look at the different subsidiaries as separate local businesses, and to keep them operationally separate. There was also a fear at HQ that some subsidiaries might become too dominant in the group.

Danke's ambitions were not in line with any of these features of the corporate strategy. It therefore decided to pursue the beer-can project with as little participation as possible on the part of corporate HQ. An important ingredient of Danke's strategy was to create an informal association, Aspabox. Initially, this group consisted of Danke, Aspi, the subsidiary in Switzerland, and two of the subsidiaries in England (England B and S). Later, other subsidiaries in Aspa joined the association. Due to its relatively strong position in Aspa, Danke became the informal leader of Aspabox and arranged regular meetings between managers at different functional levels of the participating subsidiaries.

Initially the overall purpose of the association was to exchange ideas and information between the subsidiaries regarding products, marketing and customers in the different local markets. After a while, however, Danke launched the beer-can project in Aspabox and a cooperation started between Danke and England B. This cooperation eventually resulted in the release of an identical beer-can box to customers in England. Due to the limited capacity at England (B) to serve the large British market, a certain proportion of the boxes was produced by Danke and sold through England B in the English market.

A side-effect of this project was an increase in the tension between England B and England T. The latter subsidiary was much larger than England B and England S. As a consequence it had been appointed by HQ as a regional center for the British market. In many ways England T was the only subsidiary in Aspa strong enough to challenge Danke's position in the Aspa-group as the most important subsidiary. At one time during the development process of the beer-can box Danke tried to involve England T in the project with a view to acquiring a larger customer base. However, England T did not want to participate in the project, referring to the special needs of its own customers and its role as a regional HQ.

The Aspabox association was created and established by Danke without involvement or initiative from the corporate HQ. Later, at the time when Danke and England B were well ahead with their cooperation on the beer-can boxes, Aspabox was recognized and acknowledged by corporate HQ, but without being authorized as a part of the formal organization.

These events demonstrate the tensions between different interests in the embedded MNC. Danke's strategy was to grow beyond its local business and to achieve a higher level of scale economies. Its ambition was to become more international and to reach customers outside the home country. It is quite possible that this strategy would be sub-optimal from Aspa's point of view, if it ended in more pronounced competition between Aspa's subsidiaries for the same country-markets but with less customized products. In any case, Danke's ambitions were not in total accordance with the corporate HQ strategy. Nor was it in line with the interests of England T, albeit for rather different reasons.

Due to the relatively strong position that it gradually developed in Aspa, in constant interaction with its partners in the business network, Danke succeeded in launching and carrying out a project that in turn affected other subsidiaries. The project did not involve the corporate HQ, and might not have been supported even if HQ had been involved from the beginning. Danke managed to realize its intentions despite lack of support from the corporate level or from England T, whose interests to some extent clashed with the project.

The case also demonstrates that Danke's intra-organizational power to pursue its own interests was not without its limits. From Danke's point of view, involving England T in the project would have meant greater potential for a larger market for the product. However, England T was not interested, but was not strong enough to prevent Danke from involving England B, one of its own subordinates. However, England T's position in its own market and within Aspa was strong enough to allow it to refuse to take active part in the project. And Danke had no possibility of forcing it to participate.

The case of the beer-can box is an example of knowledge transfer within the Aspa corporation. Transfer between the subsidiary managers within Aspabox was possible as the subsidiaries had relatively similar technologies, although some subsidiaries, such as Danke, had developed their capabilities somewhat more than others. Also, competition between the subsidiaries was relatively weak, i.e. on principle they did not operate in the same markets, which thus provided an incentive for knowledge transfer.

However, some years later Aspa was bought up and integrated into another corporation, and a new group of top managers was established at corporate HQ. They wanted to formalize the role of Aspabox as they needed information about the development processes in Aspa. The new managers thus demanded formal reports and wanted to participate at meetings. According to the subsidiary managers, Danke's central role and the informal dynamics and flexibility in Aspabox were consequently reduced.

SUMMARY

In this chapter we have proposed that an MNC is a loosely coupled organization with heterogeneous resources and embracing conflicting interests. Underlying this character lies the dual role of the subsidiaries in an MNC. On the one hand a subsidiary belongs to the MNC as a business actor with its own formal and informal organization. The subsidiary is part of the corporate context and has a role to fulfill in that context. But the subsidiary is also embedded in a business network, with business relationships developed over a long period of time. Although there is no 'master-mind' in such a network, the subsidiary has a role to fulfill there. There is nothing given, to tell us that these two roles might coincide. On the contrary, tension between the roles is common, because actors in the subsidiary contexts have different interests and diverging views about how the subsidiary should act.

More precisely, an embedded business relationship has been defined as a relationship characterized by a high degree of mutual, long-term adaptation in terms of relation-specific investments. The Embedded Multinational thus signifies an MNC whose subsidiaries operate in different business networks that, to a notable extent, consist of highly embedded relationships.

This conceptualization depicts a situation in which different subsidiaries can and will exert varying types of influence within the MNC, depending on their positions. The chapter has included a case demonstrating how Danke and England B had sufficient power to carry out a particular project, more or less without support from Aspa's corporate HQ. The case indicates that the position of subsidiaries in MNCs is dependent on the kind of business relationships that they enjoy with important others in their business networks. How, and to what extent, the subsidiaries are embedded in their business network is a crucial factor in the analysis of the MNC. The concept of embeddedness will therefore be explored further in the next chapter, supported by data from 98 subsidiaries belonging to 20 divisions in Swedish MNCs.

8. The Embedded Multinational – an empirical illustration

In Chapter 7 the Embedded Multinational was presented. An important feature of the Embedded Multinational is the closeness of the business relationships in which the different sub-units are engaged. In Chapter 8 we explore this feature further by analysing, defining and operationalizing the concept of business embeddedness at the relationship and subsidiary levels. The discussion is underpinned by an empirical illustration, using data from a set of 98 subsidiaries in 20 MNC divisions belonging to twelve MNCs.

NETWORK EMBEDDEDNESS AND INTEGRATION

One main issue in the management literature about the MNC is the managers' need to reach the right balance between local adaptation and global integration (see e.g. Doz 1986; Porter 1986; Bartlett and Ghoshal 1989; Dicken 1992). But according to our argument as presented in earlier chapters a business network develops over a long period of time and a subsidiary's role in such a network is formed by interaction with customers, suppliers, regulators and competitors. It is shaped by management as well as by history. Therefore, if local adaptation can be analysed as mainly a question of management *decisions*, local business embeddedness cannot. While the former concept is often related to the adaptation of products and services to the specific needs of consumers in a certain country, the latter concept identifies the long-lasting structural consequences following such an adaptation. The issue of global integration within the MNC itself has thus also been somewhat reformulated. It is not primarily a question of deciding about the right balance between local adaptation and global integration within the multinational, but rather of continuous attempts on the part of HQ to achieve economies of scale and scope among subsidiaries that are embedded in different networks. These networks are not specifically suited to integration, because they differ in terms of activities, actors, resources and history. The differences are partly reflected in different interests and aspirations at the subsidiary level, which render HQ's ambition to attain global integration within the multinational more difficult to implement. One example can illustrate this.

In one of the largest Swedish multinationals, the cost of R&D is enormous. It is therefore of the utmost importance to coordinate the different subsidiaries' R&D activities to avoid the duplication of investments and to achieve large-scale economy in production and development. The ability to integrate R&D is assumed to be one of the most critical competitive forces among the main competitors in the industry. But the driving-forces behind product development are, to a large extent, local. Specific customers demand special product adaptations that sometimes result in more or less customized R&D activities at the subsidiary level. From the subsidiary's point of view there can be good reason to commence such activities, especially for a large customer. From the perspective of the HQ, what is important however, is whether or not the results anticipated from such investments have a wider application to the group as a whole.

One of the largest subsidiaries of this group is located in Italy. Italy is one of the firm's biggest markets and this subsidiary has always been very profitable. The subsidiary has an important role in the group's R&D function, both as a developer of so-called standard applications, that is applications suitable for several markets, and market applications, meaning those applications suited to the Italian market only. But market applications have always been dominant in the Italian subsidiary. Changes in the organization of R&D within the group, initiated by the HQ to increase the proportion of standard applications, have not led to any profound change in the situation. One important reason for this is that almost every request from one very dominant Italian customer is defined and handled by the subsidiary as a request for a market application. This is due to the old and strong commercial and social link between the subsidiary and the customer, an important and profitable relationship for both parties. From the subsidiary's point of view, it is more important to maintain and develop this relationship by servicing the customer's special needs than to initiate the development of products that are applicable to customers in other countries, even though that would be more beneficial for its sister companies in the group.

This case illustrates that a subsidiary's interest and behavior is shaped by its business network. But the case also illustrates that the behavior is affected by the depth of its business relationships. The deeper the relationships in terms of the mutual adaptation and importance, the greater its impact on the subsidiary's behavior compared with the impact from HQ. One important aspect of the basic nature of the MNC is the degree of embeddedness of every individual subsidiary in its own business network. This is our main concern in the following section.

THE CONCEPT OF NETWORK EMBEDDEDNESS

The concept of embeddedness appeared originally in Polyani (1957) and was developed further in Granovetter (1985), reflecting the view that economic exchanges are 'embedded' in social and cultural exchanges. The basic idea behind the notion of embeddedness is that social structure plays a significant role in economic behavior. Granovetter has used the concept of embeddedness to illuminate two major drawbacks in traditional economic theory, in that it does not recognize the social element of economic exchange nor the problems of temporal and structural reductionism. The first problem means that economists tend to underestimate the extent to which economic transactions between actors are affected by the history of the transaction, and the mutual expectations on future exchange that has become a constitutive part of the relationship between the two parties. The second problem refers to the failure to realize that an economic transaction is affected by other, connected, exchanges in a wider network of transactions (Granovetter 1992).

The concept of embeddedness, as developed by Granovetter, is very much in line with important features of the business network theory presented in Chapters 2–5. In business network theory the relationship between two business actors is often characterized by trust, mutual adaptation of resources over time and expectations regarding the actors' future behavior. This was illustrated in Chapter 3 by Danke's relationships with Aspi and Bitte, which developed over time from relatively arm's-length exchange to business relationships that included intensive social interaction and cooperation about product developments, etc. These notions correspond to the temporal dimension of economic life.

But business network theory also contains the argument that such a relationship, in its turn, is dependent on other relationships that are connected to the focal relationship through the wider network. For instance, Danke's relationship with Aspi was greatly influenced by the ongoing transactions between Danke and Fenster, but in its turn it also influenced the transactions between Aspi and Bill (see Chapter 4). This illustrates the point made by Granovetter, that all economic life has a structural dimension, that is, a certain relationship can be understood only if we include other relationships with which it is connected.

Inherent in the concept of embeddedness, as applied by Granovetter and other scholars, is the assumption that the antithesis to a high degree of embeddedness is arm's-length market exchange. In the second case, the exchange itself is mainly limited to price data, which supposedly distills most of the information needed to make efficient decisions. The relation between the partners is more a matter of self-interested, profit-seeking behavior than of intentional commitment and long-term trust. The level of adaptation of resources between the counterparts is low, and they tend to switch to new counterparts to take advantage of new entrants or to avoid dependence (Uzzi 1997). But these characteristics can be more or less manifest in a relationship, as can trust and adaptation. It is therefore reasonable to assume that a high degree of embeddedness and arm's-length exchange can be analysed as two opposite ends on a continuum rather than as distinctive features. This also means that a relationship, and therefore a network, can be characterized as more, or less, embedded.

A subsidiary's environment consists primarily of a set of direct exchange relationships with other business partners, as well as indirect exchange relationships connected with direct relationships. This is illustrated in Figure 8.1.

The figure illustrates three important features of the networks surrounding the subsidiaries of an MNC. First, the networks consist of both direct and indirect relationships. Second, the relationships, both the direct and the connected, differ in their 'profundity' as regards trust, adaptation, importance and, thus, substitutability. A mixture of arm's-length relations and highly embedded relationships occurs both within the MNC and outside it. Third, different subsidiaries have different types of network with respect to the above dimensions.

One way of defining the degree of embeddedness in such a set of relationships is to estimate the number of actual connections relative to the number that would be possible, often referred to as 'density' (Aldrich and Whetten 1981; Ghoshal and Bartlett 1990). The density measure, therefore, reflects the extent to which every actor is linked to every other actor in the set. Although this measures the tightness of the set of relationships, and therefore also to some extent a specific actor's degree of embeddedness in its network, there are two major problems connected with this definition. First, it does not cover the attributes of the exchanges in terms of activity interdependence and adaptation between the actors. The stronger the specific activity interdependence between the subsidiary and the other actors, the more this reflects close, trustful relationships rather than arm's-length exchanges. The attributes of the relationships cannot thus be excluded if we want to estimate the degree of embeddedness in a specific network. That is, not only the number but also the profundity of relationships has to be estimated in Figure 8.1.

Second, the concept of density assumes that it would be possible to estimate the number of actors and connections in a business network 'from above'. But,

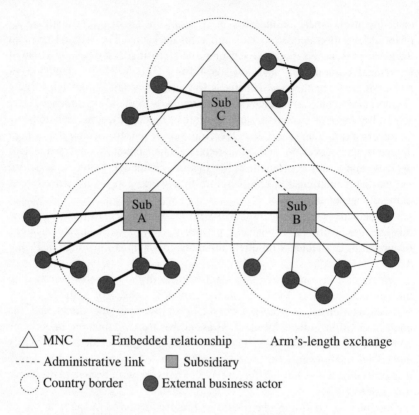

△ MNC   —— Embedded relationship   —— Arm's-length exchange
----- Administrative link   ▣ Subsidiary
◌ Country border   ● External business actor

*Figure 8.1   The MNC subsidiary environment: direct and indirect
relationships*

as we noted in Chapter 2, business networks are primarily enacted. They can
only be subjectively defined from an actor's viewpoint, and the boundaries of
such networks are vague when it comes to the number of relevant business
partners. A subsidiary's degree of embeddedness should thus be defined by its
own estimation of its relevant direct and indirect business partners, and the
attributes of its exchange with these partners in terms of interdependence and
adaptation.

It follows from the above discussion that the more visible the business
partners are in the eyes of the subsidiary concerned, the more the subsidiary's
behavior and activities are likely to be influenced by these particular network
actors. The more dependent the subsidiary is on specific business partners for
the pursuit of its activities, and the more adapted it is to them, the more
embedded it will be. If these business partners in their turn are dependent on,
and adapted to, the subsidiary, this is likely to strengthen the latter's degree of

embeddedness, since interdependence is more prone to produce long-term relationships. Consequently, the more pronounced the interdependence and adaptation between the subsidiary and these other parties, the more embedded the subsidiary is in its business network.

As Figure 8.1 indicates, both direct and indirect relationships constitute a subsidiary's degree of embeddedness. Whereas we can speak of direct embeddedness in customer and supplier relationships, actors such as customers' customers, suppliers' suppliers, complementary suppliers, etc. may also influence the subsidiary's direct relationships. The more prominent such indirect relationships are in the activities of the subsidiary, the tighter the structure of the network and thus the embeddedness of the subsidiary.

To sum up, we can conclude that a low level of local embeddedness means that the subsidiary's relationships with other actors in the network are more of the 'arm's-length' type, in the sense that the level of adaptation between the resources and activities of the parties involved is relatively low, which means that the relationships are relatively easy to replace. A high degree of embeddedness means that the subsidiary's relationships are difficult to replace, because over time, both sides have adapted their resources and activities to each other to such an extent that every relationship has become unique and commands a diversity of resources for activation.

Given our conceptualization of embeddedness, it is not easy to estimate precisely the degree of embeddedness of a focal network. It is no easy task to measure variables such as adaptation, trust and interdependence. But in order to conceive the heterogeneity of the MNC, and the way the different networks surrounding the subsidiaries affect its strategy and management, we have to tackle the concept on the empirical level as well. The following sections in this chapter will thus look more deeply into data about subsidiaries belonging to some large Swedish MNCs, in order to see how embeddedness can be measured. Our aim is to illustrate how embeddedness can be estimated in real situations, and to analyse the degree of embeddedness of many subsidiaries in a large number of Swedish multinationals.

SUBSIDIARY EMBEDDEDNESS IN SWEDISH MULTINATIONALS

The total data set consists of the business networks of 98 subsidiaries, of which the majority are located outside Sweden. Data about these subsidiaries has been collected from extensive interviews with managers at different levels in the subsidiaries and from managers at the parent level in Sweden. The investigation focuses on the divisional level of the MNC, which means that every subsidiary investigated belongs to a certain division and that the parent perspective is equivalent to the perspective held by the divisional managers. For a fuller description of how the data has been collected, see Appendix I.

The subsidiaries belong to 20 divisions in 12 Swedish multinationals. These divisions represent a broad spectrum of Swedish industry and involve big, well-known companies in industries such as pulp and paper, telecommunications equipment, petrochemical products, power distribution, hard metal tools, gas applications for industrial use, saws and chains, welding consumables, industrial equipment, transportation, software and management training.

The size of the divisions, in number of employees and turnover, varies. Except for two service companies that both have less than one thousand employees and a turnover around 500 million Swedish kronor, the divisions are fairly large with a turnover ranging from 1.7 to 23 billion Swedish kronor. The largest division has more than 27000 employees and the smallest about one thousand. All the divisions are highly internationalized. In ten cases more than 50 percent of the employees work outside Sweden, and in all the divisions except one more than 50 percent of the turnover comes from units abroad. Profits arise mainly from foreign units. The size of the subsidiaries investigated varies between 50 and 5000 employees. In general, the most important subsidiaries according to the divisional HQ's estimation have been included in the study, which means that the sample is dominated by subsidiaries that have been part of the division for quite a long time and have their own production and development activities.

The subsidiaries are predominantly located in Western Europe, reflecting the main location of Sweden's trading interests. The companies, divisions and subsidiaries, with the size of the subsidiaries and the product/service of each and one, are listed in Appendix 1.

SUBSIDIARY EMBEDDEDNESS – A MULTIDIMENSIONAL CONCEPT

Embeddedness is a multidimensional concept. A subsidiary can be embedded in its business network by way of different activities. For instance, a subsidiary can have a profound relationship with another actor concerning product development or the development of new production processes, but without any sales or marketing activities. Or certain relationships in the network can be of vital importance for a subsidiary seeking new markets for its existing products, but not for developing new products. This makes it difficult to define embeddedness, since a subsidiary exhibiting a high level of interdependence in several dimensions is clearly more embedded than a subsidiary that adapts itself in one dimension only. But there are too many dimensions to assume a strong correlation between them. Consequently, we have to choose one dimension of embeddedness at a time.

We concentrate below on embeddedness regarding technology development, since – as we have indicated above – the investigated subsidiaries belong to the most important and fully-fledged units within each division, which means that in their case, technology development is a relevant and important function. Business network theory also postulates that the development of new products and processes is an activity proceeding primarily in relationships *between* business actors rather than *within* the actors themselves. Embeddedness in terms of technological development is thus of crucial interest from a network perspective. We will therefore concentrate below on technological embeddedness in the network of 98 subsidiaries.

More precisely, technological embeddedness is measured as the degree of adaptation practised by the subsidiary and its business partners with respect to two distinct functions: product development and production development. Appendix I provides a detailed description of the measurement technique, which was limited to the investigation of a maximum of six relationships. This limitation was due mainly to the large amount of data needed to establish and assess each relationship, but it can also be justified on the grounds that generally speaking there are relatively few business relationships to which companies tend to attach much long-term importance (Cowley 1988; Håkansson 1989; Perrone 1989). Nevertheless, it has to be borne in mind that the omission of some of the business actors in a subsidiary's network means that the assessment of embeddedness is always incomplete. However, altogether 516 customer/supplier relationships have been investigated among our 98 subsidiaries, i.e. an average of 5.27 relationships per subsidiary.

Another bias in our measurement concerns the focus on what the subsidiary managers consider to be the relationships that are most important to the activities of their own subsidiaries. This certainly means underestimating the arm's-length character of the subsidiary's network, which means in turn that our measurements are more suitable for comparisons between subsidiaries than for assessing the absolute level of embeddedness in the 'whole' networks of the subsidiaries.

Embeddedness at the Relationship Level

Table 8.1 reveals the degree of embeddedness among the 516 most important customer and supplier relationships. As indicated above, our assessment of embeddedness concerns the degree of mutual adaptation regarding product and production process technology between a focal subsidiary and its opposite number in each relationship. In Table 8.1 the degree of relationship embeddedness is interpreted on a five-point scale in accordance with the measurements used during interviews with subsidiary managers (see Appendix I). Some important conclusions can be drawn from the table.

Table 8.1   Embeddedness in (important) subsidiary business relationships

Degree of embeddedness	Corporate relationships		External relationships		All relationships	
	(No.)	(%)	(No.)	(%)	(No.)	(%)
Very high	6	5.1	3	0.8	9	1.8
High	18	15.5	55	13.8	73	14.2
Medium	41	35.0	139	34.8	180	34.9
Low	27	23.1	114	28.6	141	27.3
None	25	21.4	88	22.1	113	21.9
Total	117	100.0	399	100.0	516	100.0

First, the degree of embeddedness varies quite a lot between individual relationships, ranging from no adaptation at all to a very high degree of adaptation. Second, about half the relationships are embedded to some extent at least (a medium level), and of these almost a third reveal a high level of embeddedness, while the other half exhibit more of an arm's-length character with a low level of adaptation, or with none. Third, the overall picture seems to hold also when the relationships are separated into two categories, i.e. those with external customers or suppliers on the one hand and those with corporate customers and suppliers on the other – although there is a slight predominance of relationships embedded on the corporate side. The main impression, though, is that the distribution and average embeddedness in business relationships is similar externally and internally. Fourth, external relationships predominate quite markedly among the relationships that are considered important according to the subsidiary's own judgment. Whereas 399 of the important relationships investigated were external to the MNC, 117 were within it.

The overall picture strongly supports the relevance of our business network perspective. A large proportion of the relationships are embedded to some degree (a medium level), and 15–20 percent to a high or very high degree. More importantly, relationship embeddedness is a phenomenon in both the business and the corporate contexts of the subsidiary. Our data contradicts the traditional picture of the business firm as an organization that is internally coordinated and integrated, but engaged externally with a more or less anonymous group of customers and suppliers. It is clear that close relationships with external counterparts are important and, consequently, the external environment of the subsidiary is of crucial importance to its business.

But what does embeddedness in the business network look like at the subsidiary level? This question will be addressed in the following section.

Embeddedness at the Subsidiary Level

Figure 8.2, which is based on Appendix III, characterizes the studied subsidiaries according to their corporate and external embeddedness. The estimation is based on the *highest* relevant value. Thus, if a subsidiary has two important corporate relationships, it is the one with the highest embeddedness value that determines its level of corporate embeddedness. The same reasoning defines external embeddedness. Measurements were based on the subsidiaries' and their business partners' respective adaptations regarding product *and* production technology, and were given on a five-point scale, where one meant no adaptation at all and five meant a very high level of adaptation. The average values of relationship embeddedness thus ranged from 1 to 5. The highest degree of mutual adaptation in corporate and external

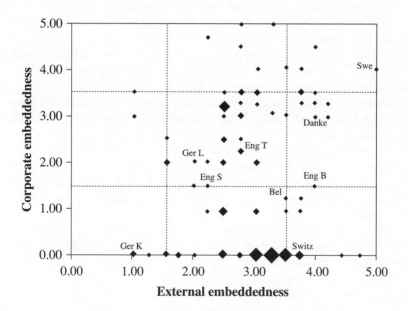

Figure 8.2   External and corporate embeddedness at the subsidiary level (low, medium and high)

relationships (one corporate and one external relationship) was chosen to represent the particular subsidiary's corporate and external embeddedness. In Figure 8.2 values below 1.5 are regarded as indicating a *low* level of embeddedness, while values between 1.5 and 3.5 would indicate a *medium* level. A value of 3.5 or higher represents a *high* level of embeddedness. Some subsidiaries have the same position, which is indicated by the size of the marks. The number of subsidiaries ranges from one (the smallest mark) to six (the largest mark).

Figure 8.2 reveals a remarkable difference between subsidiaries. It shows that 3 percent have a low level of embeddedness in both their corporate and their external relationships (i.e. these are of arm's-length character), while 7 percent have a high level of embeddedness in both their corporate and their external relationships. The figure also shows that 40 percent have a high level of embeddeness (3.5 or over) in one or both contexts – corporate, external or both. The overall picture reveals that although relatively few subsidiaries are embedded in both the corporate and the external contexts (7 percent), many are embedded in either one *or* the other.

Another striking feature is that 43 percent of the subsidiaries exhibit a low level of corporate embeddedness but medium or high level in the external context. Of these a majority, 32 percent, have not identified any important relationships at all with corporate sister units. The total share of subsidiaries lacking any important corporate relationships is 35 percent, which means that corporate embeddedness is equal to zero in Figure 8.2. In contrast, no subsidiary is without some important external relationships, which means that the lowest value for external embeddedness in Figure 8.2 is 1.0. Further, in only 2 percent of the cases did corporate embeddedness predominate, such that a low level of external embeddedness was combined with a high or medium level in the corporate context. The embeddedness at the subsidiary level is summarized in Table 8.2.

The analysis shows that external embeddedness at the subsidiary level is common, and often more noticeable than the corporate kind. This is also reflected in the fact that there were 58 highly embedded external relationships in Table 8.1 (a value of 3.5 or over), as against a total of 24 for corporate relationships.

Several subsidiaries in the Aspa corporation are indicated in Figure 8.2. The figure shows that Germany K is the least embedded subsidiary (see also Chapter 6). It lacks important corporate relationships and its external relationships also reveal a low level of embeddedness. The Belgium subsidiary and the one in Switzerland have developed a high level of embeddedness in their external markets, while their emebeddedness vis-à-vis the Aspa corporation has remained low-level. The Swedish subsidiary and Danke show the highest levels in both external and corporate embeddedness.

Table 8.2   Embeddedness at the subsidiary level

Subsidiary embeddedness	Percent of cases ($n = 98$)*
Low corporate embeddedness *and* low external embeddedness	3
High corporate embeddedness *and* high external embeddedness	7
High corporate embeddedness *or* high external embeddedness	40
Low corporate embeddedness *and* medium/high external embeddedness	43
Absence of important corporate relationships	35
Low external embeddedness *and* medium/high corporate embeddedness	2

Note: *The combinations of corporate and external embeddedness described in the table do not necessarily exclude each other. Therefore the percentage of cases totals more than 100.

Overall, there is no significant positive correlation between corporate and external embeddedness at the subsidiary level. As indicated in Figure 8.2 the correlation is no more than 0.09. Even if we exclude subsidiaries that have no corporate relationships at all (34 out of 98 subsidiaries), the correlation between external embeddedness and corporate embeddedness remains insignificant (0.19). This implies that external embeddedness does not drive corporate embeddedness, or vice versa.

What, then, does drive subsidiary network embeddedness? A reasonable assumption would be that the type of operation in terms of products, markets and/or technology has a profound effect on the way a subsidiary's relationships develop. It has been suggested, for instance, that service firms, or firms whose products have a high service content, are forced to develop more interactive and interdependent business relationships (Majkgård 1998). Another common assumption is that more standardized products correspond to a more market-like context, with arm's-length exchange predominating over close business relationships. It thus seems reasonable to expect the variation in embeddedness between subsidiaries to be considerably lower *within* divisions than in the group of subsidiaries as a whole. After all, divisions are supposed to reflect a high degree of within-division similarity in terms of products, markets and technology, although its member subsidiaries differ in their size, location, etc.

Our next step will thus be to look at the variation in embeddedness among subsidiaries *within* divisions.

VARIATION IN SUBSIDIARY EMBEDDEDNESS WITHIN DIVISIONS

Figures 8.3a and 8.3b display the subsidiaries' corporate and external embeddedness *within* each division (A–T). A first glance also suggests a remarkable variation within the 20 divisions. Most divisions have an obvious mixture of subsidiaries representing low, medium and high levels of embeddedness, irrespective of whether the embeddedness is external or corporate. Of the 16 divisions (A–P) where our study included at least four subsidiaries, only K exhibits a fairly low level of variation, referring to external embeddedness only, since K has no corporate relationships. Thus the Aspa corporation, for example, which corresponds to division A in Figure 8.3a and which was analysed in greater depth in Chapter 6, reveals substantial differences between its nine subsidiaries. We have already noted that Germany K, which corresponds to subsidiary 1, exhibits the lowest level of embeddedness. No important corporate relationships were identified (giving it a very low degree of corporate embeddedness), and its managers declared that the technical adaptations in its most important external business relationships were also on a very modest scale. In contrast, subsidiaries 8 and 9 reveal a high degree of technical adaptation in their corporate and external relationships. Danke (i.e. subsidiary 8) has a long-standing history of becoming embedded in business relationships, both inside and outside the MNC (see Chapters 3–4). The Swedish subsidiary (subsidiary 9) was acquired by Aspa in its early expansion stage (see Chapter 6) and reveals a similar history of relationship development, resulting in a high level of both corporate and external embeddedness. The other subsidiaries in the Aspa group land somewhere between these two extremes on the embeddedness scale. We can conclude that although Aspa's subsidiaries reveal a high degree of similarity in industrial terms (the packaging industry), they differ a lot in their business networks – at least as these are characterized by our embeddedness concept. A similar pattern is also obvious in the other divisions, although not always as markedly as in division A.

Figures 8.3a and 8.3b also indicate that the variation is considerable in both the external and the corporate contexts, confirming that there is no obvious correlation between the two in the divisions as a group. Some divisions have subsidiaries exhibiting a low level of corporate embeddedness but a high level of external embeddedness, or vice versa. For instance, Division O has two subsidiaries with a low level of corporate embeddedness combined with a high level of external embeddedness, as well as one subsidiary in the opposite situation, i.e. with a high degree of corporate embeddedness and little external embeddedness. A fourth subsidiary has much the same average degree of embeddedness in both dimensions. Some other divisions – C and I for

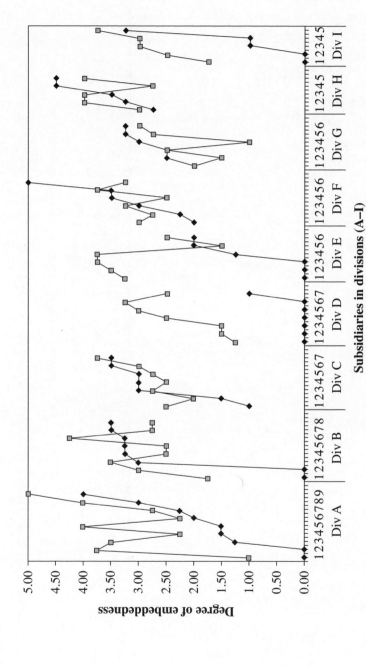

Figure 8.3a Difference in corporate and external embeddedness in divisions (A–I)

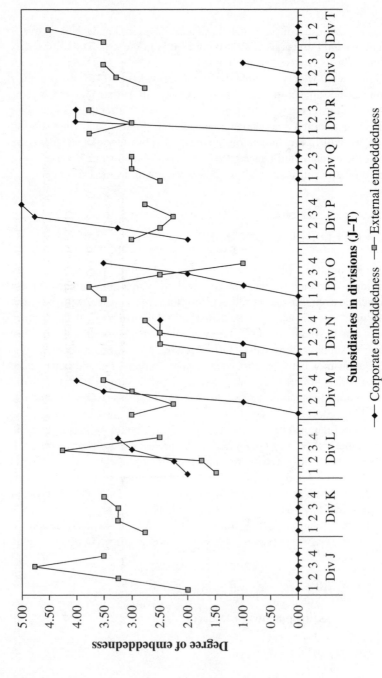

Figure 8.3b   Difference in corporate and external embeddedness in divisions (J–T)

118

instance – seem to have a positive correlation between the two types of embeddedness.

All in all, we can conclude that the variation in embeddedness between subsidiaries *within* divisions is as striking as it is in the group of subsidiaries as a whole. This is crucial, because it means that the MNC HQ has to deal with subsidiaries with widely varying business-network contexts, despite their belonging to the same corporate 'family'. As we will demonstrate in Chapters 9–11, this has far-reaching consequences for the MNC, affecting its system of control, influence and knowledge management. In the following section, however, we will first complete our analysis of subsidiary embeddedness by analysing the extent of influence from *connected* relationships (the impact of connected relationships was addressed at some length in the Danke case, see Chapter 4).

CONNECTED RELATIONSHIPS

So far our analysis has focused on the subsidiary's *direct* business relationships. We noted earlier, however, that an evaluation of embeddedness should include even those other relationships that are *connected* with the direct relationships. For instance, a subsidiary's relationships with a specific customer can be more, or less, influenced by its relationships with other customers or suppliers, *or* it can be influenced by 'second-order' relationships, that is relationships between a focused customer or supplier and other actors in the network (third parties). Whereas direct embeddedness concerns the degree of mutual adaptation in relationships with business partners, connected embeddedness concerns the degree of *influence* of indirect relationships on a focal business relationship (see also Figure 4.5 in Chapter 4). It is reasonable to suppose that, other things being equal, the greater the influence from such *connected* relationships, the more embedded the subsidiary will be in its network. Figures 8.4 and 8.5 illustrate our two-step analysis of embeddedness.

In order to demonstrate the importance of a subsidiary's connected relationships we have assessed the degree of influence on the subsidiary's direct external relationships stemming from other customers, suppliers, customer's customers, supplier's suppliers and competitors. An average value

Figure 8.4   Direct embeddedness

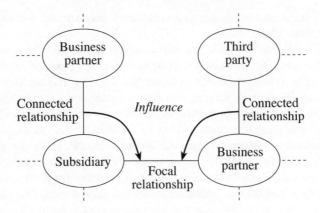

Figure 8.5   Connected embeddedness

of influence from these external relationships has been calculated for each subsidiary. See Appendix I for a more detailed description of the method.

Figure 8.6 reflects the combination of direct embeddedness and connected embeddedness among the investigated subsidiaries. (As in Figure 8.2, Aspa subsidiaries have been marked and the size of the marker indicates a number of subsidiaries (one to four) in a certain location.)

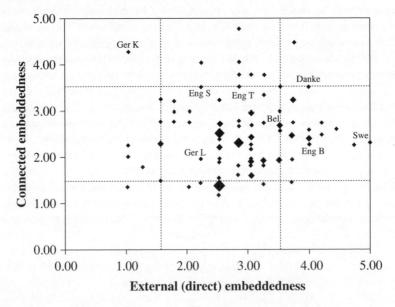

Figure 8.6   Subsidiaries' external and connected embeddedness (low, medium and high level)

Figure 8.6 reveals no apparent correlation between direct embeddedness and connected embeddedness among the subsidiaries (the correlation coefficient is low, 0.075). It seems that whether or not a subsidiary and its particular business partner become specifically adapted to each other, has little to do with the extent of influence from other direct or indirect relationships.

First we can see that the average connected embeddedness is low in about 15 percent of the cases, and high in about 12 percent. This means that the degree of connectedness is 'medium' in more than 70 percent of the cases. In almost all of these, the level of external direct embeddedness is medium or high. Or, to put it differently, it is quite common that a medium or high level of direct embeddedness is combined with a medium level of connected embeddedness. Several Aspa subsidiaries belong to this group, although there is some variation. Whereas Belgium, England B and in particular Sweden, have a higher level of external direct embeddedness, for England S and T it is the connected embeddedness that is higher.

Second, only one or two subsidiaries combine a low level of direct embeddedness with a low level of connected embeddedness (the lower left-hand corner in Figure 8.6). In this situation, which applies to 2 percent of all subsidiaries, arm's-length exchange dominates the external network – the direct and the connected. Within Aspa the activities of the German subsidiary, Germany L, come closest to this description. Given its focus on the efficient production of 'brown boxes', Germany L has not developed a high level of embeddedness in its direct business relationships. Influence on its direct relationships stemming from other relationships is also perceived as modest.

Third, the subsidiaries in this last group can be compared with those in the opposite situation (the upper right-hand corner), that is to say subsidiaries with high levels of direct and connected embeddedness. Very few subsidiaries belong to this group, but Danke is one of them. Besides the specific technical adaptations it has made in its business relationships, an important characteristic of Danke's network is also that some of its relationships – those with Aspi, Bitte and Fenster for instance – have had a considerable effect on the development of other relationships (see Chapter 4).

Finally, only one subsidiary is identified in the position combining a low degree of direct embeddedness and a high degree of connected embeddedness (upper left-hand corner). This suggests that direct embeddedness is not a necessary condition for connected embeddedness. One interpretation of this is that a subsidiary's arm's-length exchange with a customer or supplier can be greatly influenced by other relationships, even though their direct exchange is not being conducted within an embedded relationship. This could apply, for instance if activities in indirect business relationships in a subsidiary's network have a powerful effect on its direct exchange with customers and suppliers. However, this does not mean that a focal subsidiary and its customers and suppliers will start investing in specific mutual technical solutions, such as would increase the direct embeddedness of the subsidiary concerned. It is equally possible that the influence of indirect relationships may mean that the subsidiary conducts new business and finds technical solutions that are generally applicable to market actors. Or, to put it differently, developments in the surrounding business network may impose new technical or business-related procedures, without necessarily raising the level of the subsidiary's embeddedness in its direct relationships. Germany K represents such a situation. This subsidiary exhibits a very low level of external embeddedness in its direct business exchange. And yet the influence from its indirect relationships on the direct business exchange is considerable. Thus, despite a similar history as regards ownership and technology, Germany K and Germany L differ when it comes to their external embeddedness (direct and connected), as well as their corporate embeddedness (see also Figure 8.2).

To sum up, it seems that there is also a relatively high degree of variation between subsidiaries when connected embeddedness – as expressed by influence on the direct relationship stemming from other relationships – is taken into account. In general we would argue that a subsidiary's overall embeddedness increases to the extent that connected embeddedness adds substantially to the direct embeddedness. Our analysis shows that 12 percent are greatly affected by connected relationships, and that 85 percent are affected to a 'medium' level at least. However, although connected embeddedness is an important feature of the business network structure, it is not altogether clear how direct and connected embeddedness can be combined into a measure of total subsidiary embeddedness. Thus, in order to simplify our analysis of the impact of embeddedness on control, influence and knowledge management in the MNC, (see Chapters 9–11), we will limit ourselves to direct embeddedness. It should be remembered, however, that direct embeddedness does not tell the whole story of a subsidiary's business network.

SUMMARY

This chapter has dealt with subsidiary embeddedness in MNCs. The concept of embeddedness stems essentially from the original idea of both Polyani and Granovetter that economic exchanges occur in a social and cultural context, which means that transactions have a history and are linked to other transactions. The concept of embeddedness is therefore consistent with the view that business markets can be described as networks of more or less long-lasting relationships. We have argued that in seeking to understand not only the strategic behavior of the MNC but also its internationalization and the possibility of integrating different operations and controlling the subsidiaries and the power structure in the MNC itself, the embeddedness – both direct and connected – of its subsidiaries is an important explanatory factor.

But the chapter has also demonstrated that embeddedness is a complicated concept when it comes to operationalization. This is because business networks are enacted, which means that the limits of the network are vague and have to be analysed from a particular actor's point of view. But it is also because a subsidiary's activities vary in their interdependence vis-à-vis other actors. The embeddedness of a certain relationship, and thus of the network as a whole, is therefore a multidimensional concept.

As an empirical illustration of subsidiary embeddedness we have used data from 98 subsidiairies belonging to Swedish multinationals. It has been shown that the degree of embeddedness, defined as mutual adaptation in product and production development, differed considerably from one relationship and one subsidiary to another. About 40 percent of the 98 subsidiaries considered their own business networks to be fairly highly embedded or 'non-market', in the sense that the majority of the important relationships observed in the network revealed quite far-reaching adaptation between the subsidiary in question and its customers and/or suppliers. About 16 percent, in contrast, exhibited a more 'market-like' network structure.

It has also been shown that the variation in embeddedness between subsidiaries *within* each division is as marked as it is in the group of subsidiaries as a whole. Thus, differences in terms of industry, products, technology and so on do not seem to provide an obvious explanation of variations in embeddedness. In a network-theory perspective, time suggests one obvious underlying factor. It takes time to develop embeddedness; and the age of the relationships concerned are thus an obvious indicator of the importance attaching to time. There is a highly significant correlation between the average age of a subsidiary's relationships, and its degree of embeddedness. The average age of the relationships in the sample as a whole is over 17 years. Irrespective of the forces underlying embeddedness, however, the variation within divisions suggests that the MNC management has to deal with subsidiaries that are embedded in quite different types of networks, even though they all belong to the same corporate 'family'.

A separate analysis has also been made of the extent to which the subsidiary's relationships with external customers and suppliers were influenced by other direct or indirect relationships, or what are known as connected relationships. It has been shown that, between subsidiaries, connected embeddedness varies as much as direct embeddedness, and that there is no apparent correlation with direct embeddedness.

This chapter has presented the empirical grounds for our view of the MNC as a heterogeneous and loosely coupled organization whose subsidiaries differ considerably as regards their business network context inside and/or outside the MNC. In the three following chapters we will analyse various management issues associated with control, power structure and knowledge transfer in the Embedded MNC, in which the differences in subsidiary embeddedness play a major part in the models to be presented.

PART III

Management of the Embedded Multinational

9. Control and influence in the Embedded Multinational

In Chapter 8 the concept of business embeddedness at the subsidiary level was introduced and analysed. The following chapters are devoted specifically to 'classical' managerial issues in MNCs, namely the control exerted by corporate HQ over the subsidiaries, the role of the subsidiaries in the strategy process, and knowledge management. The model of the multinational firm outlined in the preceding chapters will be frequently referred to in the analysis, in which the network embeddedness of the subsidiaries is an important variable. In Chapter 9 we propose a model of the sources of influence to be found in MNCs and use it to analyse the conditions for the control exerted by corporate HQ. A distinction is drawn between HQ's formal control and its actual influence. This model is tested with data from 98 subsidiaries in 20 MNC divisions.

This book is built on the fundamental assumption that the various units in an MNC are embedded in business networks. In seeking to understand the way control and influence are shaped within the corporation and distributed among the different organizational actors, it is important that these networks should be taken into account. Each subsidiary operates within a particular network of business relationships that in turn constitutes a large proportion of the resources on which the individual subsidiary bases its position in the MNC. This conclusion applies regardless of whether we focus on relationships with external customers, suppliers, etc. or on similar relationships with other corporate units. Both types of relationship are part of the subsidiary's network, and the structure and processes within the network define the type of influence that the network actors exert upon one another. The more central a subsidiary's position in the network, the stronger its chances of influencing the behavior of another network actor. This contention holds irrespective of whether this actor is a corporate or a non-corporate unit: it is business relationships rather than ownership relationships that matter.

This is not to say that other types of relationship do not matter. Influence and control within the MNC are also dependent on administrative and hierarchical relationships between corporate units. For instance, the higher a subsidiary's formal position in the organization, the greater its chances of exerting influence on other corporate units. This claim does not rest solely on an ingrained conception that units higher in the hierarchy have a legitimate right to give orders to units lower down (Bacharach and Lawler 1981). It is also based on the assumption that a higher formal position also means better opportunities for surveying the environment and handling uncertainty (Hickson et al. 1971; Pfeffer 1981). Access to information about the environment means power – something that few people would deny.

A pertinent question, however, is whether a higher formal position always coincides with more accurate information, and what is the information about? In the business network perspective that we are applying to MNCs, knowledge about the resources and capabilities of other business actors is of central importance when it comes to power. The hierarchical and formal position in itself does not automatically produce such knowledge. Rather, the basic source is the set of direct and connected relationships that the unit has with these actors, often built up over a long period of time. These relationships constitute the unit's overall position in the network. In most work produced under the contingency view (see, for example, Ghoshal and Nohria 1997; Egelhoff 1988), information about the organization's environment is assigned an important role. On the other hand, this view pays surprisingly little attention to environmental characteristics, except in rather imprecise terms such as dynamism, complexity or the degree of competition. The environment is remarkably 'face-less', but still sufficiently comprehensible for the corporate HQ to decide upon such things as an efficient degree of formalization and centralization.

In our view, knowledge about the relevant business network and about specific relationships is what matters. The environment has got 'a face'. Or, to put it another way, any particular unit's influence within an organization is dependent on knowledge about the strategic resources that the organization has at its disposal (Pfeffer 1981). If these resources are largely embedded in business relationships – as assumed in our perspective – it follows that first-hand knowledge of these relationships is a crucial source of power. Such first-hand knowledge is created primarily in the course of ongoing (daily) interactions with other business actors in the network.

Thus, the business network perspective does not accept the view that a hierarchical position automatically implies basic knowledge about the business networks in which the different corporate units are embedded. Such knowledge may be found at the top of the organization, but it has to be *acquired* in much the same way as at lower levels. In many cases this is an insurmountable task for top managers in large dispersed organizations like MNCs.

Thus, while not totally denying the ability of higher hierarchical levels to survey a 'greater' part of the environment, the above line of argument suggests that the power of the top management levels in most MNCs boils down to the question of the legitimate right to give and implement orders in the organization. This power should not be underestimated. It is rooted in our culture that formal authority matters, and that a subordinate should obey orders and instructions. Thus, a corporate executive officer of an MNC apparently enjoys considerable power through hierarchical authority. However, our point is that this authority does not provide fiat as the dominant or even 'last resort' mechanism of influence in the MNC. Rather, our view implies that authority and knowledge about business networks coexist as sources of power. The top management level primarily represents influence through formal authority, while the subsidiary represents influence primarily through network knowledge. If we recognize that knowledge about business networks can also be found in the higher echelons, the basic model can be described as in Figure 9.1.

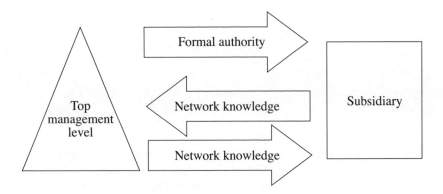

Figure 9.1   Sources of influence in the MNC

Influence through formal authority is one-sided and based on the legitimized right to make decisions and to implement them at lower levels. Influence through network knowledge is reciprocal and based on access to resources in business networks in which the different subsidiaries are operating. The figure indicates that control through formal authority can be either reinforced or counterbalanced by influence through network knowledge. If it is counterbalanced there is no given limitation to the dominance of a subordinate unit. The net effect may very well be that the higher levels are more dependent on a subsidiary than the reverse, since power based on network knowledge does not differ qualitatively from power based on formal authority. Both sources of power generate dependencies, and which power will dominate remains an empirical question.

CONTROL EXERTED BY HEADQUARTERS OVER SUBSIDIARIES IN AN MNC

The above argument implies that the possibilities for a corporate HQ controlling the different subsidiaries is dependent on its own legitimacy and its willingness to exert formal control, and on factors emanating from the business networks in which the subsidiaries are embedded. This overall situation regarding control is illustrated in Figure 9.2.

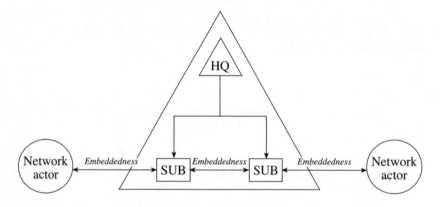

Figure 9.2   The network context of HQ-subsidiary control in the MNC

In earlier chapters we have emphasized the dual role of the subsidiary. One role is shaped by the corporate context of the MNC. The subsidiary is expected to fulfill its role in accordance with the corporate strategy, as developed and promoted by HQ. The arrows from HQ to the subsidiaries in Figure 9.2 symbolizes this role.

An equally important role derives from the subsidiary's position in the business network. This role has developed over time and is shaped by the expectations of other network members. The more the various activities and resources are adapted by both parties, the more pronounced will these expectations be. The concept of network embeddedness introduced and analysed in Chapter 8 goes a long way towards capturing these network characteristics, as symbolized by the two-way arrow between the subsidiary and its external and internal business network partners.

When it comes to the control exerted by HQ this duality of roles in the MNC has two important consequences. First, it cannot simply be presumed that these roles will coincide. On the contrary, the expectations among network partners may be quite different from those at the HQ. In contrast to HQ's search for integration we can posit the involvement of the subsidiaries in business activities with their external business partners, based on successive and reciprocal adaptations. The classic conflict between national responsiveness and global integration (Doz 1986) is in fact an example of this problem of dual roles. For instance, the subsidiary's interest in developing products and services specifically for customers in its own local market comes up against HQ's desire to involve them in the centralized development of products for global use.

Second, the dual roles imply that HQ is not alone in exercising control. Other actors also want to influence the behavior of the subsidiaries, and they too possess sources of power, which they can exploit more or less successfully. Embeddedness offers one such source of power: the more a subsidiary adapts to the activities of other network actors, and vice versa, the more dependent the subsidiary becomes on these actors. For instance, if a subsidiary has adapted its production facilities very extensively to a particular customer, as in the Danke case for example, then this customer is likely to have a say regarding the subsidiary's future behavior, thus competing with HQ for control. It has also been shown empirically that the higher a subsidiary's external embeddedness, the lower the level of control by HQ, as the subsidiary perceives it (Andersson and Forsgren 1996).

However, the negative impact of a subsidiary's external embeddedness on the control exerted by HQ can be counteracted by other factors. The most important of these is HQ's own knowledge regarding the subsidiary's business, including the latter's own business network. The more top management knows about the resources possessed by the subsidiary and the activities it undertakes, the greater the possibility of exerting control over the subsidiary's daily operations.

CONTINGENCY THEORY AND CONTROL FROM HEADQUARTERS: SOME RESERVATIONS

It could of course be argued that, ultimately, the formal authority exercised by HQ will always dominate as a control mechanism. Knowledge about business networks would then be less important in an analysis of sources of power, regardless of whether the knowledge is to be found at corporate HQ or at the subsidiary level. The only effective source of power is HQ's formal authority. This is a somewhat extreme position, but it seems to be the fundamental assumption of those applying contingency theory to the question of control in MNCs, even if they also assign a certain role to information in their analysis. Ghoshal and Nohria (1997), for instance, do not seem to query HQ's ability to decide about the appropriate levels of centralization and formalization for every individual subsidiary – about what they refer to as differentiated fit. At the same time they acknowledge that 'HQ cannot effectively make all the decisions in the MNC because it does not possess extensive knowledge of the subsidiaries and must consequently depend on the subsidiaries for that' (Ghoshal and Nohria 1997, p. 116). According to these authors, effective decisions about formalization and centralization do seem to be among the decisions that *can* be made by HQ, despite its lack of knowledge. Why this is so is not discussed by the authors, but appears to be taken for granted. The obvious contradiction is left unsolved.

According to a related view that diverges from the coalition model of organizations (Cyert and March 1963), it could be argued that goal congruence is the dominating mechanism in an MNC. If goal congruence dominates, the distribution of knowledge and competence in the organization is less important in a control context. All the units in the organization are aware of the common goal, and all are striving in the same direction. This is the basic assumption behind the 'shared value approach' and the idea of 'normative integration'. The emphasis here lies on creating a common understanding of goals, values and practices, in order to influence how subsidiaries perceive their own interests and the way they act (Ghoshal and Nohria 1997, p. 114).

However, the 'shared value approach' can be questioned on several grounds. Values and interests at the subsidiary level are rooted in the business contexts of the individual subsidiaries, of which HQ's understanding is incomplete. These contexts will have developed over a long period of time in interaction with various business network actors. They are context-specific and vary from one subsidiary to another; they are also difficult to change. The possibility of replacing such differentiated value structures by a common value, created and implemented by HQ, is probably as much wishful thinking as it is a real possibility.

Further, even more than in the case of decisions about efficient levels of formalization and decentralization, HQ's chances of creating an *efficient* 'shared value' are limited. This approach suffers from a classic dilemma: everyone can agree upon a goal, provided it is general enough. To be efficient, a goal has to reach a certain level of specificity. But at that level it is difficult to reach a common understanding about the goal itself. (In Chapter 11 we will return to the issue of 'shared values' as a mechanism for integration in MNCs.)

In sum, there are several reasons for doubting formal authority as the dominant source of power and for querying the 'shared value approach'. Instead, in line with what is known as the 'resource dependence perspective' (Pfeffer and Salancik 1978), we suggest that the impact of formal authority stemming from HQ is challenged by the impact of critical knowledge possessed by units at the subsidiary level in the MNC. In a business network perspective a crucial part of that knowledge is reflected in relationships with business actors. In line with the resource dependence perspective we argue that the various subsidiaries will use their knowledge in different ways to support their own values. The focus is on a 'differentiated value approach' rather than a 'shared value approach'.

A BUSINESS NETWORK MODEL OF HQ CONTROL

Starting from the assumptions of fundamental sources of power as illustrated in Figure 9.1, we suggest that HQ control can usefully be separated into two dimensions: formal control and actual influence. 'Formal control' refers first of all to the level at which formal decisions are taken, that is to say the degree of centralization. This dimension refers to HQ's right to exert formal authority and its desire for integration. However, in line with the resource dependence perspective, the configuration of the formal decision system is dependent not only on HQ's ambition to exert control but also on the subsidiaries' ambition to avoid HQ control, and/or on influence exerted by other stakeholders in the subsidiary business network. The degree of centralization is not solely the business of HQ.

'Actual influence' refers to the extent to which HQ manages to intervene in the operations of the subsidiary, irrespective of how far formal decisions are centralized. For instance, the formal decision to make a large investment in a subsidiary can be taken by the CEO, without any involvement in the process of actually shaping the suggested investment. A high degree of centralization may be combined with a relatively low level of actual influence. But the opposite situation is also possible. Even if HQ has decided to decentralize the formal decisions to the subsidiary level, HQ's actual influence may be high on account of the knowledge it possesses about the subsidiary's operations or the subsidiary's dependence on resources at the HQ level.

Three points need to be emphasized. First, the two dimensions – formal control and actual influence – both refer to *HQ control*. HQ will definitely exert some control through the centralization of decision-making, but to evaluate the extent to which the behavior of the subsidiary is affected by HQ requires that influence from other sources of power also be accounted for. Second, the configuration of the formal system is in itself an object of influence emanating from these sources. For instance, we would expect that if the subsidiary is heavily dependent on HQ's resources, this would have a positive impact on the degree of HQ's actual influence on the subsidiary's operations and on the degree of centralization of decision-making. Third, there is no reason to expect the impact of the sources of power to be similar, depending on whether the influence is formal or actual. For instance, the impact emanating from external network actors via the subsidiary's network embeddedness is probably greater on HQ's actual influence than on the way the formal decision-making is designed.

This line of argument implies that HQ's control over the subsidiaries in an MNC network is subject to forces and counterforces. Against HQ's aspirations to exert control there is the subsidiary's own interest in achieving a certain degree of autonomy and the aspirations of other network actors to shape the subsidiary's operations. The strength of HQ's aspirations increases with the need for integration within the MNC; its ability to exert control increases with the subsidiary's dependence on the resources that HQ can offer. The subsidiary's aspirations to avoid control from HQ are dependent on the demands of other network actors to exert influence on the subsidiary via its network embeddedness. The subsidiary's possibilities for achieving its aim, however, are reduced by its dependence on the resources possessed by HQ.

The impact of HQ's knowledge about the subsidiary's operations is more complicated. First, in line with contingency theory, the conclusion would be that HQ will decentralize decision-making to the subsidiary level in so far as it lacks knowledge itself about the subsidiary's business (Ghoshal and Nohria 1997). This is the classic way of reducing the need for information-processing at the HQ level (Egelhoff 1988). A basic assumption behind the theory is that HQ is reluctant to decentralize formal decision-making to lower levels, but will decide to do so if the distance between the locus of decision-making and the locus of knowledge becomes too great (Galbraith 1973). Consequently, what follows from this view is an expected positive relationship between HQ's knowledge about the subsidiary's operations on the one hand and, on the other, the degree of centralization due to HQ's tendency to keep control over the formal decision-making whenever its knowledge allows it to do so.

The conclusion is different if business network theory and the resource dependence perspective are applied in combination. While contingency theory emphasizes the formal control mechanisms, it is the distinction between formal control and actual influence that is crucial in the resource dependence perspective. The knowledge possessed by HQ is primarily a source of power enabling HQ to exert actual influence over the subsidiary's behavior. The more HQ's control is exerted through actual influence, the less need there will be to use formal decision-making as a control mechanism. Or to put it another way: the less knowledge HQ has regarding the subsidiary's operations, the more important will formally centralized decision-making be as a control mechanism. If HQ does not understand much about the subsidiary's business or technology, then it can get at least some insight into why a particular investment is needed by keeping the formal investment decisions at the corporate level. In such a case HQ would thus be reluctant to 'give up' its formal control in terms of decentralization, since in terms of knowledge it is in a weak position. Consequently, in sharp contrast to the claim of contingency theory, we posit that a lack of knowledge on the part of HQ is positively associated with centralization, not with decentralization. The argument is summarized in Figure 9.3.

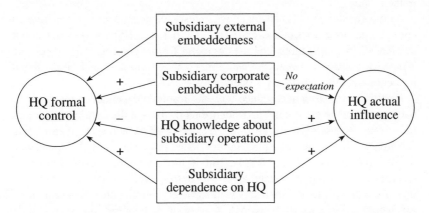

Figure 9.3   The expected relations between sources of power and HQ's formal control and actual influence over subsidiaries

In line with our argument about the dual role of the subsidiary, we expect the subsidiary's external network embeddedness to have a negative impact on HQ's degree of formal control (centralization) and on HQ's actual influence. The impact will probably be strongest on the actual influence, since the external network actors with whom HQ competes for control over the subsidiary are mainly interested in the way the subsidiary actually fulfills its role in the business network, rather than in the level at which the formal decisions are taken.

Corporate embeddedness reflects the need for integration with other MNC units. As integration is supposed to be one of HQ's major occupations, its access to formal decision-making power will be important whenever integration between units becomes a crucial issue.

It is therefore reasonable to expect that the degree of centralization will be greater, the greater the degree of corporate embeddedness. The impact on actual influence is more difficult to predict. On the one hand, the actors in the

corporate network can be regarded in the same way as actors in the external
network, i.e. as competitors for influence over the focal subsidiary, which
means that we would expect a negative relationship between actual influence
and corporate embeddedness. On the other hand, if we consider these actors as
corporate units rather than units external to the MNC, we may expect to find
HQ exerting more actual influence over the subsidiary's behavior via its
relationships with sister units. Or to put it another way: organizational
boundaries matter in a control situation. Thus, an analysis of corporate
embeddedness and actual HQ influence is likely to reveal both forces and
counterforces, which is why no specific prediction about causality is included
in the model.

As indicated in the discussion above, a resource dependence perspective on
control leads us to expect a *negative* relation between HQ's knowledge about
the subsidiary's operations and the degree of formal control, while expecting
a *positive* relation between the same independent variable and HQ's actual
influence over the subsidiary's operations.

Finally, and also in accordance with the resource dependence perspective,
we expect that the greater the dependence on the part of the focused subsidiary
on resources possessed by HQ, the greater is HQ's ability to control that
subsidiary. First, it creates a platform for actual influence through dependence
(Cook and Emerson 1979, 1984). But it probably also means that HQ's
chances of securing a certain level of control over formal decisions will
improve, and will reveal themselves in stronger centralization. Consequently,
we would expect to find positive relationships between the subsidiary's
dependence on HQ's resources on the one hand, and formal control and actual
influence on the other. The second relationship in particular is fully consistent
with the resource dependence perspective and can therefore be expected to be
specially strong.

METHODS

The Sample and the Collection of Data

The model presented in Figure 9.3 was tested on a sample of 98 subsidiaries
in a total of 20 MNC divisions. But before elaborating upon this, we will
describe the methods and the data regarding all the variables included. HQ's
formal control and actual influence over subsidiaries are tested with the help
of a regression analysis.

Every variable is based on underlying indicators (see Appendix 1),
measured on a five-point Likert scale where 1 means 'none at all' (or very
low level) and five means 'very much' (or very high level). In interviews

the respondents (HQ and/or subsidiary managers) were asked to estimate the indicators. The values of each indicator were added together to create a mean value for each variable. This was done after checking for the internal consistency between indicators, which secured a so-called Cronbach's alpha value of over 0.60. Most variables used in Chapters 9–11 are in fact composed of several underlying indicators, and in all cases the Cronbach's alpha values lie between 0.604 and 0.795 (see also Appendix I).

Dependent Variables

To acquire a measure of HQ's formal control over decisions we asked subsidiary managers about the extent to which HQ had centralized decision-making with regard to three strategic issues, namely control over the suppliers available for the subsidiary to choose from, control over the products that the subsidiary could introduce in the domestic market, and the same control regarding the international market.

To acquire a measure of the other dependent variable, namely HQ's actual influence over subsidiary operations, we asked subsidiary managers about the extent to which their particular subsidiary makes concessions to the HQ managers. The question was addressed to the subsidiary's top manager, the sales manager, and the purchasing managers. Figure 9.4 reflects the distribution of HQ control and influence in the 98 subsidiaries.

Figure 9.4 shows that HQ's formal control varies substantially, ranging between a very low and a very high degree of control. Thirty-two percent of the subsidiaries perceive strategic decision-making as being centralized at HQ to a high or a very high degree. At the same time 43 percent regard themselves as enjoying a high or very high degree of decision-making autonomy. Overall,

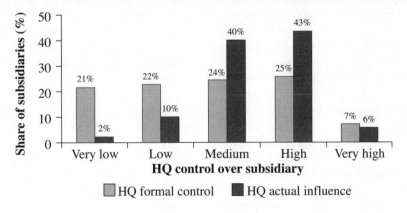

Figure 9.4   Level of headquarters' control and influence over subsidiaries

the picture indicates that the formal control exercised by HQs differs markedly from one subsidiary to another.

The actual influence exerted by HQs reveals a different pattern. Only 12 percent of the subsidiaries claim that HQ enjoys a low or very low level of influence, whereas 49 percent claim that its level of influence is high or very high. Altogether, a picture emerges implying that HQs can often influence their subsidiaries even though decisions are not centralized at the HQ level. There is a moderate but negative (Pearson) correlation of –0.32 between the two dimensions. This negative correlation supports the conclusion that we drew in the previous section, namely that HQs are more reluctant to decentralize the formal decision-making when their actual influence is slight, and vice versa.

Independent Variables

The external and the corporate network embeddedness of the subsidiary have been conceptualized and measured in accordance with the lines laid down in Chapter 8. Embeddedness has thus been estimated as the mutual adaptation of product development and production-process development in the subsidiary's six most important customer and supplier relationships. An average value for each subsidiary vis-à-vis external business partners (external embeddedness) and sister units (corporate embeddedness) has been calculated. (For a more detailed description of the measurements, see Appendix I.)

The remaining independent variables, HQ knowledge about the subsidiary's operations and the subsidiary's dependence on HQ were estimated as follows. Regarding the first of these, HQ representatives were asked to assess their knowledge about the respective subsidiary's day-to-day operations and the extent to which it was possible to understand the subsidiary managers' way of thinking. Subsidiary dependence on HQ was measured by calculating the mean value of seven indicators: the importance of HQ for the subsidiary's activities, product development, production-process development, security in delivery, business volume, technological information, and new important business contacts. The questions were answered by HQ managers.

Figure 9.5 shows that 36 percent perceive the degree of dependence on HQ as low or very low, whereas only 12 percent regard it as high or very high. Most subsidiaries, about 52 percent, perceive their dependence as lying somewhere between the two extremes.

The figure also reveals that relatively few (11 percent) of the HQs claim that the level of their knowledge of subsidiary operations is low, while 62 percent lay claim to a high or very high level of knowledge. Nonetheless, it should also be pointed out that 27 percent of the HQs – i.e. a relatively large group – claim that they have medium-level knowledge only.

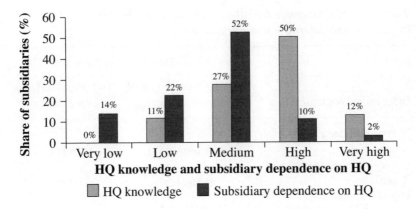

Figure 9.5 *Degree of HQ knowledge regarding subsidiary operations, and degree of subsidiary dependence on HQ*

AN ANALYSIS OF HQ CONTROL – FORMAL CONTROL AND ACTUAL INFLUENCE

Using the data and defining the variables as described in the preceding section, the model in Figure 9.3 has been tested in a couple of regression analyses. The result of this test is summarized in Table 9.1.

The overall result is consistent with the model proposed in Figure 9.3. First, network embeddedness seems to affect the amount of influence that HQ can maintain over the subsidiary's operations. There is a significant negative relation between the external embeddedness of the subsidiary and HQ's actual influence. This result supports the posited idea of a 'struggle' between different stakeholders. The greater the subsidiary's involvement in profound, long-lasting business relationships with external actors, the more difficult it is for HQ to exert influence over the subsidiary concerned. The HQ is not alone in the arena, and the external actors have an interest in exerting influence on the subsidiary's behavior, as well as the power to do so. It is also interesting to see that the impact of external embeddedness on formal control, albeit pointing in the same direction, is not significant. This also supports the proposition that actual influence rather than the level of formal decisions is what matters to the external network actors.

The positive relation proposed between subsidiary corporate embeddedness and formal control is not significant, although the coefficients point in the suggested directions. It is interesting to note, however, that the impact on actual influence seems to be non-existent, as the above discussion suggested.

The impact of HQ's knowledge of the subsidiary's operations is also consistent to some extent with the above analysis. There is a strong negative

*Table 9.1   Headquarters formal control and actual influence over
           subsidiaries – a regression analysis[1]*

Independent variables	Dependent variables	
	HQ formal control over subsidiary	HQ actual influence over subsidiary
External embeddedness of subsidiary	–0.18 (–1.49)	–0.29 (–2.12)*
Corporate embeddedness of subsidiary	0.15 (1.50)	0.02 (0.17)
HQ knowledge about subsidiary activities	–0.36 (–3.68)***	–0.03 (–0.32)
Subsidiary dependence on HQ	0.27 (2.82)**	0.36 (3.46)***
Subsidiary relative size[2]	0.07 (0.60)	0.17 (1.41)
R^2	0.29	0.18
Adj-R^2	0.25	0.13
F-value	7.08***	3.64**

Notes:
1 Regression coefficients, t-statistics in parentheses, R-squares and F-values. Significance levels:
  * = t<0.05, ** = t<0.01, *** = t<0.001.
2 Subsidiary relative size is used as a control variable.

impact of HQ's knowledge on the degree of formal centralization. When HQ has limited knowledge, the importance of formal decision-making as a means of HQ control is relatively greater. On the other hand, when HQ does know quite a lot about the subsidiary's operations, this knowledge is perceived as an important source of its power, and it then appears much easier for HQ to accept some decentralization of the formal decision-making to the subsidiary level.

Note that this result is in total conflict with contingency theory, which suggests that a lack of knowledge at the HQ level is dealt with by some form of decentralization. The main reason for this contradictory result, it seems to us, is that the contingency theory approach largely ignores any influence stemming from sources of power other than the formal organization. The theory disregards the fact that such sources can substitute for the formal organization in HQ's efforts to control the subsidiaries.

However, the expected positive relation between HQ's knowledge and its actual influence is not confirmed by the results. At first sight this is a surprising outcome from a resource dependence point of view, but should perhaps be considered together with the apparently strong impact of the subsidiary's dependence on HQ's resources. As Table 9.1 has shown, a subsidiary's dependence on HQ makes a strong and significant impact. A possible explanation of this result is that in the case of actual influence it is primarily the subsidiary's dependence rather than HQ's knowledge that counts. Although knowledge in itself is an important source of power, unless the subsidiary is dependent on HQ's resources (including knowledge), HQ's actual influence will be limited. This conclusion is in fact more in line with the main thrust of the resource dependence perspective, whereby power is treated primarily as something connected with relationships between actors rather than with the actors themselves (Dahl 1957; Hatch 1997). The possession of knowledge may be effective in controlling other units, particularly if the knowledge is needed by the units concerned.

By and large the result of this test indicates that control is a multifaceted phenomenon imbued with forces and counterforces. Clearly, though, a combination of the business network approach and the resource dependence perspective, is appropriate. The business network approach helps us to identify other actors apart from HQ who want to have a say regarding subsidiary behavior. It also helps us to consider the factors that are important in this context, and to recognize the sometimes varying impacts of these factors on formal control as opposed to actual influence.

The result also lends support to the view that dependence may be the strongest determinant of control.

SUMMARY

In this chapter we have suggested that control in MNCs is associated with formal authority and with influence based on resource-dependence. Starting from a combination of the resource dependence perspective and our own business network theory, we posit that HQ's ability to exert control over its subsidiaries is contingent not only on the degree of centralization of decision-making but also on the subsidiary's dependence on HQ's resources, and even on the type of business network in which the subsidiary is embedded. This last point indicates the extent to which the HQ has 'competitors' among other business actors who also want to influence subsidiary behavior. The more firmly the subsidiary is embedded in profound, crucial and long-lasting relationships with specific suppliers and/or customers, the more interested will these actors be in influencing the subsidiary's behavior – and sometimes in directions other than those intended or desired by HQ.

We have suggested a model of HQ's control over its subsidiaries in which the dependent variables are HQ's formal control (degree of centralization of formal decision-making) and its actual influence, while the independent variables are the subsidiary's business network and its dependence on HQ and HQ's knowledge about its daily operations. The model has been tested with data from 98 subsidiaries in Swedish MNCs, with the use of regression analyses. Relatively strong support for the model has been found. First, when a subsidiary is deeply embedded in its external business network, this appears to have a negative effect on HQ's control, in terms of its actual influence. Substantial external embeddedness means that when a subsidiary takes action there are certain external actors to whom it must pay attention, and who are thus very important to it. In so far as control is a zero-sum-game, this means in turn that HQ has less influence over the subsidiary in such situations than it would have if the subsidiary's external embeddedness were less profound.

Second, a powerful explanatory variable regarding both formal control and influence, is the subsidiary's dependence on HQ's resources. This is fully consistent with the fundamental assumption of the resource dependence perspective, namely that dependence generates power. On the other hand, HQ's knowledge about the subsidiary's business does not seem to offer any explanation of HQ's actual influence. It is sometimes said that knowledge generates power. On the basis of our analysis here, we would add that this applies only if the knowledge concerned is needed by somebody else. If the subsidiary does not need the knowledge that HQ possesses about its products or markets (probably because it already has that same knowledge itself), then HQ's knowledge is of limited use as a source of power. What counts then is the extent to which the subsidiary is dependent on other resources, such as financial capital, that are controlled by HQ.

Third, an interesting finding concerns the negative correlation between degree of centralization and HQ's knowledge. That is, the *less* HQ knows about the subsidiary's operations, the more reluctant it appears to be to decentralize the formal decision-making. Or to put it differently, if HQ only has a limited knowledge of what the subsidiary is doing, it will fight to keep control over the formal decision-making by way of centralization, since this gives some insight at least into the subsidiary's business. This contradicts the usual assumption in contingency theory that limited knowledge on the part of HQ leads to decentralization.

The focus of this chapter has been on HQ's control over the subsidiary rather than the subsidiary's influence over HQ and the rest of the MNC. Rather, the subsidiary's influence has been implicitly treated as a question of *avoiding* control from above. In the next chapter, instead, we will look at the factors that affect the level of the subsidiary's influence on the rest of the MNC. That is to say, we focus on the arrow directed away *from* the subsidiary in Figure 9.1. Again, we base our argument on the resource dependence perspective and our own business network approach.

10.   Subsidiary power in the Embedded Multinational

Chapter 9 focused on the conditions for exerting control from the point of view of corporate HQ. In the present chapter we turn to the subsidiary's ability to exert influence 'from below'. Our argument is based on the same sources-of-power model described at the beginning of Chapter 9. A distinction is drawn between the subsidiary's influence on strategic decision-making and its own functional importance, thus reflecting two types of sub-unit power in MNCs. Determinants of these two types of power are discussed below and tested against the same data as that used in Chapter 9.

In the previous chapter we maintained that HQ's formal control and its actual influence over its subsidiaries' behavior are a matter not only of authority but also of control over other critical resources on which the subsidiaries are dependent. We also argued that the actual influence is reciprocal in that a subsidiary is not only affected by HQ, but in its turn also *affects* the behavior of HQ and other corporate units. This means that a subsidiary can exert influence over strategic investments above and beyond its own local undertakings, and may sometimes find itself in confrontation with the intentions of corporate HQ.

In the following pages we discuss two types of subsidiary power that can be found in MNCs. The first and more traditional type of power is conceptualized here as net dependencies between parties, that is to say between a focal subsidiary and other units in the MNC. Net dependencies are defined, in line with the resource dependence perspective (Pfeffer and Salancik 1978), as the reciprocal need for resources controlled by the other parties involved.

The second type of power has more to do with the position of a unit in a functional system. The greater a subsidiary's involvement in the MNC as a functional system, the greater its functional importance to that system. Its involvement endows the subsidiary with a certain power within the system. However, this second type of power is of a different kind, in that it cannot be exerted unidirectionally, since the subsidiary would probably be unable to function without the system. So net dependence is replaced here by interdependence in a work-flow system, and the subsidiary's power is reflected in other parties' perception of its importance, rather than in its actual influence on decisions made by others.

In the two following sections these two types of power will be further explored.

SUBSIDIARY INFLUENCE BASED ON CONTROL OF CRITICAL RESOURCES IN A BUSINESS NETWORK SETTING

The literature of intra-organizational power offers various definitions of what constitutes a critical resource (Pfeffer 1981). Different types of resource, e.g. formal position, access to information, capability to handle uncertainty, network position, etc. are supposed to function as sources of power (Hinings et al. 1974; Astley and Sachdewa 1984; Krackhardt 1990). Many researchers, however, have adopted a more straightforward definition: a critical resource is one on which someone else apart from the unit controlling it, is dependent. This is consistent with the resource dependence perspective, which suggests that if actor A is more dependent on actor B than B is on A, then B can exert influence on A rather than the other way round. This is known as a net-dependence argument, implying that power is a relational concept associated with directional dependencies (Astley and Zajac 1990).

Thus, resource dependence theory tells us that power is about dependence. Essentially, all the units in an MNC are dependent on one other, simply because, at least financially, they are assumed to be contributing to the same corporate system. Thompson would call this pooled dependence (Thompson 1967). Consequently, units that contribute less are more dependent on those that contribute more. For instance, a large and/or profitable subsidiary is more influential in the MNC, other things being equal, than a small or less profitable subsidiary would be.

We have frequently noted in this book that a subsidiary's business network is one of its most important resources. Its relationships with customers, suppliers, etc. constitute a valuable resource since they enable the absorbing, developing and commercialization of new knowledge from the environment (Håkansson and Johanson 2001; Lane and Lubatkin 1998). We have also shown elsewhere that a subsidiary's market performance is positively related to the extent of embeddedness in its relationships with external customers and suppliers (Andersson et al. 2001, 2002). Consequently, we posit that a subsidiary's external embeddedness is an important – if not the most important – indicator of a valuable resource over which it exerts control. It is also a resource that can provide a platform from which the subsidiary can exert influence on the strategic behavior of the MNC as a whole (Andersson and Forsgren 2000). Consequently, we claim that a subsidiary's external business network is a source of power, irrespective of the kind of relationship it enjoys with the rest of the MNC, because there is at least a pooled-interdependence situation.

This type of influence can be reinforced, however, if the subsidiary also does business with other sister units. Through its role as supplier and/or customer of other corporate units the subsidiary has access to intra-organizational channels through which it can exert influence, irrespective of its own resources or its market performance. There is reason to assume that the stronger these relationships are in terms of age and the mutual adaptation of resources, the greater the possibility of exercising influence through the subsidiary's intra-corporate business network. Consequently, we posit a positive relationship between corporate embeddedness and subsidiary influence.

As we suggested above, however, influence is primarily a question of who is dependent on whom. If the subsidiary is heavily dependent on the rest of the MNC, while no sister unit is dependent on the subsidiary, its platform for exerting influence in the MNC is a weak one, irrespective of the actual structure of its business network. On the other hand, if other corporate units and/or corporate HQ perceive themselves as being heavily dependent on the subsidiary in question while the latter perceives its own dependence as slight, then its ability to exert unidirectional influence will increase. What really counts is thus the net dependence between the subsidiary and the rest of the MNC. We can conclude that the greater the corporate net dependence vis-à-vis the focal subsidiary, the greater the influence exerted by that subsidiary on decisions reached in other corporate units. The discussion is summarized in Figure 10.1.

Later in this chapter we will investigate the extent to which this model explains the influence of subsidiaries on strategic decisions in MNCs. The analysis will be based on the same data as we used in Chapter 9 (data from 98 subsidiaries in 20 divisions in Swedish MNCs; see Appendix I).

First, however, we will introduce another more complex view of subsidiary power. In the next section we will thus consider power not as a question of net dependencies between two parties, but as a question of interdependencies in a functional system. We call this type of subsidiary power 'systemic power'.

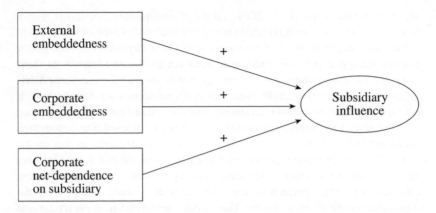

Figure 10.1   Determinants of subsidiary influence in MNCs in a business network setting

THE SUBSIDIARY'S SYSTEMIC POWER IN A BUSINESS NETWORK SETTING

In the preceding section we looked at the subsidiary's influence within the MNC as a consequence of net-dependencies in resource exchanges between units. The greater the dependence of other corporate units on the focal subsidiary the more influence does that subsidiary possess. This implies that a subsidiary's influence is greater when there is a big difference between the level of dependence of its sister units and its own dependence on them. The differences in power among units are a function of imbalances or 'net exchange' differences between units in dyadic relationships (Anderson and Narus 1990; Blau 1964; Emerson 1962). This represents an 'asymmetric' view of power.

However, a unit's power can also be conceived as contingent on its functional role in the overall system of work-flows created by an organization's division of labor (Astley and Zajac 1990). In such a perspective the emphasis falls on non-directional interdependencies in a unit's relationships with other units, rather than on net dependencies. This power is associated with a unit's nature as a 'cog in the wheel', in that the system is dependent on the focal unit and that the unit cannot function without the system. This type of power has therefore been dubbed 'systemic power' (Astley and Zajac 1991, p. 403).

There is a fundamental difference between these two types of power. Power derived from net dependencies has to be explained ultimately in the context of decision-making processes. Through the asymmetric resource dependencies in dyadic relationships a subsidiary can be expected to influence the actual decision-making processes of its exchange partners in accordance with its own interests. This is a case of realized rather than merely potential power.

Systemic power is of another kind. A subsidiary achieves systemic power not by creating a favorable balance of resource exchange vis-à-vis its sister units, but by performing tasks that are essential to the functioning of the MNC as a whole. It is manifested in its 'functional importance' for the overall system, not by its influence over the decisions of other units.

An example can perhaps clarify the distinction between influence stemming from asymmetric dependencies on the one hand, and systemic power on the other. Through its connections with particular local suppliers, a subsidiary may have access to a unique resource that is important to its own performance. Further, by its very uniqueness, the resource is also useful as input into the operations of other MNC units. This creates a favorable position for the subsidiary, in that it functions as a bridgehead for other subsidiaries seeking access to this unique resource. The other subsidiaries become highly dependent on their favored sister unit – a dependence that is not counterbalanced by its equivalent in the other direction. Due to this favorable net dependence, the focal subsidiary can to a great extent 'dictate' the strategic investments that the MNC will make, where it will locate its production, what firms will be acquired, etc.

Compare this situation with the case of a subsidiary possessing a specific role in a vertically and/or horizontally integrated production system. In some MNCs, for instance in the forest industry, subsidiaries are linked to each other in vertically integrated production systems across borders, which creates serial dependencies between the units. In other MNCs the subsidiaries may produce particular qualities of a certain product, while marketing the whole quality range in their local markets. Such a situation creates a system of mutually dependent flows of products and of information about future markets. In both these cases it is difficult to decide which is the unit possessing the ultimate power and, thus, the ability to exert influence on the decisions of other subsidiaries. No single unit emerges as the most powerful one, with the possibility to 'dictate' the behavior of other units, because even if the MNC cannot function without the presence of any one subsidiary, a single subsidiary cannot function without the MNC either. Such a subsidiary is not powerless, but its power is of a different kind. It is not unidirectional. That is to say, it must be exercised in interplay with other subsidiaries possessing a similar type of power. It is systemic power rather than net-dependence power.

The empirical manifestation of such power is the subsidiary's 'functional importance', as assessed for example by the corporate HQ. Functional importance can be expected to reflect the consequences to the corporate system of the subsidiary's withdrawal from the system. The more serious these consequences are likely to be, the greater the functional importance of the subsidiary and, thus, its systemic power. From this follows that while a subsidiary's influence on the strategic decision-making can be analysed as a function of favorable net-dependencies vis-à-vis sister units, its functional importance can be analysed in terms of its integration with these units. The greater the subsidiary's integration with other MNC units in terms of mutual resource flows, the greater also its functional importance. Such importance is also a source of power, but it is much more complicated for the individual subsidiary to exploit this type of power than to exploit power based on net dependencies. For instance, the view that one subsidiary has greater functional importance than another does not automatically make it easier for that subsidiary to lay down conditions for action. In bargaining about investments, subsidiaries always have to remember that they are part of a system and that their ability to function outside it is limited. In fact the greater their functional importance, the more remote by definition is this possibility. The possession of functional importance will certainly ensure a subsidiary a prominent role in the bargaining processes, but the outcome of such processes is far from certain.

In the previous section on subsidiaries' influence, corporate embeddedness and external embeddedness were introduced as independent variables. Corporate embeddedness was assumed to offer the subsidiary better opportunities for exerting influence on the decisions of its sister units, since business relationships with sister units provide channels for influence of this kind. External embeddedness, on the other hand, was assumed to reflect the critical resources on which the subsidiary's influence is based in the first place.

Corporate and external embeddedness are also relevant independent variables when it comes to a subsidiary's functional importance or systemic power. Corporate embeddedness reflects the 'cog-in-the-wheel' dimension, i.e. the degree of a subsidiary's involvement in the functional system of the MNC. The greater the corporate embeddedness, the stronger the interdependencies between the subsidiary and the corporate system and, consequently, the greater the functional importance of the subsidiary. However, the 'cog' needs resources in order to fulfill its role in the system, and the subsidiary's external embeddedness is one important source for such resources. This leads us to conclude that there is also a positive relationship between a subsidiary's external embeddedness and its functional importance.

The subsidiary's business network thus promotes not only its resource-dependence power but also its systemic power within the MNC. Instead, the main difference between the two types of power is reflected in the third independent variable in Figure 10.1, namely 'corporate net dependence on the subsidiary'. Corporate net dependence reflects the degree of asymmetry between the subsidiary and its sister units, in terms of the resources needed by each side. Although this is expected to provide a powerful explanatory variable as regards the subsidiary's influence on the strategic decisions of sister units, it does not automatically generate a stronger perception of the subsidiary's functional importance. Rather, a high degree of asymmetry indicates that although the subsidiary is important to other sister units, these units are not important to the subsidiary. Or to put it differently, the subsidiary's integration in the MNC system is only partial. For this reason we would expect the impact of corporate net dependence on the subsidiary's systemic power to be only slight or moderate. Our discussion of systemic power is summarized in Figure 10.2.

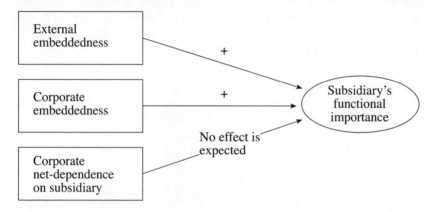

*Figure 10.2   Determinants of a subsidiary's functional importance
(systemic power) in a business network setting*

The models proposed in Figures 10.1 and 10.2 are tested with the same data set that was used in the preceding chapter. The methodology applied is presented below.

METHODS

The Sample and the Collection of Data

The analysis of the models presented in Figures 10.1 and 10.2 is based on the same sample as in Chapters 8 and 9. In the sections that follow we describe the methods and data applying to every variable in the model and use a regression analysis to test the extent to which the variables explain the degree of influence and the extent of functional importance that the subsidiaries enjoy in the MNC.

Dependent Variables

'Subsidiary influence on corporate decisions' was measured by asking HQ
managers about the influence of subsidiaries on strategic investments
undertaken at the divisional level in the MNC. Our primary interest here is that
the influence of a subsidiary should concern significant investments of long-
term importance for the MNC. Influence on four kinds of decisions were used
as indicators. These concerned investments in R&D, production capacity,
product lines and acquisitions. The four indicators constructed the average
measure presented and interpreted in Figure 10.3. The figure shows that the
share of subsidiaries possessing a very high degree of influence and those
possessing a very low degree is the same, i.e. 5 percent in both cases. The
figure also reveals that 25 percent perceive the degree of subsidiary influence
to be high, while 39 percent perceive it as 'medium'.

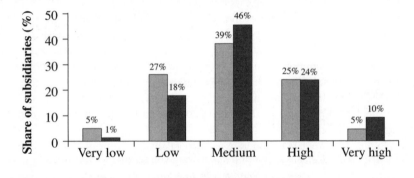

☐ Subsidiaries' influence on decisions ■ Subsidiaries' functional importance

Figure 10.3   Subsidiaries' influence and functional importance

Figure 10.3 also shows the functional importance of subsidiaries within the
MNC. This is measured in terms of the average values for a subsidiary's
importance to the product and production development, the technological
information, the information about market activities and new important
business contacts of other MNC units. Representatives of the divisional HQ
were used as respondents. The figure shows that 10 percent of the subsidiaries
possess a very high degree of importance, which suggests that these
subsidiaries may be regarded as 'centres of excellence' or 'strategic leaders'
(Holm and Pedersen 2000; Bartlett and Ghoshal 1989), who make a strong
impact on the development of the MNC. Twenty-four percent possess a high
degree of importance, while 18 percent have a low degree only. However, the
great majority of the subsidiaries (80 percent) are of 'medium', 'high', or

'very high' importance to the rest of the MNC, which indicates that relatively few subsidiaries are unrelated to other MNC units.

The variable 'corporate dependence on subsidiary' reflects the degree of net dependence of the MNC organization vis-à-vis the individual subsidiary. As Astley and Zajac (1990) point out, a unit's power can be described as a function of imbalances or 'net exchange' differences between units in dyadic relationships. In the present case we assume that dependence in power relations of this kind is reflected in the adaptations that actors are willing to make in relation to one another. Thus, by questioning subsidiary managers and using a five-point Likert scale we measured net dependence in terms of the scope of the adaptations made by the sister units vis-à-vis the focal subsidiary as regards product and production-process technology, minus the scope of adaptations undertaken by the subsidiary itself regarding the same activities. A high positive value reflects a high net-dependence on the part of the MNC vis-à-vis the subsidiary. Correspondingly, a high negative value reflects a high net-dependence on the part of the subsidiary vis-à-vis the MNC.

Figure 10.4 shows the results. It is suggested that equal dependence reflects a situation whereby the subsidiary and the MNC have a net value for dependence spanning from –1 to +1. Moderate dependence ranges from –4 to –2 (the subsidiary adapts and is moderately dependent) or from 2 to 4 (MNC units adapt and are moderately dependent). Values below –4 or above 4 reflect a high degree of dependence on the part of the subsidiary and the MNC respectively.

Figure 10.4 reveals a moderate net-dependence in favor of the subsidiary in 13 percent of the cases. In 52 percent of the cases the subsidiary and the rest of the MNC are equally dependent on each other. In more than a third of the cases the subsidiary is moderately or highly dependent on the MNC. Thus, not

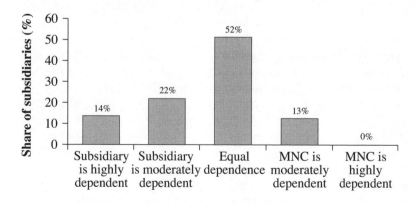

Figure 10.4   The MNC (net) dependence on subsidiaries

surprisingly, the overall picture implies that the subsidiary is more dependent on the MNC than vice versa.

The following section offers an analysis in which the external and corporate embeddedness of subsidiaries and the subsidiaries' corporate dependence are used to explain the subsidiaries' influence on corporate decisions and their functional importance in the MNC.

ANALYSIS OF SUBSIDIARY INFLUENCE AND FUNCTIONAL IMPORTANCE IN THE MNC

The statistical analysis was conducted in the same way as the corresponding test in Chapter 9.

In Table 10.1 the results of the regression analyses are depicted. Subsidiary relative size has been used as a control variable in both equations. The first regression concerns the effects of external embeddedness, corporate embeddedness and corporate net-dependence on subsidiary influence. The second regression deals with the effect of the same variables on subsidiary importance (systemic power).

Somewhat surprisingly, the degree of external embeddedness is not significantly related to influence, while corporate embeddedness is. One interpretation of this could be that a subsidiary needs to have channels into the

Table 10.1 Subsidiary influence and importance in the MNC – a regression analysis[1]

Independent variables	Dependent variable	
	Subsidiary influence	Subsidiary importance
External embeddedness of subsidiary	0.08 (0.64)	0.46 (3.67)***
Corporate embeddedness of subsidiary	0.36 (3.32)***	0.49 (4.62)***
Corporate net-dependence on the subsidiary	0.26 (2.56)**	0.08 (0.79)
Subsidiary relative size[2]	0.34 (3.05)**	0.01 (0.12)
R^2	0.29	0.28
Adj-R^2	0.26	0.24
F-value	8.32***	8.15***

Notes:
1 Regression coefficients, t-statistics in parentheses, R-squares and F-values. Significance levels: * = t<0.05, ** = t<0.01, *** = t<0.001.
2 Subsidiary relative size is used as a control variable.

MNC in terms of business relationships with its sister units in order to exert influence over them. A strong source of power in terms of external embeddedness is not enough. Compare this result with the result reported in Chapter 9 regarding HQ's control. External embeddedness had a significant negative impact on HQ's actual influence over the subsidiary (see Table 9.1). The results indicate that it is much easier for a subsidiary enjoying a high degree of external embeddedness to *avoid* control from HQ than it is for it to use its position as a base for intra-organizational influence.

Consideration of functional importance suggests that external embeddedness and corporate embeddedness are both statistically significant. This is in accordance with our expectation. Corporate embeddedness reflects the degree of interdependence in the MNC as a workflow system, and should consequently have a positive impact on the subsidiary's functional importance in that system, as perceived by HQ. It corresponds to the 'cog-in-the-wheel' dimension. External embeddedness reflects the extent to which the subsidiary can contribute to the system, thus having an impact on the activities of other MNC units.

A comparison between net-dependence and corporate embeddedness highlights the difference between power stemming from resource dependence (influence) and systemic power (functional importance). While the first variable seems to be a relatively strong predictor of influence, it is of no significance as regards functional importance. Corporate embeddedness, on the other hand, is also significant with regard to functional importance, because it reflects the interdependence dimension. The more a subsidiary integrates its business with that of other corporate units, the greater its perceived functional importance within the MNC will be.

The difference is also reflected in the result for the control variable 'relative size'. While size is significantly related to influence, it is not related to functional importance. Through its size the subsidiary has some chance of exerting influence because of the resources that size in itself implies, even if there are no other business connections between the subsidiary and the rest of the MNC. However, a subsidiary can never be functionally important as a result of size alone. In order to be functionally important some degree of business integration is needed between the subsidiary and its sister units.

SUMMARY

Thus the intra-organizational power of the subsidiaries appears to be a multidimensional concept. A subsidiary's influence and its functional importance are both present, and both seem to be relevant aspects of intra-organizational power. They also appear to differ in the way they are determined by other variables. While subsidiary influence is affected by corporate embeddedness, by the MNC's net-dependence on the subsidiary and by the subsidiary's relative size, functional importance is primarily affected by the whole network to which the subsidiary belongs. Neither imbalance in terms of resource-dependencies nor the relative size of the subsidiary seems to matter. The 'cog-in-the-wheel' dimension is more important to systemic power, while asymmetric dependencies are crucial to resource-dependence power. While the second of these allows more room for the subsidiary to look after its own interests by influencing decisions made by other corporate units, the first cannot be used as easily in the same way. Involvement in the affairs of a corporation or a group or a family does not always mean you can dictate or set the rules for the other members -particularly if withdrawal from the system is not a serious option. However, such involvement does lead to systemic power or, to put it differently, to a natural place at the negotiation table where decisions about future investments are taken.

11. Transfer of knowledge in the Embedded Multinational – the role of shared values and business networks

> The importance of shared values as mechanisms for control in MNCs has been emphasized by many scholars. The view presented in this book, however, is that business networks are more important than shared values. In Chapter 9, the possibility of creating shared values in an MNC was questioned. In the present chapter we scrutinize the assumption of shared value as an important mechanism in somewhat greater depth. In doing so, we compare the importance of shared values between the HQ and the subsidiary with the importance of factors such as the subsidiary's business network and HQ's knowledge about this network. The analysis is underpinned by data from the 98 subsidiaries used in the two preceding chapters.

In Chapter 9 we touched upon the idea of 'shared value' as a 'glue' holding the whole MNC together. We argued that values and interests at the subsidiary level are rooted in the subsidiary's own business context, of which HQ has only partial understanding. Values and interests of this kind have been a long time in the making, through interaction with other business network actors. They are context-specific; they differ from one subsidiary to another; and it is difficult to change them. The possibility of replacing this differentiated value structure by a common culture created and implemented by HQ, is probably more problematic than is usually assumed.

The importance of shared value as an integrating mechanism in MNCs has been noted by several authors. Ghoshal and Nohria (1994, 1997), for instance, argue that the presence of shared values between HQ and subsidiaries has a beneficial effect on the performance of the MNC. Others have stressed the importance of shared values as a factor affecting the performance of an

MNC as well as communications within it (Wiener 1988; Ghoshal et al. 1994).

The basic idea behind the 'shared-value' approach concerns the impact of common views on cooperation. It is expected that a large dose of shared values will favor cooperation and, thus, the level of MNC performance. Or to put it another way, the more views a subsidiary and its HQ hold in common, the more inclined will that subsidiary be to work together with other subsidiaries. Cooperation between subsidiaries can thus be regarded as an intermediary variable between shared values and performance. The extent to which the focal subsidiary is important to the operations of other subsidiaries will thus provide our first indication or 'test' of the relevance of the 'shared-value approach'. If shared values improve the cooperation between subsidiaries, it will probably also be positively related to MNC performance.

In the preceding chapters we have demonstrated the important role of the business network when it comes to HQ's ability to control subsidiaries, as well as the subsidiaries' possibility of influencing the strategic behavior of the MNC, but we did so without including the concept of shared values. Instead, our analysis was built on the assumption that it is structural, or maybe operational, conditions that matter. It was shown that factors such as the subsidiary's external network embeddedness, its corporate embeddedness and its perceived resource dependence are powerful predictors of control and influence within the MNC. We focused on 'hard' factors such as business relationships, rather than 'soft' factors such as norms and values.

However, the business network perspective as presented in this book does not imply that 'soft' factors are irrelevant. What it suggests, though, is that business comes first, and shared values second. A business relationship is developed gradually, fostering in its turn shared values among those involved. From this follows that the possibility to use shared values as a normative mechanism in an MNC is circumscribed by the business in which the subsidiaries are engaged and by the structural factors of such business. The business network model thus means that the current business relationships in which the subsidiary is embedded are more important as integrative mechanisms than the values that the subsidiary shares with HQ or with other subsidiaries.

However, since shared values and business networks have both been noted as important integrating factors, it seems relevant to confront the two variables with one another. In the present chapter we will therefore analyse the relative merits of the 'hard' and 'soft' factors as variables in explaining the degree of cooperation in MNCs. More specifically, we explore how far the existence of shared values between the subsidiary and HQ can explain the scope of knowledge transfer inside the MNC, when network embeddedness, resource dependence and HQ's knowledge about the subsidiary's operations have also been accounted for. Such a model will be offered in the next section.

A MODEL OF KNOWLEDGE TRANSFER IN MNCs

A model of knowledge transfer within MNCs should thus, in line with the argument above, contain two groups of independent variables: one reflecting the business network in which the different subsidiaries are embedded, and a second reflecting the scope of shared values in the MNC. The first of these represents the 'hard', structural variables rooted in the ongoing business of the MNC and its subsidiaries, while the other reflects the socialization between the individual subsidiary and HQ, irrespective of the subsidiary's business. The latter are 'soft' factors, which it is assumed that HQ can use as integrative mechanisms.

In our earlier research we demonstrated that a subsidiary's external business network affects the extent to which it transfers knowledge to its sister subsidiaries (Andersson et al. 2001, 2002). The closeness of the relationships with external customers and suppliers generates a capability for absorbing and developing new products and new production processes. Some of these new products and processes then 'spill over' into other subsidiaries in the MNC by way of knowledge transfer.

However, irrespective of the level of external embeddedness, the extent of the subsidiary's involvement in business relationships with its sister units will probably help to promote its transfer of knowledge to these units. There are two reasons for this. First, other corporate units are more likely to recognize the capability of a particular subsidiary if it has already cultivated business relationships with one or more of their own kind. Second, in themselves such business relationships provide important channels for the transfer of knowledge, for instance in the joint problem-solving activities with suppliers and customers. We would thus expect corporate embeddedness to have a positive impact on the transfer of knowledge between a particular subsidiary and its sister units.

A subsidiary's embeddedness, be it external or corporate, reflects the kind of structural or 'hard' factors that underpin knowledge transfer within the MNC. However, according to received theory, the importance of factors relating to HQ's ability to stimulate coordination and integration within the MNCs also has to be recognized. We have after all no grounds for assuming any kind of automatic knowledge transfer from one subsidiary to another. There are in fact a variety of obstacles to such a thing, due either to the 'sender's' willingness (or otherwise) to engage in knowledge transfer or the 'receiver's' readiness (or otherwise) to employ solutions that have been developed elsewhere (cf. the so-called 'not-invented-here' syndrome). HQ can thus play an important part by overcoming or reducing these obstacles.

In line with the resource-dependence argument we suggest that the greater HQ's opportunities are for influencing subsidiary behavior due to its control of critical resources, the more likely it is that it can stimulate knowledge transfer among the corporate units. In Chapter 9 we demonstrated how a subsidiary's recognition of its own dependence on HQ goes a long way towards explaining its subjection to influence from HQ. Consequently, it seems reasonable to expect that this variable – resource dependence – will also affect HQ's opportunities for stimulating knowledge transfer within the MNC. HQ can exploit a subsidiary's dependence as a way of 'forcing' it to share its expertise with other MNC units.

However, HQ's capability in this respect is also dependent on its own expertise. We have already claimed that the subsidiary's external network embeddedness is a crucially important factor, in that it constitutes an essential base from which the subsidiary can develop a unique competence in the first place. But only if HQ is aware of the development of this competence in the subsidiary's interaction with external business actors, can this be exploited to stimulate knowledge-sharing in the MNC. A major indicator of such awareness is the extent to which HQ conducts relations of its own with the external business partners of the subsidiary concerned. Such relations make it much easier for HQ to evaluate the possibilities and the difficulties associated with the transfer of knowledge between the subsidiary and its sister units.

Finally, assuming that shared values are indeed 'the glue that holds an organization together' (Wiener 1988) we argue that the presence of values held in common by HQ and the subsidiary in question would have a positive effect on the subsidiary's willingness to share its expertise with others. If the subsidiary entertains the same goals, norms and visions as HQ, then it is less likely to resist sharing any knowledge it possesses with others. In fact, the existence of shared values in an organization implies that knowledge will be transferred almost automatically, because sharing HQ's values will also involve an interest in coordinating and integrating knowledge within the MNC. The argument can be summarized in the model in Figure 11.1.

The Sample and the Collection of Data

The analysis of the model in Figure 11.1 is based on the same sample that we used in Chapters 8, 9 and 10. The following sections describe the methods and data for each variable in the model. In a regression analysis we then test the extent to which the variables explain the scope of the knowledge transfer among subsidiaries. For details of the methods, see Chapter 9 and Appendix I. For an empirical description of the variables 'external and corporate

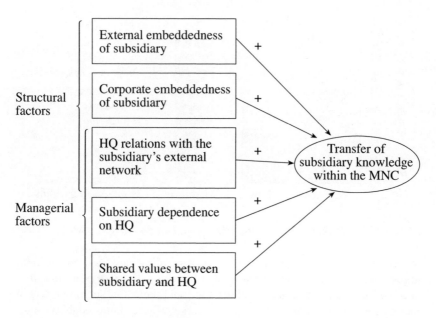

Figure 11.1   A model of knowledge transfer in MNCs

embeddedness', and 'subsidiary dependence on HQ', see Chapter 9. Below we describe the measurement and distribution of the four remaining variables.

'Transfer of subsidiary knowledge in the MNC', which is the dependent variable, was measured by asking both HQ representatives and the managers of a specific subsidiary about that subsidiary's importance to the activities of other corporate subsidiaries. Our primary interest here is that the knowledge in question should reflect both technology-related and market-related activities. Five indicators have been chosen from interviews and are given on a five-point scale referring to the subsidiary's importance to the following aspects of their co-subsidiaries' operations: product development, production-process development, technical information, information about market activities and new major business contacts. To reduce the problem of common-method bias and to create consistency with the measurement of shared values, we included the answers of both subsidiary and HQ managers. Thus, starting from these answers we went on to create an average value for the transfer of subsidiary knowledge. The average values were interpreted and distributed as shown in Figure 11.2. The figure indicates that subsidiaries with 'very high' or 'very low' levels of knowledge transfer are uncommon (i.e. 1 and 2 percent of the subsidiaries, respectively).

A dominating share of the subsidiaries, i.e. 60 percent, exhibit a 'medium' level of knowledge transfer, while about one-fifth exhibit levels that are low

Management of the embedded MNC

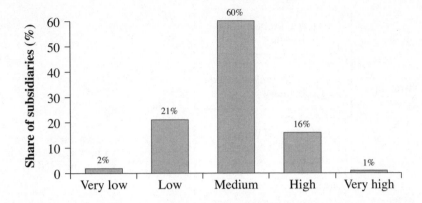

Figure 11.2   Transfer of subsidiary knowledge in the MNC

or very low. Some (16 percent) of the subsidiaries, however, are of great importance when it comes to knowledge transfer. Thus it appears that it is uncommon for subsidiaries to be either very unimportant or very important in the context of technology-related or market-related knowledge transfer, suggesting that links do exist between most subsidiaries in this area, but that only a minority of them have developed any very extensive roles.

Figure 11.3 shows the extent of HQ relations with the subsidiary's external network partners. Subsidiary managers first identified their most important relationships as those with external partners, after which HQ managers were asked to evaluate the extent of the direct contact they had developed with the subsidiaries' business partners. The extent of such relations was measured on a four-point scale (Blankenburg and Johanson 1992). The variable 'HQ

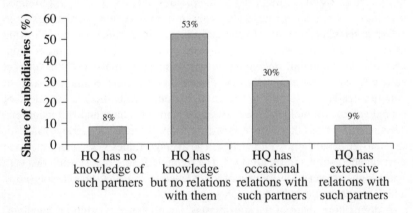

Figure 11.3   HQ relations with the subsidiaries' external network partners

relations with the subsidiary's external network partners' thus ranges from 'no HQ knowledge of the existence of such partners' to the development of 'extensive HQ relations with such partners'.

Figure 11.3 shows that in 9 percent of the cases HQ has developed extensive relations with their subsidiaries' important business partners. We can speak of an HQ-subsidiary-business partners triad, implying that HQ learns about the network activities, about the subsidiary itself and about these external partners. In the majority of cases (53 percent) we can speak of an 'open triad', implying that HQ knows about the existence of an external business partner but has no relationship of its own with the partner in question. In 8 percent of the cases HQ has no knowledge at all of the existence of the subsidiary's most important external business partners.

We also need to examine the variables of shared values. The issue of shared values is a delicate one. It implies that two or more actors have similar norms, goals and/or visions. These dimensions are general in their nature and complicated to capture (Hofstede et al. 1990), but they are manifested in cooperative behavior, which in practical business means that the interests of one actor are consistent with the interests and behavior of another actor (Ghoshal and Nohria 1997). Thus, the effect of shared values in the MNC will be reflected in a low level of diverging interests, and we will thus treat such values as an indication of shared interests in business activities. In contrast to most research on this issue, our focus concerns the practical level, i.e. investments in various business activities rather than the actors' sharing of general ambitions and vision (Tsai and Ghoshal 1998). We argue that MNC subsidiaries may have similar visions, but may still prefer to pursue totally different activities in order to achieve them. For instance, investment in some particular R&D activities may be consistent with the visions of one subsidiary, but irrelevant or even contrary to those of others.

Further, most research has been based on a single-respondent measurement. This is problematic since not only do MNCs consist of several geographically dispersed subsidiaries, but business interests are also deeply rooted in the long-term experience of business relationships within and outside the firm. To ask only one actor in such a system will increase the risk of bias and speculation. In the present study, subsidiary managers and HQ managers have both answered questions about the extent of their shared interests.

Five questions were put to the managers concerning the degree to which they perceived themselves as having identical interests. The questions concerned investment in R&D, marketing, purchasing, product design and production. On a five-point scale ranging from a very low degree to a very high one, the subsidiary and HQ respondents evaluated the extent of their identical interests as regards each one of the five activities.

Two steps were taken to create one measure out of the two perspectives involved. First we checked the Cronbach's alphas for the subsidiary and HQ measures, which proved to be good (0.720 and 0.702 respectively). Then we checked the Cronbach's alpha for all ten indicators, which was 0.705. There was thus good internal consistency between subsidiary and HQ responses. This was further confirmed by the fact that in 70 percent of the cases the two groups agreed on the degree of their shared interests, claiming this to be 'very high' or 'high'.

Nonetheless, we also looked at the extent of the difference regarding the five indicators in each subsidiary–HQ relationship, checking for instance whether the subsidiaries and the HQs held the same opinion (see Figure 11.4). If a subsidiary claimed a very high or very low degree of shared interests, for example, how far did this differ from the view of the HQ representatives?

We can say immediately that extreme asymmetrical opinions were uncommon, and opinions regarding the extent of shared interests were the same in 32 percent of the cases. In 38 percent of the cases there was a slight difference between the two perspectives. In 15 percent of the cases both parties claimed a modest difference. Finally, in 13 percent of the cases was the degree of difference 'high', while in only 1 percent was it 'very high'. It is interesting to note that a big difference in opinions occurred mainly when the subsidiary managers had claimed a 'high' level of shared interests (about 11 percent). When HQ representatives claimed a high (or very high) level of shared interests, opinions on the subsidiary side differed markedly in 3 percent of the cases only. Thus, it seems that subsidiary managers are more inclined to claim a high level of shared interest with the HQ than the other way around.

However, the overall picture reveals considerable consistency among the ten indicators. Cronbach's alpha was satisfactory and in 70 percent of the cases the two respondent groups have equal or only slightly diverging opinions about the level of shared interests. We have therefore added the answers from both parties together in the following regression analysis, which means that a high subsidiary value may be added to a low HQ value (or vice versa). It should be noted, however, that asymmetry appears in 10–15 percent of the cases.

When combining subsidiary and HQ answers we found no cases of a 'very low' level of shared values, and only one percent of the cases showed a 'low' level. The majority of cases show a 'high' level (62 percent) or a 'medium' level (30 percent). In relatively few cases, however, a picture of a 'very high' level of shared values does emerge (7 percent). Overall, we can say that the degree of shared values is seldom low or very low. But we should also stress that the sharing of values is far from complete.

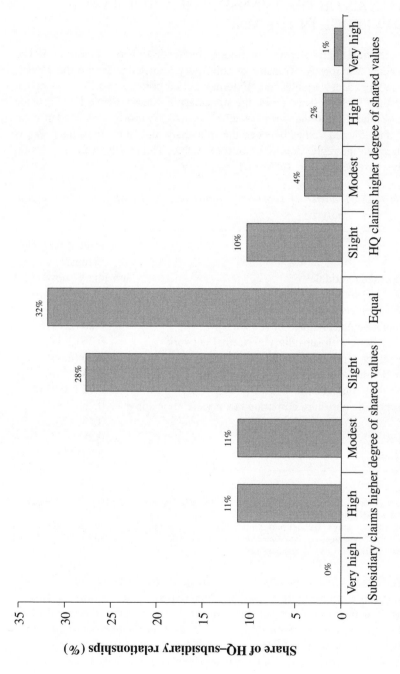

Figure 11.4   Difference between the opinions of subsidiaries and HQ on the degree of shared values

ANALYSIS OF THE TRANSFER OF SUBSIDIARY'S KNOWLEDGE IN THE MNC

The statistical analysis corresponds to the model described in Figure 11.1. The dependent variable is 'Transfer of subsidiary knowledge within the MNC'. The independent variables are 'External and corporate embeddedness of the subsidiary', 'HQ relations with the subsidiary's external network', 'Presence of subsidiary corporate business relationships', 'Subsidiary dependence on HQ' and 'Shared values between the subsidiary and HQ'. Subsidiary size is included in the regression as a control variable. The results of the regression analysis are depicted in Table 11.1.

Table 11.1   Transfer of subsidiary knowledge in the MNC – a regression analysis[1]

Independent variables	Dependent variable (Transfer of subsidiary knowledge)
External embeddedness of subsidiary	0.42 (3.44)***
Corporate embeddedness of subsidiary	0.28 (2.18)*
HQ relations with subsidiary's external network	0.26 (2.49)*
Subsidiary dependence on HQ	0.26 (2.49)*
Shared values between subsidiary and HQ	–0.04 (–0.46)
Subsidiary relative size[2]	–0.02 (–0.21)
Presence of subsidiary corporate business relationships[2]	0.26 (1.87)†
R^2	0.45
Adj R^2	0.38
F-value	6.84***

Notes:
1 Regression coefficients, t-statistics in parentheses (significance levels: † = $t<0.10$, * = $t<0.05$, ** = $t<0.01$, *** = $t<0.001$).
2 Subsidiary relative size and presence of subsidiary corporate business relationships are used as control variables. The latter variable is a dummy, where 0 = no corporate relationships and 1 = presence of corporate relationships.

The results of the regression analysis are quite clear. The 'business network' factor seems to be more important than shared values as an explanatory variable with regard to knowledge transfer. External network embeddedness and corporate network embeddeddness are both positively and significantly related to the subsidiary's role as a provider of competence to other MNC units. The corporate HQ's own relationships with the subsidiary's external business partners also seem to have a positive effect on that role. On the other hand, the variable shared values between subsidiary and HQ is clearly insignificant.

These results are somewhat surprising in view of the importance that various scholars attach to shared values in the context of cooperation and integration within an organization (Deal and Kennedy 1982; Wiener 1988; Hofstede et al. 1990; Schein 1996; Ghoshal and Nohria 1994, 1997; Nahapiet and Ghoshal 1998). Apart from differences in the conceptualization and measurement of shared values there are several possible reasons for the gap between our result and what we have referred to as the 'shared-value approach' above.

First, even if we assume the importance of corporate culture as a 'glue' in the organization, the position of shared values as the core of corporate culture can still be questioned. Hofstede among others, for instance, has pointed out that organizational culture makes its impact on the behavior of sub-units by way of shared *practices* (Hofstede et al. 1990; Kilduff 1992). According to this view, measuring shared values in terms of common norms, interests, etc. does not cover the essential contents of the 'glue'. Shared values may or may not be the same at different organizational levels, but what counts is whether the same routines, conventions, habits or rituals are being applied. Or to put it differently, above a certain level of shared values in an MNC, perhaps secured by the principles for recruiting subsidiary managers, no 'additional' shared values will have any substantial effect on knowledge transfer. What does affect the transfer process is the extent to which a common culture has become manifested in common practices.

It has also been pointed out that a major barrier to knowledge transfer arises from differences in the *business logics* employed by different sub-units in an MNC, for instance between marketing-oriented and production-oriented people. An innovation introduced by the marketing people is of no interest to the production team, who may not even be able to identify it on account of their different ways of looking at things (Ståhl 2004). These cognitive differences can arise even if the units share the same goals or interests. Thus, shared values do not capture similarities or dissimilarities in business logics.

Second, the content and structure of the ongoing business of sub-units has seldom been included in analyses of the importance of shared values. Ghoshal and Nohria (1997), for instance, use a model implying that the level of shared values between subsidiaries and HQ, and the degree of fit in terms of centralization and formalization, are the only independent variables included in their investigation of the impact on MNCs' performance. The strength of the subsidiaries' operational integration is not taken into account in their analysis. If we assume that an important underlying variable with regard to knowledge transfer is the way in which units are related in business terms, then a large part of the relevant context is being excluded from the model, which may lead in turn to an overemphasis on the importance of shared values.

Third – and this is related to the first point above – to conceptualize shared values in an MNC in terms of common norms, goals and visions between HQ and the subsidiaries can be misleading. If cooperation and knowledge transfer are primarily a question of the relationships between subsidiaries rather than those between the subsidiaries and their HQ, it follows that 'horizontal' shared values are more important than the 'vertical' kind. The more common interests that the subsidiaries share, the greater will be their knowledge exchange, irrespective of their relationships with HQ. If we assume that shared values between two units are built up gradually in the course of business interactions, it follows that business relationships actually capture shared values. This explains, then, why corporate network embeddedness is such a strong predictor of knowledge transfer in our model.

This line of reasoning reflects a more skeptical view of the role of HQs than that adopted in certain works on shared values. The impression is given in some research that if an HQ creates shared values among its subsidiaries in accordance with its own values, the MNC as a whole will achieve a higher level of coordination and, consequently, will perform better (see, for example, Bartlett and Ghoshal 1989; Ghoshal and Nohria 1994, 1997). Apart from the acknowledged difficulty that anyone – including HQ – will encounter when it comes to changing basic human values (see, for example, Hofstede et al. 1990), there is also good reason to question the image of the HQ as *the* coordinator in an MNC. We might agree that this is perhaps HQ's most important role, but it is quite another matter whether HQ succeeds in fulfilling it. Or to put it another way, we can question whether HQ is actually the main actor in the knowledge transfer processes of the MNC.

Inherent in the business network perspective that we have been applying in this book is the idea of an MNC as a loosely-coupled, federative organization with dispersed power and interests. The extent to which knowledge exchange occurs in such an organization depends more on the relationships between the sub-units than on those between them and the HQ. Consequently, the level of shared values between HQ and the individual subsidiary is not such a crucial issue as is usually assumed. The insignificant result in our model regarding shared values between the HQ and its subsidiaries is not therefore so surprising.

SUMMARY

In this chapter we have followed up a topic touched upon in Chapter 9, namely the importance of shared values as an integrative mechanism in MNCs. We have done so by analysing the impact that values shared between an HQ and a subsidiary have on the transfer of knowledge from that subsidiary to the rest of the MNC. The main purpose of the chapter has been to investigate the extent to which shared values – as opposed to 'hard factors' such as business networks and resource dependencies – can explain knowledge transfer in MNCs. A model has therefore been described in which knowledge transfer within the MNC is the dependent variable, while the independent variables are the subsidiary's network embeddedness, HQ's knowledge about the subsidiary's external business partners, subsidiary dependence on HQ, *and* shared values between HQ and the subsidiaries.

The result of the statistical analysis based on 98 subsidiaries indicates that the 'hard' rather than the 'soft' factors explain variations in the knowledge transfer from the subsidiary to the rest of the MNC. Values shared between the subsidiary and the HQ had an insignificant impact, while the subsidiary's network embeddedness – including HQ's knowledge about the external parts of that network – and resource dependence variables, were all significant and explained almost half the variation in the dependent variable. Thus, our results, unlike those reported in some recent influential works, cast some doubt on the relevance of shared values as a crucial factor in the 'life' of the MNC. The chapter ends with some reflections on the reasons why shared values are not such strong predictors of knowledge transfer as is usually assumed.

The result of our analysis in this chapter further emphasizes the important role of the business network in knowledge transfer, and consequently in learning, in the MNC. For knowledge to be transferred, however, it has to have been produced in the first place. Consequently learning includes the development of knowledge, not simply its transfer. In the next chapter we will focus on how corporate embeddedness is conceptually related to learning and knowledge management in the MNC, by making a distinction between problem-solving activities and knowledge-transfer activities.

12. Learning in the Embedded Multinational

In the present chapter, the thread of the argument from Chapter 11 will be picked up again, but from a somewhat different angle. We will now extend the analysis on two fronts. We will look at relationships between sister units, that is to say corporate embeddedness, while also distinguishing between two kinds of relationship, namely those in which the parties conduct complementary activities, and those in which their activities are similar. This should give us a better understanding of learning as manifest in the generation of innovations and their dispersal in the Embedded MNC.

In the following analysis we will first demonstrate two examples of learning processes in the Aspa corporation that are connected with the activities of Danke (see Chapter 3). In a subsequent step we present our theoretical argument suggesting among other things that the operational relationships between subsidiaries can be divided into two categories with regard to the interdependence of their activities, namely similarity and/or complementarity. We argue that the innovation transfer process is completely different between the two categories. We even claim that the expression 'transfer of innovations' (best practice, knowledge) is misleading in the second case, which is more concerned with mutual problem-solving between subsidiaries in their role as customers and/or suppliers.

TWO EXAMPLES OF LEARNING PROCESSES IN ASPA

As described in Chapter 7, one of Danke's innovations consisted of a new type of beer-can box. This innovation stemmed from a relationship with one of its biggest (external) customers. The motivation behind the innovation was the customer's desire for a box providing more efficient storage facilities combined with a more attractive commercial appearance. While the first of the qualities would reduce the customer's costs, the second was aimed at increasing the volume of sales. The technological challenge was thus a matter of design. This meant that Danke had to find out about storing, loading and transporting beer-can boxes, knowledge that they acquired from interacting with the customer. Later, when the resulting box solution was introduced to the customer with good results, Danke also launched it to the Aspa box group of subsidiary managers (see Chapter 7 on the role of the Aspa box group). In principle the new technology could be used by other subsidiaries in the Aspa corporation, since their existing technologies were already similar. One sister subsidiary, namely England B (see Chapter 6 for a description of this company) also had customers operating in the beer industry. When these met at an Aspa box meeting, they were given details of the new product technology. Subsequently the technology was adopted in England, although the product's commercial appearance (printing, pictures and colors) was modified to fit the local customer. This learning process is illustrated in Figure 12.1.

A second example of a learning process occurred when Danke engaged in the development of their white-top paper quality (see Chapter 3). This process involved their customer, Bitte, and their corporate supplier, Aspi. In this case the customer, Bitte, raised the original requests regarding the need for a white-top quality, while Aspi was the actor who was to develop and produce the requisite quality. The white top was then used as input material in the production of boxes, which Danke sold to Bitte. Danke's role was thus to develop a new box using the new paper quality. This meant that Danke had to coordinate the two relationships, serving as a link in the development process in which the three actors had dissimilar but complementary capabilities. This

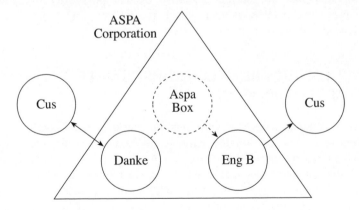

Figure 12.1   Learning from transfer

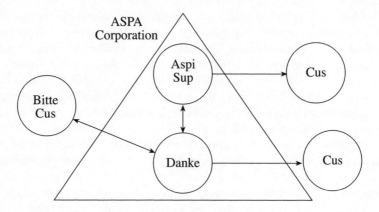

Figure 12.2   Learning from problem-solving

is illustrated in Figure 12.2. Aspi was later to sell paper with white-top quality and Danke was later to sell boxes including white-top quality paper.

Both cases illustrate a kind of learning in an MNC that signified a shift in competencies among the corporate subsidiaries. The two examples are similar in that the new technologies depended on relationships between a subsidiary, Danke, and its business partners. The beer-can box case illustrates how an external development process can lead to an internal transfer of knowledge that is subsequently used by a subsidiary in another market. The second example is somewhat different. Here, the change in competencies within Aspa was not based on a transfer between units conducting similar business in different country markets, but on vertical business relationships (one internal and one external), in which Danke functioned as a connecting link. The development was not driven primarily by the possibility of re-using technology developed by another subsidiary, but more by cooperation and interdependence between the two business relationships.

RELATIONSHIPS BETWEEN SUBSIDIARIES AND ACTIVITIES IN MNCs

The two examples above indicate that the basic activities performed by different units, and the way the activities are related to each other, have a profound influence on the conditions for learning in an MNC. In order to capture the actual learning, it is necessary to take a step back and consider the activities that are going on in the MNC, and how these activities are related to each other. One way of doing this is to look upon the MNC as an industry on its own, with more or less related activities, and to apply models that are used to characterize industries. In a seminal article about the organization of industry, Richardson (1972) offers such a model. He wrote:

> It is convenient to think of industry as carrying out an indefinitely large number of *activities*, activities related to the discovery and estimation of future wants, to research, development and design, to the execution and co-ordination of processes of physical transformation, the marketing of goods and so on. And we have to recognize that these activities have to be carried out by organizations with appropriate *capabilities*, or, in other words, with appropriate knowledge, experience and skill. The capability of an organization may depend upon command of some particular material technology, such as cellulose chemistry, electronics or civil engineering, or may derive from skills in marketing of and knowledge of and reputation in particular markets. Activities that require the same capability for their undertaking I shall call *similar activities*. But the organization of industry has also to adapt itself to the fact that activities may be *complementary*. I shall say that activities are complementary when they represent different phases of a process of production and require in some way or another to be coordinated. Now it is clear that similarity and complementarity, as I have defined them, are quite distinct; clutch linings are complementary to clutches and to cars but, in that they are best made by firms with a capability in asbestos fabrication, they are similar to drain-pipes and heat-proof-suits. Similarly, the production of porcelain insulators is complementary to that of electrical switchgear but similar to other ceramic manufacture. (Richardson 1972, emphasis in original)

If we apply the business network perspective on the MNC with a bundle of more or less interdependent sub-units, the 'organizing of industry' metaphor is useful. MNCs evolve through different phases of strategic change, acquisition periods, etc. (see Chapter 6), which means that at any point in time the sub-units represent different products, markets, specialties and capabilities in more or less the same way as a whole industry does. The activities of two subsidiaries can either be built on the same type of capability, or can be related to each other in terms of product or service flows, e.g. as customers and suppliers. In the first case the subsidiaries are dependent on a similar type of competence for their operations, but they are not dependent on each other in their ongoing business. In the second case they are forced to coordinate their business, but the business in each subsidiary can be based on totally different types of capabilities.

The concepts of similarity and complementarity are seen as two independent variables, which means that there can be more or less similarity in terms of capabilities and complementarity in terms of required (and potential) coordination between the sub-units in an MNC. The model can be illustrated in the following way: consider an MNC with three subsidiaries; C, A and B as illustrated in Figure 12.3. Subsidiary C serves as a supplier to both A and B and has thus a complementary relationship with them both. In contrast, subsidiaries can be similar, as illustrated through the relation between A and B. In such a case the subsidiaries base their operations on the same type

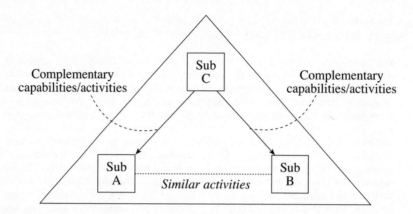

Figure 12.3 The MNC conceptualized as a pattern of industrial activities

of technology and skill. For instance, subsidiaries in different countries can produce and market the same type of product or service for the local market. The required capabilities are similar because the products/services are similar. However, the degree of similarity between capabilities can vary, for instance due to adaptations of the products/services to the local markets, difference in technology, experience, etc. Some subsidiaries may have been in business for longer, and have accumulated knowledge that other subsidiaries do not have.

In the same way complementarity between subsidiaries due to activity links can also vary. Every company/subsidiary takes on the form of a complex activity structure, and some of these activities are linked to activities in other subsidiaries. The linking of activities reflects the need for coordination and will affect when and how the various activities are carried out. Some of the activity links are standardized or relatively easy to replace with other linkages, while others call for constant interactions and adaptations of activities on both sides. The breadth and depth of activity linkages can be summarized together in the concept of complementarity.

This model implies that both similarity and complementarity can exist in MNCs in different ways, including that of not existing at all. Two subsidiaries in totally different businesses may not show any resemblance in their capabilities. However, being at the far ends of the scale is probably as unusual as two subsidiaries being identical in terms of their capabilities. There is probably always some degree of similarity, depending on the way the activities on both sides are defined. For instance, different marketing activities can be built on the same type of knowledge, even though the products and markets concerned are completely different. In the same way, two subsidiaries with identical products and markets may still differ in their capabilities due to such things as personnel, history, etc. (or in the extreme case they are probably organized as one subsidiary).

Similarly, two subsidiaries may have no connections whatsoever as regards customer/supplier relationships. And yet, since every subsidiary represents a complex activity structure, there is probably always the possibility of developing future linkages with the activities of sister units. There is always a possibility, in principle, for more coordination or adaptation of the activities on both sides of a relationship.

CONDITIONS FOR LEARNING IN MULTINATIONAL CORPORATIONS

This very simple model of activity interdependence in terms of similarity and complementarity can be used to shed some new light on the conditions for learning in MNCs. We posit that the two relationship dimensions have a profound influence on knowledge-sharing between subsidiaries, but in very different and sometimes contradictory ways.

Take first the similarity dimension. It has been argued that prior knowledge is essential if it is to be possible to absorb new knowledge from the environment. This proposition applies at both the individual and the organizational levels (Cohen and Levinthal 1990). Prior knowledge facilitates, or is sometimes even a necessary condition for, the assimilation of innovations in subsequent periods. This view is based on the concept of learning as a cumulative process, in which 'learning to learn' is an important ingredient. Developing knowledge within a certain field, and developing the absorptive capacity related to that field, go hand in hand. Or, as Cohen and Levinthal put it:

> First if the firm does not develop its absorptive capacity in some initial period, then its beliefs about the technological opportunities present in a given field will tend not to change over time because the firm may not be aware of the significance of signals that would otherwise revise its expectations. As a result, the firm does not invest in absorptive capacity and, when new opportunities subsequently emerge, the firm may not appreciate them. (Cohen and Levinthal 1990, p. 136)

Similarity between activities lies at the heart of this reasoning, although it can be argued that prior knowledge must include some portion of diversity to safeguard against the risk of the firm's absorptive capacity becoming too 'narrow-minded' and over-focused. The more two subsidiaries acquire similar knowledge as a result of performing the same type of activity, the more their absorptive capacity will be directed towards similar types of innovation. Thus, two subsidiaries possessing the same type of prior knowledge, and having developed the same type of absorptive capacity, can also be assumed to share knowledge more easily than other subsidiaries would do. The transfer of innovations between units requires a common 'language' and a mutual understanding of the technology on which the innovation is based. It should be emphasized that this claim is built not on an assumption of an established operational or business relationship between the subsidiaries, but only on the possession of similar knowledge. Similar capabilities, to use Richardson's terminology, would therefore be conducive to the transfer of innovations between units in MNCs.

What, then, about complementary activities? This class of activity is closely related to an essential element in our approach, namely that business relationships are important sources of knowledge, chiefly because one company's activities are dependent on capabilities possessed by others (Håkansson and Snehota 1995). The capabilities possessed by one company are confronted with those of others via relationships arising between the partners concerned. As Richardson (1972) sees it, these relationships arise to answer the need to coordinate activities that are highly complementary and yet dissimilar. This coordination requires the matching, both quantitatively and qualitatively, of individual firms' plans.

It should be added that customer–supplier relationships explicitly include different levels of mutual problem-solving and, consequently, technical development as well (von Hippel, 1988; Håkansson 1989). The problem-solving can be more or less relation-specific, depending on whether or not the solution is well adapted to the customer's special needs. The crucial issue here, though, is that this problem-solving is an interactive process between the parties that involves the configuration of problems and possible solutions. The more intensive this process, the more the two parties can learn about each other's capabilities. Or, to put it differently, the greater the corporate embeddedness.

This does not imply that the capabilities of both sides become more like one another. On the contrary, the effectiveness of the customer–supplier interaction process depends on the possibility of one party offering a competence that the other party does not have. Mutual problem-solving in complementary relationships is thus contingent on dissimilarity rather than similarity in the capabilities of both sides. Typically, a supplier and a customer may share some mutual problems, for instance the need to adapt or develop a particular component of the supplier's that must be able to function in the customer's production process. This means that each party may have to learn about the other's technological qualities, limitations, possibilities and requirements. In the course of their interaction the parties undergo a process of adaptation during which the component delivered by the supplier and the production process of the customer will evolve. In this case there is thus no principal sender or receiver of knowledge in the transfer process. Rather, the learning means that both parties develop their respective technologies via problem-solving in an interactive process.

Thus it seems that when it comes to learning in MNCs, we can distinguish things from two directions. On the one hand, similarities between subsidiaries facilitate learning, since the knowledge that one subsidiary already possesses will have a profound influence on its capacity and readiness to pick up further knowledge already in possession of some other subsidiary. On the other hand, it can be argued that learning is primarily something that occurs in a process of interaction between complementary activities/subsidiaries that offer *dissimilar* capabilities.

It may seem tempting to suggest that if the MNC optimizes either similarity or complementarity in terms of its capabilities, the conditions for knowledge transfer within the organization as a whole would be maximized. Such a conclusion, however, would be misleading. On the one hand, in every industry and every MNC, division of labor is vital to the whole concept of efficiency, so that by its nature every organization involves complementary chains of activity comprising a wide variety of activities and companies or sub-units. On the other hand, each organization tends to group similar activities and/or capabilities under one umbrella, which implies the duplication of operations, both geographically and operationally (Zander 1999). This in turn leads to the separation of markets or products, rather than a division of labor. These two tendencies go hand in hand, serving to shape the 'organization of industry' within the MNC.

There is reason to believe that both similarity and complementarity affect learning in the MNC, but in two different ways. This is illustrated in Figure 12.4.

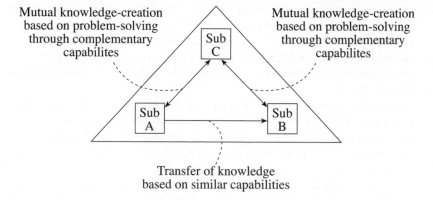

Figure 12.4   Similarity-induced and complementarity-induced learning in the MNC

Take first the similarity dimension, i.e. the relationship between A and B in Figure 12.4. We can speak of a 'student–teacher' situation in which one particular subsidiary (A) owns an innovation that, under certain circumstances, can be transferred to another subsidiary (B) for adoption and commercialization on a larger scale. Whether or not this will happen depends on the absorptive capacity of the 'student side' and on similarities in knowledge-processing and the dominant logics of both sides (Lane and Lubatkin 1998). Other important barriers include the degree of motivation on the 'teacher side' to participate in knowledge-sharing within the MNC, the non-codifiability of the knowledge, the communication and technical gap between the source and the receiver (Szulanski 1995, 2000) and the 'perception-gap' between the teacher and the student concerning the two subsidiaries' competence (Birkinshaw et al. 2000). However, although there are a number of obstacles to the transfer of innovations, the amount of similarity between the activities and the earlier experiences of both sides plays a crucial role. Similarity is important in a 'teacher–student' situation.

Another feature of this case is that the creation of the innovation precedes its transfer. Or, to put it in another way, transfer is seldom conceptualized as a prerequisite for the innovation. Although the 'teacher' can learn from the way the innovation is applied in a new context, the transfer is useful primarily to the receiving subsidiary.

The underlying principle for complementarity between subsidiaries is based not on the separation of markets but on the division of labor. Two subsidiaries are related to each other because they occupy different positions in a particular value chain (C's relationships with A and B in Figure 12.4). The different positions are based on a certain degree of specialization on both the supplier and the customer sides. Complementarity is associated with the scale dimension, because a large output is resource-saving and allows fixed capital to be used more efficiently. Complementarity due to scale-efficiency requires a certain standardization of both input and output, which means that certain capabilities on both sides are emphasized at the expense of other capabilities, albeit also at the expense of a certain reduction in resource-diversity (Håkansson, 1992).

A supplier–customer relationship will also include what is sometimes called a 'heterogenizing' element, that is a tendency to find new ways to combine activities and resources in the business relationship (ibid.). This tendency is closely connected to problem-solving in the relationship, whereby demands or problems on the customer side are confronted by possibilities on the supply side in a never-ending, interactive process. Such a process implies that the two subsidiaries enjoy a close relationship involving intensive interaction, and probably also a high degree of adaptation regarding resources and activities, that is to say, a high degree of embeddedness. Although the underlying motivation is division of labor in a chain of activities and roles, the mutual interaction between the subsidiaries leads to greater increased awareness of the capabilities on both sides through the process of mutual problem-solving.

Greater awareness of mutual capabilities should not be confused with an increase in similarity between two organizations. On the contrary, awareness of the capabilities existing on the two sides is likely to improve the ability of both to benefit from combining dissimilar resources in new ways (Zander and Kogut 1995).

Thus, whereas the learning process associated with the similarity dimension concerns learning in terms of the transfer of a certain (fixed) innovation from one subsidiary to another, the complementarity situation implies interactive problem-solving in which the two subsidiaries are involved in different ways. In an MNC context the expression 'transfer of knowledge' is consequently misleading, in so far as we are dealing with complementary activities between subsidiaries. Learning is not primarily a question of transferring an asset (a best practice) from one subsidiary to another. Rather, it means that two subsidiaries are engaged in mutual problem-solving with a view to creating and implementing a new asset (a new best practice). It is a case of combining capabilities between equals rather than of a student–teacher situation.

However, whether or not such learning between complementary subsidiaries does occur will depend on the type of relationship. To put it simply, if the relationship between the subsidiaries is more of an arm's-length type due to some standardization of outputs or inputs, there will be less common problem-solving, since the important thing will not be learning but will concern rationalization and economies of scale. If the relationship is characterized by closeness, involving adaptation of existing resources and agreement on the importance of the specific relationship for the business of those concerned, there will probably be a more pronounced tendency to try to solve common problems together.

Thus, while barriers to the transfer of best practices between subsidiaries are a question of absorptive capacity, lack of motivation (on both sides), non-codifiability and communication gaps between a source and a receiver, the barriers to problem-solving in a complementary (customer–supplier) relationship depend on the ability of the subsidiaries to combine their heterogeneous resources in such a way that new solutions will emerge. This ability is contingent on the type of operational or business relationship between the subsidiaries. Closeness, expressed in the age of the relationship, the degree of mutual adaptation of resources and activities, and the degree of trust, will be positively related to the ability to understand the capabilities of the other party.

The distinction between the transfer of best practice and problem-solving in complementary relationships resembles the distinction between know how and know what. While the transfer of best practice involves the problem of picking up knowledge about a new way to do things (a new production technique, a new product, etc.), the essential problem in the complementarity case is to learn *what* the other party can do (not *how* it is done) in order to solve a problem that has been identified by both parties. The second case concerns a combination of capabilities while the former concerns an *equalization* of capabilities.

It should be pointed out that most learning processes in a subsidiary-to-subsidiary context include elements of equalization *and* combination of capabilities simultaneously. In reality there is rarely a pure process of the transfer of best practice without some element of the combination of capabilities, or vice versa. Our point here, however, would be to build a simple model making a fundamental distinction, when learning in MNCs is being focused. The model would be based on the simple fact that the operational relationships between units in an MNC will vary. The model could be seen as a first step towards a more specific understanding of the kind of learning processes that exist and, in particular, what we mean by the oft-used but inadequately defined concept of knowledge-sharing in an MNC.

LEARNING IN THE EMBEDDED MNC

The analysis so far has been limited to the relationships between subsidiaries *within* the MNC. A crucial issue for the Embedded MNC, however, is the role of the subsidiaries' external business networks. The model presented above should therefore be complemented by including these networks. Following Richardson's terminology and his thinking on industrial organizing, a subsidiary's external relationships can also be classified into two types: relationships based on similar or on complementary capabilities. Although similarity and complementarity may be found in all kinds of relationships, we suggest that a separation on Richardson's lines offers a constructive distinction for identifying the principal kinds of learning process in the MNC. Similar capabilities are best represented by a subsidiary's competitors, which base their products and activities on the same type of technology as the focal subsidiary. Complementary capabilities are best represented by business relationships with customers and suppliers. These relationships imply that the subsidiary's activities are complementary in relation to other companies outside the MNC.

By adding the subsidiaries' external relationships to Figure 12.4, we get the model shown in Figure 12.5.

The model demonstrates that both learning through transfer and learning through problem-solving represent external *and* internal processes of the MNC. It also shows that the external and internal learning processes are

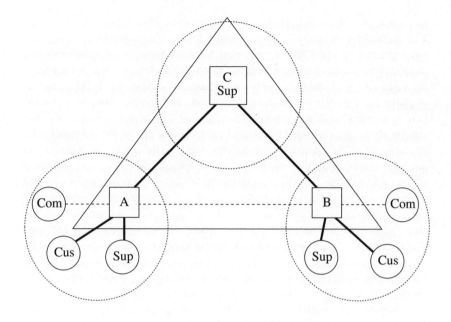

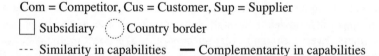

Com = Competitor, Cus = Customer, Sup = Supplier

☐ Subsidiary ⬚ Country border

--- Similarity in capabilities   ▬ Complementarity in capabilities

Figure 12.5   A model of learning in the Embedded Multinational

related to each other. Innovations that are created through problem-solving in the interaction between subsidiary A and its external customers/suppliers, for example, can later be transferred to a sister unit, B, which has similar business in another country and which thus has a certain amount of absorptive capacity for such an innovation. Or an innovation that a subsidiary has picked up through its communications with a competitor, could be used in its problem-solving process with an internal supplier, C.

The model in Figure 12.5 (and the case examples in the introduction to this chapter) indicate that the learning processes in an MNC can be combined in several possible ways, along the external/internal and similarity/complementarity dimensions. However, it seems reasonable to assume that an important archetype in this context is provided by an MNC consisting of subsidiaries using a similar technology (because of similar products but different local markets), embedded in complementary business relationships, whereby the external relationships do more to create the difference between the subsidiaries than the corporate relationships do. This is illustrated in Figure 12.5, in which subsidiary A and subsidiary B have a common internal supplier but each has its own distinct external business network of customers and suppliers. In such a situation learning through problem-solving is located in the value chains in which A and B are partners, while learning through transfer is primarily a matter of communication and information flows between the two of them. Following our line of reasoning in Chapter 8 and in the last section above, we posit that the crucial issue for learning on the 'external side' is closeness in the business relationships, since closeness is conducive to an ability to use and combine the other party's capabilities in new ways. Learning on the 'internal side', however, is of two kinds. First, there is learning through problem-solving occurring between subsidiaries that are complementary to each other, such as A and C or C and B in Figure 12.5. As on the 'external side', closeness in the relationship is positively related to such learning. Second, there is learning through transfer between subsidiaries that are similar to each other, such as A and B. Such learning is more dependent on the existence of efficient information systems linking the subsidiaries to one another.

However, our model also reveals a more generic difference between learning through problem-solving and learning through knowledge transfer, namely the imperative to learn through problem-solving is much stronger than the imperative to learn through transfer. This is due to the basic logic of business. Every firm, and every subsidiary, is dependent on the efficiency of the value chain to which it belongs. Business is what compels the subsidiary and its customers and suppliers to cooperate in order to make the whole network as efficient as possible. This is a fundamental assumption of business network theory. And mutual problem-solving is an important and natural ingredient in the process. It is not primarily a result of administrative control by corporate HQ or the design of control systems, but rather of drivers representing business as such. The subsidiary and its business partners cooperate and learn about new products or new production processes because the conditions of business drive them to do so, and not because corporate HQ tells them to do so.

In principle there are no such drivers in the case of relationships between subsidiaries with similar capabilities. Subsidiaries that produce and sell the same type of product or service in different local markets, will give priority to their relationships with complementary rather than similar capabilities. Or, to put it another way, our line of reasoning suggests that sharing knowledge with similar sister units is not regarded as a prerequisite for the subsidiary's business. On the contrary, the subsidiary may find it to be an obstacle to problem-solving in business networks, due to limited managerial resources at the subsidiary level. Consequently, we posit that in relationships based on similarity, the transfer of knowledge is dependent not only on efficient information systems and other administrative devices, but also on the motivation on both sides in favor of such transfer. We need only recall how the transfer activities were broken down in Aspa when motivation wobbled in the subsidiaries and the new Aspa HQ called for a change in the routines for Aspa box meetings (see Chapter 7). A general conclusion arising from our model is thus that learning in MNCs is dominated by problem-solving rather than knowledge transfer, although both types of learning are possible and can occur.

From a management point of view the critical issues are also different. In the similarity case the most important thing is to create an organizational context that stimulates communication and the exchange of knowledge between the subsidiaries, for example with the help of the performance-evaluation system, by giving some subsidiaries a mandate to become centers of excellence with a special responsibility to share best practices with others, or by creating project groups, teams, etc. In the complementarity case the overall managerial concerns are how the subsidiaries should be related to each other operationally and how much discretion they should have in choosing customers and suppliers. The more standardized and market-like the supplier–customer relationship between two subsidiaries, for instance, the less the scope for creating new knowledge through common problem-solving. The discussion above is summarized in Table 12.1.

Table 12.1   Learning in the embedded MNC

Type of relationship	Underlying principle	Type of learning process	Critical factor for learning	Major barriers to learning	Critical management issues
Similar capabilities	Division of markets	Transfer of innovations	Absorptive capacity	Lack of motivation	Administrative systems
Complementary capabilities	Division of labor	Mutual problem-solving	Closeness of business relationships (embeddedness)	Distrust	Value-chain policy

Our model indicates that the question of learning in MNCs implies a contradiction in purpose that management has to address. On the one hand, management may emphasize learning in the MNC as a question not only of transferring innovations but also of developing them through mutual problem-solving. Close relationships are conducive to mutual problem-solving and should therefore be encouraged. On the other hand, if management also stresses the need for cost-efficiency, then closeness in relationships has lower priority than the standardization of easily replaceable activity links. Cost efficiency, thus, stands against learning in complementary relationships.

This line of reasoning leads to the conclusion that the subsidiary's external network must fulfil two purposes at the same time. On the one hand a certain degree of business embeddedness is necessary for the subsidiary if it is to be able to contribute to the creation of innovations through problem-solving in business relationships. On the other hand, a certain degree of standardization in its relationships is also necessary if a certain level of scale efficiency and profitability is to be reached. This indicates either an external network consisting of a mixture of close and arm's-length relationships or of specialization among the subsidiaries, whereby some of them give priority to learning through close relationships and others to (short-term) profitability through more arms-length relationships. The subsidiaries that give priority to learning are more important when it comes to the transfer of knowledge to other similar units. The various administrative devices for inducing knowledge transfer should thus be directed primarily towards these subsidiaries.

SUMMARY

In this chapter we have suggested that learning in the Embedded MNC can be separated into two distinct processes: the transfer of knowledge and mutual problem-solving. This distinction is based in turn on a Richardson's view regarding the interdependence of activities in industry, whereby activities may be either similar or complementary depending on the capabilities required to perform them (Richardson 1972). By looking at the 'industrial' relationships between sub-units in the Embedded MNC in the same light it is possible to get a better understanding of the kind of learning processes to be found in such corporations. Some learning processes are directed more towards extending 'how-to-do' knowledge from one subsidiary to another with similar operations and capabilities. The extent to which such knowledge will be transferred will depend on the absorptive capacity on the receiving side and on motivational factors on both sides.

Other learning processes are directed more towards solving mutual problems between subsidiaries involved in a complementary value-chain relationship. Here it is more a question of developing new solutions by combining different capabilities residing in different subsidiaries rather than of transferring a 'fixed' solution from one subsidiary to another with similar operations and, consequently, similar capabilities. The extent to which such mutual problem-solving will occur depends to a large extent on the closeness of the relationship between the parties, that is to say on the degree of business embeddedness.

The distinction between similar and complementary activities can be applied also to external relationships, as was illustrated in Figure 12.5. We have argued that a subsidiary has complementary relationships with external customers and suppliers, and similar relationships with competitors. The subsidiary's 'external' learning in connection with problem-solving therefore occurs primarily in customer–supplier relationships, while the knowledge transfer involved in the assimilation of new solutions occurs by way of links with competitors.

In this chapter we have also discussed some managerial implications of the distinction between knowledge transfer and mutual problem-solving. While the managerial concern in the first case is primarily to implement administrative systems that will facilitate horizontal communication and motivate transfer, the question in the second is rather how to configure the value-chain in the MNC. It has also been pointed out that the question of learning in the Embedded MNC implies a contradiction between the high degree of embeddedness required in order to stimulate problem-solving and arm's-length relationships needed to achieve greater standardization and cost efficiency. Dealing with this contradiction is a matter of concern connected with both the 'external' and the 'internal' learning in the subsidiary. How this contradiction is addressed will have a profound impact on the roles assumed by the different subsidiaries in the Embedded Multinational.

13. The Embedded Multinational – an epilogue

In this last chapter we will elaborate further on the basic character of the Embedded Multinational, comparing it with some alternative MNC models. References to institutionalization theory and contingency theory will help to highlight some major differences, especially in terms of the interaction between the environment and the MNC and the role of HQ in the Embedded Multinational.

In Chapter 1 we referred to Edith Penrose's description of the model of the large MNC as 'ill-defined and ... inadequate even for analytical purposes' (Penrose 1971, p. 266). The author's concern at that time was that top managers in such firms were much more powerful in relation to owners and other interest groups than the received theory allowed. She argued that top managers were 'non-accountable in the sense that they themselves define the international public interest to be considered' (ibid., p. 267). This comment is probably as relevant today as it was in 1967. However, Penrose did not take into account that, even if MNC HQs are very powerful in their exercise of 'economic statesmanship' in society (Berle and Means 1933), their opportunities for exerting power *inside* the MNCs are another matter. In the preceding chapters we have outlined a model of the MNC as a heterogeneous, loosely coupled organization in which no unit, not even HQ, possesses full knowledge of the MNC's operations. If we assume that knowledge is crucial for the exercise of power, we can conclude that the control exerted by HQ inside the MNC is limited. So, where Penrose observed that MNC HQs, as representing organizations with large resources, possess *more* power in society than is assumed in received theory, we suggest that they have *less* power to control such resources than is usually assumed in the theory or in the public debate. It should be noted here that Penrose's statement about the greater public power of an MNC HQ and our view regarding its circumscribed internal power, are not mutually contradictory. Although it sounds somewhat paradoxical, it is quite possible to exert considerable influence on political decisions in society, without having full control over the organization on which this influence is actually based.

THE FUNDAMENTAL ORGANIZATIONAL CHARACTER OF THE EMBEDDED MULTINATIONAL

We find that the traditional way of defining MNCs in terms of their ownership systems is inadequate when it comes to understanding the kind of creature that the MNC actually is. Every day we are told by the economic press and others that corporations like General Electric, ABB, Philips and so on are all homogeneous units with clear strategies and unified behavior. This view is not concomitant with our model, which suggests that an analysis starting from individual business actors (units, firms) and moving on to the way ownership links constitute what we call 'the MNC' may sometimes be more appropriate. Or, to put it another way, the ownership system can only partly explain why MNCs behave in the way they do, for example what countries they decide to invest in and how they choose to do it. It should be emphasized, however, that our view does not preclude the idea that, as a legal ownership system, the MNC has powerful resources at its disposal. Because it certainly has. What our view does imply, though, is that the possibilities for mobilizing these resources for some specific purpose are much more complicated than is usually assumed. The Embedded MNC definitely cannot be compared with an army under a commander-in-chief. Rather, it is a complicated, non-transparent and loose structure, encompassing many conflicting interests and dispersed resources. HQ can certainly attempt to mobilize these resources for some particular purpose – and up to a point is in a position to do so – but the outcome of such attempts are difficult even for HQ itself to predict.

THE EMBEDDED MULTINATIONAL AND ITS ENVIRONMENT

Related to this overall character of the Embedded Multinational is a further implication from our model, namely that an MNC's environment consists of *several* environments, each with its own distinct characteristics. To some extent this view recalls the concept of isomorphic pull as applied in institutionalization theory. It has been argued, for instance, that because the MNC straddles different fields, it is subject to incompatible or inconsistent pulls from the environment. In line with our own perspective, institutionalization theory also offers an explanation as to why MNCs tend to be loosely coupled: it is because this represents a way of responding to the contradictory isomorphic pulls of the environment (Westney 1993).

However, there are important differences between our view and that of institutionalization theory, which conceptualizes the environment in rather general terms linked primarily to the characteristics of a particular country's institutions. It has been observed, for instance, that countries vary institutionally in their norms, legal systems and cognitive structures. An MNC, which by definition operates in several countries, has to cope with a diversity of environments due to these institutional differences (Kostova 1999). The variety of isomorphic pulls thus stems mainly from the MNC's need to adapt itself to the different institutions in the countries concerned.

In our view the actual business plays a more important part than institutional differences. The MNC has several environments because it is involved in several business contexts, in terms of products and markets. The institutional differences between countries do matter, but *how* they matter is connected with the specific business involved. One particular institutional difference between countries may be more or less relevant, depending on the nature of the business in question. Analytically speaking, in seeking to identify the forces underlying the MNC's loosely coupled structure, differences in business contexts precede institutional differences in our model.

This difference also has important implications for the character of the isomorphic pull. Institutionalization theory focuses primarily on the fact that a country's environment imposes certain patterns or structures on the MNC and its subsidiaries (DiMaggio and Powell 1983; Scott 1987; Westney 1993), for instance because they have to adapt to certain regulations or standards. Thus, while institutions are relatively stable over time, they differ between countries, which means that the MNC has to cope with a trade-off between the need to adapt to the different institutions on the one hand, and the need to standardize and integrate its subsidiaries on the other (Westney 1993).

In our model of the Embedded MNC, adaptation to the environment has quite a different character. It concerns the interactions between individual subsidiaries and their customers, suppliers and competitors and the extent to which these have developed into close business relationships. Thus, adaptation consists primarily of investments in relationships with *specific* other business actors in a particular business context. The adaptation is mutual rather than unilateral, and the relationships involved are difficult to change or replace, at least in the short run. In this specific sense the environment adapts to the MNC as much as the MNC adapts to the environment. Moreover, the subsidiary in question acquires a specific *role* in a business network that differs from the roles of other subsidiaries in their networks.

This implies that while institutionalization theory emphasizes the 'do in

Rome as the Romans do' nature of an MNC's adaptation to the environment, our approach means that 'what MNCs do in Rome, they do together with the Romans'. It is thus not primarily a question of passive adaptation to institutional differences, but more of active – often interactive – adaptation to needs and capabilities of specific business actors.

This focus on business relationships rather than on institutions affects our basic conceptualization of the MNC. Fundamental to the MNC according to institutionalization theory is that it has to cope with more than one *institutional* environment at once. Fundamental to the MNC according to our model is that it is involved in more than one *business* environment, regardless of whether or not the institutional environments are the same. Two subsidiaries in a particular MNC may be working in different business environments, as defined by their relationships with other business actors, while operating in the same country and thus being confronted by the same institutions. Or the reverse may hold: two subsidiaries may be involved in similar types of business relationships but in different types of institutions.

Both perspectives thus imply forces strong enough to produce inconsistent isomorphic pulls, but there is a fundamental difference regarding the way these isomorphic pulls can be understood and handled by the MNC. Knowledge about institutions – for instance important authorities, laws, local regulations, business norms, etc. – are at least up to a certain point objective and codifiable. Even national culture can be learnt to some extent 'from outside'. There is thus a fair possibility for an MNC's top management to acquire knowledge 'from a distance' about institutions in a subsidiary's country.

It is much more difficult, however, for HQ to learn about and understand a subsidiary's business relationships, partly because these are so specific but also because such knowledge has to be acquired through experience. To put it in simple terms, it is much easier to find out about a local regulation than about the kind of relationship the subsidiary has been developing with a local customer or supplier over a period of some years. This second kind of knowledge is embedded in the relationship, and first-hand experience of the processes that are going on in the relationship is a prerequisite for learning, especially since such relationships are constantly changing, as our Danke case in Chapters 3 and 4 has amply demonstrated.

The whole problem of the asymmetry of information between a firm's HQ and its subsidiaries is thus much more prominent in our 'Embedded Multinational approach' than when the problem is approached in terms of institutionalization theory, because HQ generally knows less about subsidiaries' business networks than about the institutions they have to deal with. Relatively speaking the management of an Embedded Multinational is thus an even more difficult task, depending to a large extent on the level and quality of HQ's knowledge about the subsidiaries' networks (see Chapter 9). In the case of the Embedded Multinational the external embeddedness of the subsidiaries is a defining characteristic of the MNC's overall environment. On the one hand it helps to particularize the environment that actually affects the MNC's behavior. The embeddedness of a multinational, unlike its institutional environment, is reflected in the presence of identifiable 'faces', that is to say specific actors with whom the subsidiaries interact and exchange resources. On the other hand, the subsidiaries' external embeddedness offers a very simple but practical tool for specifying the extent to which their operations are rooted in their various local business contexts. The stronger the external embeddedness of a subsidiary, the greater the impact of its local business on its role and the way it behaves, and the less amenable it will be to control from HQ.

In Chapter 8 we described the big differences that can be seen in external embeddedness, even between subsidiaries in the same division of an MNC. Thus, instead of defining the environment in institutional terms, our concept of embeddedness allows for differences not only at the country level but, and more specifically, at the subsidiary level. From an HQ perspective this is an important difference, since it is subsidiaries – not countries – that HQ is supposed to be managing!

INSIDE THE EMBEDDED MULTINATIONAL

Our model of the Embedded Multinational has led us to emphasize the crucial role of markets and business actors in the coordination of business activities. In this sense we can be said to have adopted a more 'industrial' or 'operational' view than that offered by either institutionalization or contingency theory. Accordingly, our view of various important characteristics *inside* the MNC reflects an 'industrial' approach. We claim that the extent to which sister units are related to each other business-wise, is more important than the way they are related to each other in an administrative or legal sense. This means that if we want to understand the role of the subsidiary in the MNC, it is important to consider corporate as well as external embeddedness. By applying the same criterion inside and outside the MNC it becomes possible to make a more reliable comparison between the subsidiary's external and internal roles, and a more accurate evaluation of its integration inside the MNC. For instance, as we observed in Chapter 8, the received view that subsidiaries are normally integrated internally but are dominated externally by arm's-length relationships, has not gone undisputed here. On the contrary, among the studied subsidiaries we found that strong external embeddeness was generally more pronounced than strong corporate embeddedness. Or, to put it another way, external integration is often more pronounced than internal integration.

Another feature of our model is that it evokes a certain doubt about the importance of normative integration and shared values in the MNC. In the more management-oriented literature in particular, a great many expectations are associated with the part played by common norms and shared values as an organizational 'glue' (Bartlett and Ghoshal 1989). In the contingency theory approach, normative integration is seen as an important complement to the necessary adaptation of the formal structure to 'inconsistent isomorphic pulls' (Westney 1993; Ghoshal and Nohria 1997). In most of the literature on this issue, the existence of shared values has been associated with the existence of a personal network. It is not clear whether this is supposed to mean that all employees participate in such a network, but there seems to be an implicit assumption at least, that enough people take part to justify speaking of *one* set of shared values in the organization.

In our view this is too much to expect. Although our model of the Embedded Multinational does not exclude the existence of shared values or similar interests among MNC units, it assumes that shared values are created and maintained primarily by the sharing of *operations* rather than by the sharing of *information*. Or to put it differently, business networks come first in our model, and personal networks later. Typically, a common understanding of each other's capabilities and a common willingness to share information with one another is something that reflects resource exchange and, consequently, resource interdependence. Corporate embeddedness is therefore a better proxy for the existence of shared values than personal networks imposed upon the organization in one way or another. Personal networks are primarily created as important ingredients in business relationships.

This line of argument leads to two important conclusions. If shared values are relationship-specific rather than organization-specific, an MNC will contain many different sets of shared values rather than one or only a few. This follows directly from our 'industrial' view of the MNC. Hence, attempts to create personal networks on grounds other than business relationships will be largely in vain. This means in turn that the importance of shared values as a glue for the whole MNC, or even for whole divisions, has a limited place in our model of the Embedded MNC.

Further, shared values are not exclusively an intra-organizational affair. If shared values are ingrained primarily in business relationships, they can be expected to play a similar role externally and internally. Subsidiaries develop shared values between themselves and important external customers and suppliers, and other business actors in their network; these shared values then strengthen the relationships concerned, making the subsidiary's local business environment even more specific to itself and different from the business environments of its fellow subsidiaries.

To summarize, we can conclude that the crucial context within which shared values will be created consists of the subsidiary's business network, irrespective of which part of the network is external or internal. This network will have a considerable impact on the behavior of the subsidiary, and there is no contradiction or conflict in principle between the external and internal parts of the network. The business network as a whole possesses a common logic, which is probably much stronger than any that could be created by HQ outside this context, for instance by means of personal networks.

HQ'S SITUATION IN THE EMBEDDED MULTINATIONAL

Our business network approach implies that the MNC's external markets are less market-like than is usually assumed in economic theory, since these markets are characterized primarily not by arm's-length transactions but by business relationships between specific actors. This was the main message presented in Chapters 2–5. Another aspect here is then the implication of a more market-like structure than usually assumed *inside* the MNC, in the sense that business relationships between relatively independent actors are important ingredients in the MNC's interior life.

Implicit to the business network perspective on markets is the assumption that knowledge about one's own and other actors' capabilities is crucial to what actually occurs in the market. This is one of the main reasons for developing business relationships. However, like the Austrian view of the market process (Kirzner 1997), our approach also implies that this knowledge is widely dispersed and is not passed on to anyone in its totality. A crucial theme in the Austrian approach is not only that business actors lack knowledge: they don't even know what knowledge it is that they lack. It is a situation of 'sheer ignorance' (ibid., p. 62) or radical uncertainty (Goodall and Roberts 2003), which in combination with entrepreneurial discovery constitutes the characteristic nature of the market process. If we accept that there are also 'markets' inside the MNC, and also that these 'markets', too, exhibit similar characteristics, then we have to conclude that every sub-unit in the MNC suffers from 'sheer ignorance'. Knowledge is not passed on to anyone in its totality, not even to HQ. And, what is more interesting, *HQ does not know what the sub-units know (or vice versa)*.

It should be noted that this view of HQ's situation deviates radically from the information-asymmetry problem in agency theory, or the uncertainty problem of contingency theory. An implicit assumption of both these theories is that HQ is able to assess any information that the subsidiary possesses but that it does not possess itself, and that it can design control systems and communication channels accordingly. In a situation of sheer ignorance these possibilities are seriously restricted, because HQ does not know what activities or assets there are for it to control. Rather than a mechanistic view of organizational knowledge based on the accumulation of empirical facts, our argument is more in line with a view of knowledge as socially embedded and action-oriented (Giddens 1984). It is a question of 'collective' knowing that is context-specific and that implies closure vis-à-vis other contexts (Goodall and Roberts 2003).

In the literature of socially embedded knowledge the particular contexts to which knowledge is assumed to be bound have often been expressed in rather general forms such as 'communities of practice' (Lave and Wenger 1991), 'networks of practice' (Teigland 2003) or 'social capital' (Nahapiet and Ghoshal 1998). In our book 'communities of practice' refers primarily to all the business networks in which the MNC's units are embedded. In these networks 'collective knowing' is created continuously in business exchanges between the members of the network. These activities reproduce the network, but they also imply that 'collective knowing' is difficult if not impossible for anyone to grasp who is not directly involved in the activities concerned. But for outsiders the problems are even worse, because they does do not even know what there is to know.[1]

A fundamental characteristic of the Embedded Multinational is that, to a large extent, HQ is an outsider vis-à-vis the business networks in which the subsidiaries are embedded. Some scholars have argued that this creates a characteristic tension between the center and the periphery in MNCs (Regnér 1999), or even that it constitutes a prerequisite for entrepreneurship at the subsidiary level (Yamin 2002; Mudambi and Navarra 2004). At any rate, if coordination of activities between subsidiaries is supposed to be one of top management's major tasks, the difficulties in fulfilling the task is obvious, because knowledge of what others know is a necessary component of coordinated action (Goodall and Roberts 2003). Note that the main reason for these difficulties is not lack of knowledge about the subsidiaries' operations as such, because this lack can be dealt with by way of decentralization, integrative organizational forms, performance evaluation and so on. Rather, the difficulties emanate from the basic fact that HQ does not know which activities and/or subsidiaries should be coordinated, or why. If HQ knows what the subsidiaries do, but not how they do it, it is still possible for it to assume a coordinating role by various organizational means. But if HQ does not know what the subsidiaries are doing, or why, then its coordinating task is rather tricky. This second type of socially embedded knowledge is acquired primarily by way of 'co-presence' in the business network.

The importance of the distinction between the HQ's 'mechanical' knowledge and 'collective knowing' was demonstrated by the empirical analyses presented in Chapter 11. The overall result indicates that what counts in terms of HQ's potential for stimulating knowledge transfer within the MNC is *HQ's own presence in the subsidiaries' networks*. It was found that if HQs had relationships of their own with the subsidiaries' most important business partners, this had a positive effect on the transfer of knowledge. If HQ was also an important actor in a subsidiary's network as regards resources, thus making that subsidiary dependent, then HQ would have a chance of influencing the subsidiary's operations. Knowledge about the subsidiary's operations was not enough to engender such influence (Chapter 9).

The problem of 'sheer ignorance' within MNCs is not of course restricted to HQ. Every subsidiary's knowledge about other units, including HQ, is also greatly restricted by the particular business network in which it is embedded. No unit has full insight into other units' lives. This situation is the main reason for the heterogeneous, loosely-coupled nature of the Embedded MNC. It can be argued, however, that even in such situations a central authority may be necessary, especially when efficiency calls for coordinated action. It has been observed that even units possessing perfect powers of reasoning may still be unable to coordinate their independently undertaken actions, or are only able to coordinate them after costly trial and error. A central authority may represent a least-cost response to such problems (Foss 1992). For instance, if it is necessary to reach an agreement about which subsidiary should take care of which market and/or country in order to avoid duplication, then an autocratic decision on the part of HQ may offer the most efficient solution, even though HQ's knowledge about what the subsidiaries are doing is severely restricted. Sometimes somebody simply has to decide.

However, this rather technical efficiency argument disregards the fact that dispersed knowledge is combined with dispersed interests in the MNCs. Dispersed interests are as socially embedded and context-specific as dispersed knowledge. The Embedded Multinational is thus much dominated by several local rationalities, all emanating from the subsidiaries' various business networks (Forsgren et al. 1995). Thus, even if dividing markets and/or countries among the subsidiaries by a centralized decision would be a rational choice from an overall point of view, the subsidiaries themselves may refuse to accept such a decision. More importantly, a dispersed-knowledge situation also gives the subsidiaries the power to offer effective resistance. This is why it is so important to analyse the sources of power in much the same way as we did in Chapters 9 and 10, if we want to understand the political processes within the MNC. As we see it, being the HQ of an Embedded MNC involves a never-ending process of seeking to understand what is going on in different parts of the organization, and a continuous struggle for influence in competition with other MNC units. It is an interesting paradox that this is what occurs just when the perception of the general public embraces the idea of a powerful and dominating HQ that exerts more or less full control over the MNC's operations. This paradox deserves a study of its own!

A LAST WORD

The message of our study of the Embedded Multinational resolves itself into a recommendation to the students and managers of MNCs to reinstate business at the center of the analysis of management and organization. The globalization of recent decades has led to an awakening interest in the cultural and institutional differences between countries, and the importance that these have for management. It is worth remembering, however, that business is an institution common to many countries, particularly those with market economies. It bespeaks a common logic that should not be forgotten in analysing business firms, be they national, international, multinational or global.

NOTE

1. To a certain extent this is a reality even for insiders, reflected in the importance of discovery and surprise in all market processes (Kirzner 1997).

Appendix I Research methods

BACKGROUND OF THE STUDY

This book has its roots in a project, *Managing International Networks*, or MIN, conducted at the Department of Business Studies, Uppsala University, during the 1990s. The focus of the project was on the importance of subsidiaries' business networks to subsidiary development and the impact of such networks on the management of the MNC. Data has been collected (personal interviews in MNC subsidiaries and headquarters) over a period of seven or eight years. The amount of the material is extensive, and its analysis continues to this day. So far, the project has resulted in four doctoral theses, several articles in international journals (see Appendix 2), and the reports presented to the participating firms fairly soon after the data-collection stage was complete. The project led us to realize that despite the growing amount of research surrounding these questions, the perception of the MNC as being embedded in networks of business relationships, both internal and external, is still in its infancy. The MIN project has addressed several issues in this field, and offers some observations that may contribute to the further development of theory in this expanding field.

FOCUS OF THE BOOK

The present book deals primarily with the following issues. First, the main idea and theme of the book build upon a recognition of the importance of business relationship embebbedness in subsidiary networks. Hence, there is a strong focus on the subsidiary level of the MNC and on the subsidiaries' network of business relationships. Given this focus, the book then distinguishes between corporate and external networks. One crucial argument is that embeddedness in relationships is essential not only to the individual subsidiary's own development but also to the impact of subsidiaries in general within the MNC. A second point thus addresses the more classical questions of business administration, such as the influence of subsidiaries on decision-making, their importance to the development of activities among sister units, and the transfer of knowledge and learning processes between them within the MNC. In our analysis of knowledge transfer, we specifically compare the effect of managerial factors such as shared values, with structural factors such as corporate and external embeddedness. We also look at HQ's control over the subsidiaries' activities, which given the impact of the corporate and external network embeddedness of subsidiaries, is of crucial importance.

Further, the book discusses the internationalization of the business firm, comparing a traditional view with a network perspective. We also explore internationalization in three dimensions: the ownership dimension, the corporate network dimension and the external network dimension.

Empirically the book opens with a case description of the development of one firm's (Danke's) most important business relationships (Chapter 3). The case illustrates the characteristics of relationships, looking at their specific importance and their interconnectedness. With the help of descriptive statistics, later chapters analyse a more extensive set of observations (98 MNC subsidiaries). The final chapters present regression analyses dealing with the main issues of the book, namely the influence of subsidiaries, knowledge transfer between them, the role of shared values, and HQ's control.

DESCRIPTION OF THE DATA

All the empirical studies in the book are based on the same database, i.e. a sample of Swedish MNCs. These firms represent a broad spectrum of Swedish industry, albeit with an emphasis on manufacturing (hard materials, paper, power, petrochemicals, retailing, transportation, services and telecommunications; see Table AI.1).

The data consists of information from 98 subsidiaries, 93 of them in Europe and 5 in North America, and all organized into 20 Swedish MNC divisions. In all but one case the divisional HQ was located in Sweden. The study comprised 2–10 subsidiaries in the different divisions, with a mean value of 4.95. The divisions belonged to 13 MNCs, seven of which included one studied division, five included two studied divisions, and one included three. This variation was the result of the number of divisions in the MNCs and the opportunities for gaining access to conduct face-to-face interviews with the managers of the HQs and subsidiaries in the divisions.

The divisions averaged 5846 employees, varying between 315 and 27600. Turnover ranged from 75 million to US$2.9 billion, with an average of about US$750 million. Most divisions are very international: five had between 14 and 42 percent of their employees outside Sweden, while 15 divisions have 50 percent or more. Altogether, the divisions had about 117000 employees and an annual turnover exceeding US$12.5 billion.

Table A1.1   The database

MNC	Division	Industry	No. of studied subsidiaries per division	Division size (employees)	Division internationalization (%)
ABB	Motors	Machinery and equipment	5	2700	85
ABB	Relays	Electrical appliances	6	4150	24
AGA	Gas	Gas manufacture	3	11000	90
Alfa Laval	Separation	Machinery and equipment	4	4700	79
Alfa Laval	Thermal	Equipment	3	3100	74
ASG	Air and sea	Transport and storage	4	315	50
ASPA*	Packaging	Paper, paperboard	10	4600	80
Garphyttan	Pumps and systems	Machinery and equipment	3	660	92
Garphyttan	Haldex	Machinery and equipment	2	720	42
Nobel	Berol	Chemicals	5	1000	15
Ericsson	Cable and network	Electrical appliances	6	12000	22
Ericsson	Radio communication	Communication equipment	4	16000	50
Ericsson	Public telecommunication	Communication equipment	8	27600	50
ESAB	Consumables	Metal products	6	3000	97
IBS	IBS	Business services	7	972	58
Mercuri	Mercuri	Education services	7	1000	88
Sandvik	Coromant	Metal products	4	6300	63
Sandvik	Saws and tools	Metal products	4	3200	69
SCA	Graphic paper	Paper	4	3400	38
SCA	Packaging	Paper, packaging	4	10500	80
Average			4.95	5846	62

Note: Aspa is a pseudonym since it is an anonymous case-study multinational used in the book.

196

In cooperation with the divisional HQs we have selected subsidiaries that are representative of the divisions' business activities, to make it easier to draw general conclusions from the data. On average, the 98 subsidiaries in the sample accounted for over 50 percent of the 20 divisions' combined operations measured in terms of the number of employees. In 25 percent of the divisions, the studied subsidiaries accounted for more than 80 percent of the divisions' total operations; the figure for the remaining divisions was between 10 and 60 percent. The size of the subsidiaries varied from 50 to over 5000 employees. The studied subsidiaries were responsible for their own production and sales, which meant that product development and production process development were important activities for them all.

DATA COLLECTION

Our initial contact with these firms was made at the divisional headquarters (HQ) level, rather than at the corporate level. There were two reasons for this. First, the divisional level of the firm is closer to the subsidiary operations, and the divisional HQ has a direct management relationship with the subsidiaries. Second, knowledge about subsidiary activities is primarily an intra-divisional issue, since the divisionalization of the MNC separates the various businesses from one another. At the initial meeting with divisional HQ managers the project was described, and suitable subsidiaries for investigation were discussed. A basic criterion was that the subsidiary should produce and deliver one or more products to market or corporate customers (users). This meant that many of the sampled subsidiaries also conducted technical development regarding their products and processes. Divisonal HQ managers arranged access to the subsidiaries for us, informed them about our project and provided us with general information about the business conducted by the division and particular subsidiaries.

Next, subsidiaries were contacted and data was collected in the course of face-to-face interviews. The interviews were divided into three sections: one with the subsidiary's top manager, one with the sales director(s) and one with the purchasing director(s). Each interview comprised four areas of investigation: one dealing with background questions connected with the activity in question; one dealing with the subsidiary's business relationships; one dealing with the subsidiary's formal and informal role within the MNC; and one dealing with managerial issues in the subsidiary–HQ relationship. For instance, the subsidiary's sales manager(s) first told us about general sales characteristics and activities. In a next step, certain relationships were selected and investigated. In a third step, the subsidiary's roles – for example, its importance to corporate sister units – were studied. Finally, in a fourth step, we investigated the management relationship between the subsidiaries' sales departments and divisional HQ. The same four-step procedure was used with the subsidiaries' purchasing and top managers. (With the top manager the study of relationships looked at other kinds apart from those with customers or suppliers, such as governmental agencies, unions, R&D departments, etc.). Three interviews altogether were held at the subsidiary level.

The choice of subsidiary relationships to be studied was critical. First, we had to limit the number of relationships to be investigated, as gathering information about all the kinds of relationship in which a subsidiary is involved would be an insurmountable task, especially as our study required face-to-face interviews in several countries. For practical and analytical reasons we thus limited the investigation to a relatively small number of each subsidiary's customers and suppliers associated with their most important field of business. Subsidiary sales and purchasing managers were thus asked to describe and assess six business relationships that they considered to be important in a general sense – three with customers and three with suppliers. In our personal interviews with our managerial respondents, we were very careful to make them select business relationships that were important not for some specified reason, but for any reason at all as long so it was important to their business activities. Specific indicators of relationship characteristics were then measured concerning such things as the importance, adaptation and connectedness of a relationship to other relationships within or outside the MNC (see Table AI.2).

It appeared that most of the relationships that were considered important were external to the MNC. Of 516 relationships chosen by the sales and purchasing managers, 399 or 77 percent were external.

After interviewing the subsidiary managers in a division, we went back to the divisional HQ managers and conducted personal interviews, using the same type of standardized questionnaire. From these interviews we collected information about the HQ's view regarding each subsidiary's characteristics – their business relationships, their formal and informal roles within the MNC, and HQ's relationships with each one of them. Every interview with HQs and subsidiaries lasted for about two hours, during which time any problems involving concepts or interpretations in the questionnaire were discussed and explained.

An important aspect of this arrangement was that we have used several indicators to measure the various theoretical constructs. We were also able to combine the perspectives of the subsidiary and the HQ managers, thus avoiding the obvious problem of common-method error. Naturally, depending on who was the most relevant respondent regarding a particular issue, the subsidiary perspective was sometimes preferable to the HQ perspective, or vice versa.

CONSTRUCTS AND MEASUREMENTS

Table AI.2 provides an overview of the constructs and indicators used in the statistical analyses in the empirical chapters. Some theoretical constructs have been used in more than one analysis. In principle, constructs have been measured by the average value of several indicators. When using several construct indicators, as occurred most frequently, consistency was checked by measuring the Cronbach's alpha value. The table shows that all Cronbach's values were above 0.60, which is satisfactory. In cases where only two indicators were used, we first checked that the correlation (rather than the Cronbach alpha value) was significant. It should be noted that the use of average measures based on Likert-type scales in regression analyses is not an optimal procedure. Thus we also created the same constructs by running the indicators (those with a satisfactory alpha value) in rotated (Varimax) factor analyses. The principal components indicating the constructs were saved and used as variables in the following regressions. However, these analyses produced the same results that we acquired when using the average values of indicators. The regression analyses presented in the book are therefore based on variables constructed by the average values of indicators. Table AI.2 shows the indicators used for constructing the constructs and the Cronbach's alpha values of these variables.

Most indicators were estimated on a five-point Likert scale, ranging from 1 = not at all (or very low) and 5 = very much (or very high). Similarly, attitudinal questions were estimated on a five-point scale, where 5 means 'totally agree' to a certain statement, and 1 means 'totally disagree' (3 means somewhere in between). The following paragraphs describe the measurement of the specific constructs used in the book.

First, 'external and corporate network embeddedness' refers to the subsidiary's relationships with its business partners in the market and the corporate networks respectively. Analytically speaking, the embeddedness of the subsidiary is difficult to delimit, as the network is boundless (Ghoshal and Bartlett 1990). In order to delimit and to be able to explore a meaningful part of a subsidiary's network, we have concentrated on a set of network relationships revolving round what the subsidiary in question sees as its most important business activity. Second, the network boundaries were drawn so as to include the three customer relationships and the three supplier relationships (i.e., six business relationships at most) that were considered by the subsidiary to be its most important. Other studies, which have shown that managers tend to regard a limited number of relationships as being of greater long-term importance than most ordinary market exchange relationships, appear to justify this restriction (Cowley 1988; Håkansson 1987; Perrone 1989).

Table A1.2   Constructs, indicators and respondents

Construct	Chapter	Indicators	Cronbach's alpha	Respondent
External embeddedness of subsidiaries	8, 9, 10, 11	Mutual adaptation in product development and production development in the subsidiary's external relationships	0.765	Subsidiary
Corporate embeddedness of subsidiaries	8, 9, 10, 11	Mutual adaptation in product development and production development in the subsidiary's corporate relationships	0.707	Subsidiary
External relationship connectedness	8	Influence from other actors on subsidiaries' external customer and supplier relationships	–	Subsidiary
Subsidiaries' dependence on HQ	9, 11	HQ's importance for subsidiaries' activities in product development, production development, reliability in delivery, business volume, technological information, important new business contacts	0.795	HQ
HQ's knowledge about subsidiary activities	9	HQ's knowledge about subsidiaries' day-to-day operations and possibility of understanding the subsidiaries' way of thinking	Pearson r = 0.456** (significant at the 0.01 level)	HQ
HQ's formal control over subsidiary	9	HQ's control over subsidiaries choice of suppliers and product introduction, domestically and internationally	0.631	Subsidiary
HQ's actual influence over subsidiary	9	Subsidiaries' concessions to HQ managers made by subsidiaries' top manager, sales manager and purchasing manager	0.604	Subsidiary

Variable	Ref.	Description	Value	Source
Corporate net-dependence on subsidiary	10	Net-adaptation between a subsidiary and its MNC sister units in product and production technology	–	Subsidiary
Subsidiaries' influence	10	Subsidiaries' influence on MNC decisions concerning investment in R&D, production capacity, product lines and acquisitions	0.775	HQ
Subsidiaries' functional importance	10	Subsidiaries' importance to product development, production development, technological information, info. about market activities, important new business contacts	0.721	HQ
HQ's relations with subsidiaries' external network	11	HQ degree of contact with subsidiaries' external business partners	–	HQ (and subsidiary)
Presence of corporate business relations of subsidiaries	11	Presence of corporate relationships with customers and suppliers (no (=0) or yes (= 1))	–	Subsidiary
HQ–subsidiary shared values	11	HQ's and subsidiaries' degree of shared interests in size and direction of investment in R&D, marketing, purchasing, product design, and production	All = 0.705 HQ = 0.702 Subsidiary = 0.720	HQ and subsidiary
Transfer of subsidiaries' knowledge	11	Subsidiaries' importance for MNC units' activities concerning: product development, production development, technical information, information about market activities and new important business contacts	All = 0.700 HQ = 0.726 Subsidiary = 0.714	HQ and subsidiary
Subsidiaries' relative size	9, 10, 11	Subsidiaries' number of employees in relation to the division as a whole	–	HQ and subsidiary

The subsidiary managers for sales and purchasing were first asked to identify not more than six important business relationships. From the 98 subsidiaries this gave us 399 external relationships and 117 corporate relationships. As regards the first of these, the numbers ranged between two and six depending on how many relationships the individual subsidiaries had identified as important. The number of corporate relationships ranged from none to four. To indicate the degree of embeddedness of the relational activities, the subsidiary managers were then asked to estimate the extent of the adaptations made by the two parties regarding their respective product development and production development processes. The values for each relationship (the subsidiary's values and the partner's values) were added together to yield a mean value for the extent of each subsidiary's mutual adaptation, reflecting the degree of embeddedness vis-à-vis external market actors and actors within the MNC (Cronbach's alphas were 0.765 and 0.707, respectively). This approach, which resembles the method used by Astley and Zajac (1990, p.490), was used in Chapters 9–11. In Chapter 8, external and corporate embeddedness was illustrated instead by the highest embeddedness value identified in one external relationship and in one corporate relationship.

'External connected embeddedness': the subsidiary sales managers described the constituent parts of each external customer relationship in terms of relations with the following external market actors: another customer, the customer's customer, a supplier and a competitor, and indicated (on a five-point scale) the extent to which each one influenced the business relationship (through indirect relations with the subsidiary or the customer organization). The same information was provided by the purchasing manager concerning influence on the relationship with specific suppliers, this time involving a customer, a competitor, another competing supplier, a supplementary supplier and the supplier's supplier. This information was gathered for all identified external customer and supplier relationships. For the measure of external connected embeddedness, an average influence value was constructed for the external (customer or supplier) relationship that revealed the highest value of embeddedness.

To measure 'HQ's formal control' over the subsidiaries decisions, subsidiary managers were then asked about the extent to which HQ had centralized decision-making on three strategic issues (Cronbach's alpha was 0.631), namely control over the choice of suppliers, control over the set of products that the subsidiary can introduce in the domestic market, and control over the products for introduction on the international market.

To measure 'HQ's actual influence' over the subsidiaries' operations, the subsidiary managers were asked about the extent to which they make concessions to the HQ managers, specifically the top manager, the sales manager and the purchasing manager (Cronbach's alpha was 0.604).

To measure 'HQ's knowledge about the subsidiary operations', HQ representatives were asked to assess their own knowledge about the respective subsidiaries' day-to-day operations, and the extent to which they find it possible to understand the subsidiary managers' way of thinking (the correlation between the indicators was 0.456**, see Table AI.2).

'Subsidiary dependence on HQ' was measured by calculating the mean value of six indicators of HQ importance to various aspects of subsidiary activities, namely product development, production development, security (reliability) of delivery, business volume, technological information, and important new business contacts. The answers were provided by representatives of HQ (Cronbach's alpha was 0.795).

To measure 'subsidiary influence on corporate decisions', which is one of the two dependent variables, HQ managers were asked about the subsidiaries' influence on strategic investments conducted within the MNC. Our primary requirement was that the influence of the subsidiary should concern significant investments of long-term importance to subsidiary and/or corporate development. Four degree-of-influence indicators were used: influence on decisions about MNC investments in R&D, on production capacity, on product lines and on acquisitions. Note that the measures concern influence at the organizational level of the MNC division, rather than at a relational level between the subsidiary and other specific corporate partners (Cronbach's alpha was 0.775).

'Subsidiary functional importance' was measured as the average values of the subsidiaries' importance to other MNC units as regards product and production development, technological information, information about market activities and important new business contacts. Estimates were provided by representatives of the HQ organization (Cronbach's alpha was 0.721).

'Corporate net dependence on subsidiaries': this variable reflects the degree of dependence that the MNC organization has vis-à-vis the individual subsidiaries. As Astley and Zajac (1990) point out, a unit's power can be described as a function of imbalances or 'net exchange' differences between units in dyadic relationships. In this case we assume that dependence in such power relations is reflected in the adaptations that the actors are prepared to undertake vis-à-vis each other. By questioning subsidiary managers we measure net dependence (on a five-point Likert scale) as the degree of adaptation undertaken by the MNC sister units vis-à-vis the individual subsidiaries regarding their product and production technology, less the degree of adaptations undertaken by the subsidiary concerned regarding the same activities. A high positive value will reflect a high degree of MNC net dependence vis-à-vis that particular subsidiary. Correspondingly, a high negative value will reflect a high degree of net dependence vis-à-vis the MNC on the part of the relevant subsidiary.

'Transfer of subsidiary knowledge in the MNC' was measured by checking the importance of a particular subsidiary to the activities of other corporate subsidiaries, as assessed by the HQ representatives and the managers of the subsidiary in question. Our primary interest here is that the knowledge transfer reflects both technology and market-related activities. Five indicators (given on a five-point scale) have been used in interviews: the subsidiary's importance to the other divisional subsidiaries' product development, production development, technical information, information about market activities and important new business contacts. Cronbach's alpha was 0.700 for all indicators, which comprised five HQ and five subsidiary estimations. (The HQ-based indicators had a Cronbach's alpha of 0.726, while that of the subsidiary-based indicators was 0.714.)

'HQ relations with subsidiaries' external network business partners': while subsidiary managers first identified their most important relationships with external business partners, HQ managers were subsequently asked to evaluate the level of direct contact that they had developed with the external business partners of the subsidiary. The extent of such relations was measured on a four-point scale (Blankenburg and Johanson 1992). Thus we consider HQ's relations with its subsidiaries' external business partners as a variable that ranges from no HQ knowledge of the existence of the business partners to extensive HQ relations with such counterparts.

'Shared values': five questions were put to subsidiary and HQ managers to assess the extent to which they perceived their interests as identical. The questions concerned the size of their investments in R&D, marketing, purchasing, product design and production. The subsidiary and HQ respondents assessed the level of their identical interests on a five-point scale, ranging from very low to very high for each of the five activities. To combine the two perspectives in a single measure involved two steps. First we checked the respective Cronbach's alpha for the subsidiary and HQ measures, and found them to be good (0.720 and 0.702). We then checked the Cronbach's alpha for all ten indicators; this was 0.705. There was good internal consistency between the subsidiaries and HQ's answers. In 70 percent of the cases the two respondents held the same or only slightly different opinions about the level of shared interests. The variable was created by adding together the answers of the two parties. A high value meant a high degree of shared values.

Table AI.2 summarizes the construct labels and their measurements, and information about the identity of the responding organizations. It also notes the chapters in which the constructs have been used in our empirical analyses.

Appendix II Publications of the MIN program

Andersson, U. (2003), 'Managing the transfer of capabilities within multinational corporations: the dual role of the subsidiary', *Scandinavian Journal of Management*, **19**, 425–42.

Andersson, U. and J. Dahlqvist (2001), 'Business – governed product development: knowledge utilization in business relationships', in H. Håkansson and J. Johanson (eds), *Business Network Learning*, Amsterdam, London and Oxford: Elsiever Science, Pergamon, pp. 53–68.

Andersson, U. and M. Forsgren (1995), 'Using networks to determine multinational parental control of subsidiaries', in Stanley J. Paliwoda and J.K. Ryans Jr (eds), *International Marketing Reader*, London: Routledge, pp. 72–87.

Andersson, U. and M. Forsgren (1996), 'Subsidiary embeddedness and control in the multinational corporation', *International Business Review*, **5** (5), Elsevier Science Ltd, 487–508.

Andersson, U. and M. Forsgren (2000), 'Integration in global MNCs: the Swedish case', in J. Larimo and S. Kock (eds), *Recent studies in Interorganizational and International Business Research*, pp. 343–65.

Andersson, U. and M. Forsgren (2000), 'In search of centre of excellence – Network Embeddedness and Subsidiary Roles in MNCs', *Management International Review*, **40** (4), 329–50.

Andersson, U. and M. Forsgren (2001), 'Integration in the multinational corporation: the problem of subsidiary embeddedness', in R. McNaughton and M. Green (eds), *Global Competition and Global Networks*, Aldershot: Ashgate, pp. 343–65.

Andersson, U. and U. Holm (2002), 'Managing integration of subsidiary knowledge in the multinational corporation – a note on the role of headquarters', in V. Havila, M. Forsgren and H. Håkansson (eds), *Critical Perspectives on Internationalization*, Series Editor P.N. Ghauri, Amsterdam, London, New York, Oxford: Pergamon, Elsevier Science, Pergamon, pp. 359–85.

Andersson, U. and C. Pahlberg (1997), 'Subsidiary influence on strategic behaviour in MNCs: an empirical study', *International Business Review*, **6** (3), 319–34.

Andersson, U., and B. Ståhl (2004), 'Relationships dynamics. Developing business relationships and creating value', in V. Mahnke and T. Pedersen (eds), *Knowledge Flows, Governance and the Multinational Enterprise: Frontiers in International Management Research*, New York: Palgrave Macmillan, pp. 130–48.

Andersson, U., I. Björkman and P. Furu (2002), 'Subsidiary absorptive capacity, MNC headquarters' control strategies and transfer of subsidiary competences', in S.M. Lundan (ed.), *Network Knowledge in International Business*, Cheltenham, UK, Northampton, MA, USA: Edward Elgar, pp. 115–36.

Andersson, U., M. Forsgren and U. Holm (2001), 'Subsidiary embeddedness and competence development in MNCs – a multi-level analysis', *Organization Studies*, **22** (6), 1013–34.

Andersson, U., M. Forsgren and U. Holm (2002), 'The strategic impact of external networks: subsidiary performance and competence development in the multinational corporation', *Strategic Management Journal*, **23**, 979–96.

Andersson, U., M. Forsgren and T. Pedersen (2001), 'Subsidiary performance in multinational corporations: the importance of technology embeddedness', *International Business Review*, **10** (1), 3–23.

Andersson, U., J. Johanson and J.-E. Vahlne (1998), 'Organic acquisitions in the internationalization process of the business firm', *Management International Review*, **37**, Special Issue 2/97, 67–84.

Birkinshaw, J., U. Holm, P. Thilenius and N. Arvidsson (2000), 'Consequences of perception gaps in the headquarters – subsidiary relationship', *International Business Review*, **9**, New York: Elsevier Science Ltd, 321–44.

Forsgren, M. and C. Pahlberg (1992), 'Subsidiary influence and autonomy in international firms', *Scandinavian International Business Review*, **1** (3), 41–51.

Forsgren, M. and C. Pahlberg (1995), 'Le Reti Internazionali Di Imprese, Roberto Cafferata, (a curadi)', *Materiali Di Studio Dell Organizzazione Aziendale*, Rome: Aracne Editrice, pp. 363–81.

Forsgren, M., U. Holm and J. Johanson (1995), 'Division headquarters go abroad – a step in the internationalization of the multinational corporation', *Journal of Management Studies*, **32** (4), 457–91.

Holm, U., J. Johanson and P. Thilenius (1995), 'Headquarters knowledge of subsidiary network contexts in the multinational corporation', *International Studies of Management & Organization*, **25** (1–2), 97–119.

Johanson, J., C. Pahlbeg and P. Thilenius (1996), 'Conflict and control in MNC product development', *Journal of Market-Focused Management*, **1**, 249–65.

Pahlberg, C. (1997), 'Cultural differences and problems in HQ–subsidiary relationships in MNCs', in I. Björkman and M. Forsgren (eds), *The Nature of the International Firm*, Copenhagen: Handelshöyskolens Forlag, pp. 451–73.

Pahlberg, C. (2000), 'The impact from business networks on MNC competence development – a case-study', in U. Holm and T. Pedersen (eds), *The Emergence and Impact of MNC Centres of Excellence: A Subsidiary Perspective*, Basingstoke, London: Macmillan, pp. 79–93.

Pahlberg, C. (2001), 'Creation and diffusion of knowledge in subsidiary business networks', in H. Håkansson and J. Johanson (eds), *Business Network Learning*, Amsterdam, London and Oxford: Elsevier Science, Pergamon, pp. 169–81.

Appendix III   Corporate and external embeddedness at the subsidiary level

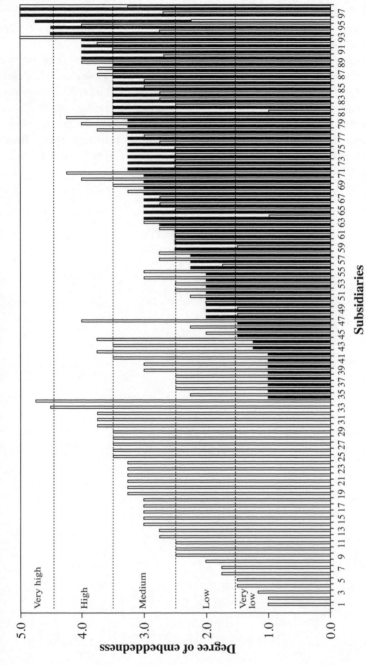

Bibliography

Aldrich, H.E. and D.A. Whetten (1981), 'Organization-sets, action-sets and networks: making the most of simplicity', in P. Nyström and W. Starbuck (eds), *Handbook of Organization Design*, New York: Pree Press, pp. 358–408.

Alter, C. and J. Hage (1993), *Organizations Working Together*, Newbury Park, CA: Sage.

Anderson, E. and B. Weitz (1992), 'The use of pledges to build and sustain commitment in distribution channels', *Journal of Marketing Research*, **XXIX**, 18–34.

Anderson, J.C. and J.A. Narus (1984), 'A model of distributor's perspective of distributor–manufacturer working relationships', *Journal of Marketing*, **48** (Fall), 62–74.

Anderson, J.C. and J.A. Narus (1990), 'A model of distributor firm and manufacturer firm working partnerships', *Journal of Marketing*, **54**, 42–58.

Andersson, U. and M. Forsgren (1996), 'Subsidiary embeddedness and control in the multinational corporation', *International Business Review*, **5** (5), 487–508.

Andersson, U. and M. Forsgren (2000), 'In search of centre of excellence: network embeddedness and subsidiary roles in multinational corporations', *Management International Review*, **40** (4), 329–50.

Andersson, U., M. Forsgren and U. Holm (2001), 'Subsidiary embeddedness and competence development in MNCs: a multi-level analysis', *Organization Studies*, **22** (6), 1013–34.

Andersson, U., M. Forsgren and U. Holm (2002), 'The strategic impact of external networks: subsidiary performance and competence development in the multinational corporation', *Strategic Management Journal*, **23**, 979–96.

Astley, G. and P. Sachdewa (1984), 'Structural sources of intraorganizational power: a theoretical analysis', *Academy of Management Review*, **9** (1), 104–13.

Astley, G. and E. Zajac (1990), 'Beyond dyadic exchange: functional interdependence and sub-unit power', *Organization Studies*, **11** (4), 481–501.

Astley, G. and E. Zajac (1991), 'Intraorganizational power and organizational design: reconciling rational and coalition models of organization', *Organization Science*, **2** (4), 399–411.

Axelsson, B. and G. Easton (eds) (1992), *Industrial Networks. A New View of Reality*, London: Routledge.

Bacharach, S.B. and E. J. Lawler (1981), *Power and Politics in Organizations*, San Francisco: Jossey-Bass.

Bartlett, C.A. and S. Ghoshal (1989), *Managing Across Borders: The Transnational Solution*, Boston, MA: Harvard Business School Press.

Beamish, P.W. and J.P. Killings (1997), *Cooperative Strategies*, San Francisco: New Lexington Press.

Berle Jr, A.A. and G.C. Means (1933), *The Modern Corporation and Private Property*, New York: MacMillan.

Birkinshaw, J. and N. Hood (1998), 'Multinational subsidiary evolution: capability and charter change in foreign-owned subsidiary companies', *Academy of Management Review*, **23** (4), 773–5.

Birkinshaw, J., U. Holm, P. Thilenius and N. Arvidsson, (2000), 'Consequences of perception gaps in the headquarters – subsidiary relationship', *International Business Review*, **9** (3), 321–44.

Björkman, I. and M. Forsgren (eds) (1997), *The Nature of the International Firm*, Copenhagen: CBS Press.

Blankenburg, D. and J. Johanson (1992), 'Managing network connections in international business relationships', *Scandinavian International Business Review*, **11** (1), 5–19.

Blankenburg Holm, D., K. Eriksson and J. Johanson (1999), 'Creating value through mutual commitment to business network relationships', *Strategic Management Journal*, **20**, 467–86.

Blau, P.M. (1964), *Exchange and Power in Social Life*, New York: John Wiley.

Blomstermo, A. and D.D. Sharma (2003), *Learning in the Internationalization Process of Firms*, Cheltenham, UK and Northampton, MA, USA: Edward Elgar.

Cannon, J.P. and W.D. Perreault Jr (1999), 'Buyer–seller relationships in business markets', *Journal of Marketing Research*, **XXXVI** (Nov), 439–60.

Cantwell, J. (1991), 'A survey of theories of international production', in C.N. Pitelis and R. Sugden (eds), *The Nature of the Transnational Firm*, London: Routledge, pp. 16–63.

Carlson, S. (1951), *Executive Behavior*, Stockholm: Strömbergs.

Caves, R. (1982), *Multinational Enterprise and Economic Analysis*, Cambridge: Cambridge University Press.

Chen, H. and T.-J. Chen (1998), 'Network linkages and location choice in foreign direct investment', *Journal of International Business Studies*, **29** (3), 445–68.

Chen, T.-J., H. Chen and Y.-H. Ku (2004), 'Foreign direct investment and local linkages', *Journal of International Business Studies*, **35**, 320–33.

Cohen, W. and D.A. Levinthal (1990), 'Absorptive capacity: a new perspective on learning and innovation', *Administrative Science Quarterly*, **35** (1), 128–52.

Contractor, F. and P. Lorange (eds) (1988), *Cooperative Strategies in International Business*, Lexington, MA: Lexington Books.

Cook, K. and R.M. Emerson (1978), 'Power, equity and commitment in exchange networks', *American Sociological Review*, **43**, 721–39.

Cook, K. and R. Emerson (1984), 'Exchange networks and the analysis of complex organizations', *Sociology of Organizations*, **3**, 1–30.

Cowley, P.R. (1988), 'Market structure and business performance: an evaluation of buyer/seller power in the PIMS database', *Strategic Management Journal*, **9**, 271–8.

Cunningham, M.T. and E. Homse (1986), 'Controlling the marketing–purchasing interface: resource development and organizational implications', *Industrial Marketing and Purchasing*, **1** (2), 3–25.

Cyert, R.M. and J.G. March (1963), *A Behavioral Theory of the Firm*, Englewood Cliffs, NJ: Prentice Hall.

Dahl, R.A. (1957), 'The concept of power', *Behavioral Science*, **2**, 201–15.

Dahlqvist, J. (1998), *Knowledge Use in Business Exchange. Acting and Thinking Business Actors*, Uppsala: Department of Business Studies.

Deal, T.E. and A.A. Kennedy (1982), *Corporate Cultures: The Rites and Rituals of Corporate Life*, Reading, MA: Addison-Wesley.

Delios, A. and P.W. Beamish (1999), 'Ownership strategy of Japanese firms: transactional, institutional and experience influences', *Strategic Management Journal*, **20** (10), 915–30.

Dicken, P. (1992), *Global Shift: The Internationalization of Economic Activity*, London: Paul Chapman Publishers.

DiMaggio, P.J. and W.W. Powell (1983), 'The iron cage revisited: institutional isomorphism and collective rationality in organizational fields', *American Sociological Review*, **48**, 147–60.

Doz, Y. (1986), *Strategic Management in Multinational Companies*, Oxford: Pergamon Press.

Doz, Y. and C.K. Prahalad (1981), 'Headquarters influence and strategic control in MNCs', *Sloan Management Review*, **23** (1), 15–29.

Doz, Y. and C.K. Prahalad (1993), 'Managing the DMNCs: a search for a new paradigm', in S. Ghoshal and E. Westney (eds), *Organization Theory and the Multinational Corporation*, New York: St Martin's Press, pp. 24–50.

Dunning, J. (1988), 'The eclectic paradigm of international production: an update and some possible extensions', *Journal of International Business Studies*, **19** (1), 1–31.

Dunning, J. (1995), 'Reappraising the eclectic paradigm in an age of alliance capitalism', *Journal of International Business Studies*, **26** (3), 461–91.

Eccles, R.G. (1981), 'The quasi firm in the construction industry', *Journal of Economic Behavior and Organization*, **2**, 335–57.

Egelhoff, W.G. (1988), *Organizing the Multinational Enterprise: An Information Processing Perspective*, Cambridge, MA: Ballinger.

Emerson, R.M. (1962), 'Power-dependence relations', *American Sociological Review*, **27**, 31–41.

Eriksson, K., J. Johanson, A. Majkgård and D.D. Sharma (1997), 'Experiential knowledge and cost in the internationalization process', *Journal of International Business Studies*, **28**, 337–60.

Ford, D. (1997), *Understanding Business Markets*, London: Dryden Press.

Forsgren, M. (1989), *Managing the Internationalization Process: The Swedish Case*, London: Routledge.

Forsgren, M. and J. Johanson (1992), *Managing Networks in International Business*, Philadelphia: Gordon and Breach.

Forsgren, M., U. Holm and J. Johanson (1992), 'Internationalization of the second degree', in S. Young and J. Hamill (eds), *Europe and the Multinationals: Issues and Responses for the 1990s*, Cheltenham, UK and Northampton, MA, USA: Edward Elgar, pp. 235–53.

Forsgren, M., U. Holm and J. Johanson (1995), 'Division headquarters go abroad – a step in the internationalization of the multinational corporation', *Journal of Management Studies*, **32** (4), 475–91.

Foss, N. (1992), '"Coase vs Hayek": Economic Organization and the Knowledge Economy', *International Journal of the Economics of Business*, **9** (1), 9–35.

Fouraker, L.E. and J.M. Stopford (1968), 'Organization structure and multinational strategy', *Administrative Science Quarterly*, **13**, 17–50.

Frazier, G.L., R.E. Spekman and C.R. O'Neal (1988), 'Just-in-time exchange relationships in industrial markets', *Journal of Marketing*, **52** (October), 52–67.

Galbraith, J.R. (1973), *Designing Complex Organizations*, Reading, MA: Addison-Wesley.

Ghoshal, S. and C.A. Bartlett (1990), 'The multinational corporation as an interorganizational network', *Academy of Management Review*, **15** (4), 603–35.

Ghoshal, S. and N. Nohria (1997), *The Differentiated MNC: Organizing Multinational Corporation for Value Creation*, San Francisco, CA: Jossey-Bass.

Ghoshal, S., T. Korine and G. Szulanski (1994), 'Interunit communication in multinational corporations', *Management Science*, **40** (1), 96–110.

Giddens, A., *The Constitution of Society*, Cambridge: Polity.

Goodall, K. and J. Roberts (2003), 'Repairing managerial knowledge-ability over distance', *Organization Studies*, **24** (7), 1153–75.

Grabher, G. (1993), *The Embedded Firm. The Socio-Economics of Industrial Networks*, London: Routledge.

Granovetter, M. (1985), 'Economic action and social structure: the problem of embeddedness', *American Journal of Sociology*, **78** (3), 3–30.

Granovetter, M. (1992), 'Problems of explanation in economic sociology', in N. Noria and R. Eccles (eds), *Networks and Organizations: Structure, Form and Action*, Boston, MA: Harvard Business School Press.

Hadjikhani, A. and P. Ghauri (2001), 'The behaviour of international firms in socio-political environments in the European Union', *Journal of Business Research*, **52** (3), 263–75.

Håkansson, H. (ed.) (1982), *International Marketing and Purchasing of Industrial Goods. An Interaction Approach*, Chichester: John Wiley and Sons.

Håkansson, H. (1987), *Industrial Technological Development. A Network Approach*, London: Croom Helm.

Håkansson, H. (1989), *Corporate Technological Behaviour: Cooperation and Networks*, London: Routledge.

Håkansson, H. (1992), 'Evolution processes in industrial networks', in B. Axelsson and G. Easton (eds), *Industrial Networks. A New View of Reality*, London: Routledge.

Håkansson, H. and J. Johanson (eds) (2001), *Business Network Learning*, Amsterdam, London and Oxford: Elsevier Science, Pergamon.

Håkansson, H. and I. Snehota (1995), *Developing Relationships in Business Networks*, Routledge: London.

Hallén, L. (1986), 'A comparison of strategic marketing approaches', in P.W. Turnbull and J.-P. Valla (eds), *Strategy for International Industrial Marketing*, London: Croom Helm, pp. 235–64.

Hallén, L., J. Johanson and N. Seyed-Mohamed (1991), 'Interfirm adaptation in business relationships', *Journal of Marketing*, **55** (April), pp. 29–37.

Hallén, L. and F. Wiedersheim-Paul (1979), 'Psychic distance and buyer–seller interaction', *Organisasjon, Marked og Samfund*, **16** (5), 308–28.

Hatch, M.J. (1997), *Organization Theory*, Oxford: Oxford University Press.

Havila, V., M. Forsgren and H. Håkansson (eds) (2002), *Critical Perspectives on Internationalization*, Amsterdam, London, New York and Oxford: Elsevier Science, Pergamon.

Hedlund, G. (1986), 'The hypermodern MNC – a heterarchy', *Human Resource Management*, **25** (1), 9–35.

Heide, J.B. and G. John (1988), 'The role of dependence balancing in safe-guarding transaction-specific assets in conventional channels', *Journal of Marketing*, **52** (January), 20–35.

Hickson, D.J., C.R. Hinings, C.A. Lee, R.E. Scheck and J.M. Pennings (1971), 'A strategic contingencies theory of intraorganizational power', *Administrative Science Quarterly*, **16** (1), 216–29.

Hinings, C.R., D.J. Hickson, J.M. Pennings and R.E. Schneck (1974), 'Structural conditions of intraorganizational power', *Administrative Science Quarterly*, **19**, 22–44.

Hofstede, G. (1980), *Culture's Consequences: International Differences in Work-related Values*, London: Sage.

Hofstede, G., B. Neuijen, D. Daval Ohayv and G. Sanders (1990), 'Measuring organizational cultures: a qualitative and quantitative study across twenty cases', *Administrative Science Quarterly*, **35**, 286–316.

Holm, U. and T. Pedersen (2000), *The Emergence and Impact of MNC Centre of Excellence: A Subsidiary Perspective*, London: MacMillan.

Hymer, S. (1976), *The International Operations of National Firms. A Study of Foreign Direct Investments*, Cambridge, MA: MIT Press.

Johanson, J. and L.-G. Mattsson (1987), 'Interorganizational relations in industrial systems: a network approach compared with the transaction cost approach', *International Studies of Management and Organization*, **XVII** (1), 34–48.

Johanson, J. and L.-G. Mattsson (1988), 'Internationalization in industrial systems. A network approach', in N. Hood and J.-E. Vahlne (eds), *Strategies in Global Competition*, New York: Croom Helm, pp. 287–314.

Johanson, J. and J.-E. Vahlne (1977), 'The internationalization process of the firm – a model of knowledge development and foreign market commitment', *Journal of International Business Studies*, **8** (1), 23–32.

Johanson, J. and J.-E. Vahlne (2003), 'Business relationship learning and commitment in the internationalization process', *Journal of International Entrepreneurship*, **1** (1), 83–101.

Johnston, R. and P.R. Lawrence (1988), 'Beyond vertical integration – the rise of the value-adding partnership', *Harvard Business Review*, July–August, 96–101.

Kilduff, M. (1992), 'Performance and interaction routines in multinational corporations', *Journal of International Business Studies*, first quarter, 133–45.

Kirzner, I.M. (1997), 'Entrepreneurial discovery and the competitive market process: an Austrian approach', *Journal of Economic Literature*, **XXXV**, 60–85.

Kogut, B. (2000), 'The network as knowledge: generative rules and the emergence of structure', *Strategic Management Journal*, **21** (3), 405–25.

Kostova, T. (1999), 'Transnational transfer of strategic organizational practices: a contextual perspective', *Academy of Management Review*, **24** (2), 308–24.

Krackhardt, D. (1990), 'Assessing the political landscape: structure, cognition and power in organizations', *Administrative Science Quarterly*, **35**, 342–69.

Lane, P.J. and M. Lubatkin (1998), 'Relative absorptive capacity and interorganizational learning', *Strategic Management Journal*, **19** (5), 461–77.

Lave, J. and E. Wenger (1991), *Situated Learning: Legitimate Peripheral Participation*, Cambridge: Cambridge University Press.

Lawrence, P.R. and J.W. Lorch (1967), *Organization and Environment: Managing Differentiation and Integration*, Cambridge, MA: Harvard University Press.

Lundvall, B.-Å. (1985), *Product Innovation and User-Producer Interaction*, Aalborg, Denmark: Aalborg University Press.

Luo, Y. and M. Peng (1999), 'Learning to compete and in a transition economy: experience, environment and performance', *Journal of International Business Studies*, **30** (2), 269–95.

Madhok, A. (1997), 'Cost, value and foreign market entry mode: the transaction and the firm', *Strategic Management Journal*, **18** (1), 39–61.

Majkgård, A. and D.D. Sharma (1998), 'Client-following and market seeking strategies in the internationalization of service firms', *Journal of Business-to-Business Marketing*, **4** (3), 1–41.

Mudambi, R. and P. Navarra (2004), 'Is knowledge power? Knowledge flows, subsidiary power and rent-seeking within MNCs', *Journal of International Business Studies*, **35**, 385–406.

Nahapiet, J. and S. Ghoshal (1998), 'Social capital, intellectual capital and the organizational advantage', *Academy of Management Review*, **23**, 242–66.

Negandhi, A.R. and R. Baliga (eds) (1980), *Functioning of the Multinational Corporation*, Oxford: Pergamon Press.

Nohria, N. and R.G. Eccles (eds) (1992), *Networks and Organizations: Structure, Form and Action*, Boston, MA: Harvard Business School Press.

Nohria, N. and S. Ghoshal (1994), 'Differentiated fit and shared values: alternatives for managing headquarters–subsidiary relations', *Strategic Management Journal*, **15**, 491–502.

Pahlberg, C. (2001), 'Creation and diffusion of knowledge in subsidiary business networks', in H. Håkansson and J. Johanson (eds), *Business Network Learning*, Oxford: Elsevier Science, pp. 169–81.

Penrose, E.T. (1959), *The Theory of the Growth of the Firm*, Oxford: Basil Blackwell.

Penrose, E.T. (1971), *The Large International Firm in Developing Countries. The International Petroleum Industry*, London: Allen and Unwin.

Perrone, V. (ed.) (1989), *Dettagli, Orizonntie Ingradimenti: Osservatorio Organizzativo*, Milan: CRORA-Bocconi University.

Perrone, V. (ed.), *Le strutture organizzative d'impressa: driteri e modelli di progettazione*, Milan: EGEA.

Pfeffer, J. (1981), *Power in Organizations*, Boston, MA: Pitman.

Pfeffer, J. and G.R. Salancik (1978), *The External Control of Organizations*, New York: Harper and Row.

Polyani, K. (1957), *The Great Transformation*, Boston: Beacon Press.

Porter, M. (1986), *Competition in Global Industries*, Boston, MA: Harvard Business School Press.

Regnér, P. (1999), 'Strategy creation in the periphery: inductive versus deductive strategy making', *Journal of Management Studies*, **40** (1), 57–82.

Richardson, G.B. (1972), 'The organization of industry', *Economic Journal*, **82**, 883–96.

Ring, P.S. and A.H. Van de Ven (1994), 'Developmental processes of cooperative interorganizational relationships', *Academy of Management Review*, **19** (January), 483–98.

Schein, E.H. (1996), 'Culture: the missing concept in organization studies', *Administrative Science Quarterly*, **41**, 229–40.

Scott, R. (1987), 'The adolescence of institutional theory', *Administrative Science Quarterly*, **32**, 493–511.

Snehota, I. (1990), *A Note on the Theory of Business Enterprise*, Uppsala: Department of Business Studies.

Ståhl, B. (2004), *Innovation and Evolution in the Multinational Enterprise*, Uppsala: Department of Business Studies, Uppsala University.

Stopford, J.M. and L.T. Wells (1972), *Managing the Multinational Enterprise*, London: Longman.

Szulanski, G. (1995), 'Unpacking stickiness: an empirical investigation of the barriers to transfer best practice inside the firm', *Strategic Management Journal*, **38** (Special Issue): 437–53.

Szulanski, G. (2000), 'The process of knowledge transfer: a diachronic analysis of stickiness', *Organizational Behavior and Human Decision Processes*, **82** (1), 9–27.

Teigland, R. (2003), *Knowledge Networking: Structure and Performance in Networks of Practise*, Stockholm: IIB, Stockholm School of Economics.

Thompson, J. (1967), *Organizations in Action*, New York: McGraw Hill.

Tsai, W. and S. Ghoshal (1998), 'Social capital and value creation: the role of intra-firm networks', *Academy of Management Journal*, **41** (4), 464–76.

Turnbull, P.W. and J.-P. Valla (eds) (1986), *Strategies for International Industrial Marketing*, London: Croom Helm.

Uzzi, B. (1997), 'Social structure and competition in interfirm networks: the paradox of embeddedness', *Administrative Science Quarterly*, **42** (1), 35–67.

von Hippel, E. (1988), *Sources of Innovation*, Oxford: Oxford University Press.

Welch, C. and I. Wilkinson (2004), 'The political embeddedness of international business networks', *International Marketing Review*, **21** (2), 216–31.

Westney, D.E. (1993), 'Institutionalization theory and the multinational corporation', in S. Ghoshal and E. Westney (eds), *Organization Theory and the Multinational Corporation*, New York: St Martin's Press, pp. 53–76.

Westphal, J.D., R. Gulati and S.M. Shortell (1997), 'Customization or conformity? An institutional and network perspective on the content and consequences of TQM adoption', *Administrative Science Quarterly*, **42**, 366–94.

Wiener, Y. (1988), 'Forms of value systems: a focus on organizational effectiveness and cultural change and maintenance', *Academy of Management Review*, **13** (4), 534–45.

Yamin, M. (2002), 'Subsidiary entrepreneurship and the advantage of multi-nationality', in V. Havila, M. Forsgren and H. Håkansson (eds), *Critical Perspective on Internationalization*, Amsterdam: Pergamon, pp. 132–50.

Zajac, E.J. and C.P. Olsen (1993), 'From transaction cost to transaction value: implications for the study of organizational strategies', *Journal of Management Studies*, **30** (1), 131–45.

Zander, I. (1999), 'How do you mean "global"? An empirical investigation of innovation networks in the multinational corporation', *Research Policy*, **28**, 195–213.

Zander, U. and B. Kogut (1995), 'Knowledge and the speed of the transfer and imitation of organizational capabilities: an empirical test', *Organization Science*, **6** (1), 76–92.

Index

absorptive capacity of subsidiary 173,
    182
acquisitions 86, 150
activity interdependence 107
activity linkages 172, 173
adaptation to business 108, 109 174, 187
administrative connection 95, 96
administrative/legal unit 78
advertising of washing powder 40
agency theory 190
alternative input material 36
American forest companies 83
American subsidiary 48
arm's-length character of network 111
arm's-length exchange 48, 49, 57, 98,
    106–7, 115
arm's-length relationships 182, 188
arm's-length transactions 22
Aspa corporation 83, 168–9, 181
    foreign expansion 83–6
    internationalization, extended
        ownership 86–7
    subsidiaries 114, 121
    subsidiary roles 99–102
Aspi 41, 44, 47, 48, 53, 59,
Aspi and Danke 46, 52, 121
    business expansion halted 38
    subsidiaries, export and import 88
    supplier to Danke 33, 34, 36–7
asset transferring 177
asymmetric view 146, 154, 187
Austrian approach 190
authority 129, 133
autonomy 99, 134
    and power 72

bargaining 3, 99
barriers 64
    to internationalization 73
beer-can box 100, 101, 102, 169, 170
Belgium 86, 114, 100

best practice 177, 178
Bill 41
    arm's-length relations 47
    foreign supplier to Danke 34, 35, 55
    forest industry 38
biotechnology network 25
Bitte 42, 44, 53, 59.169
    demanding customer 38–40
Bitte and Danke 33, 46, 52, 66
Bitte relationship 48, 121
bleaching 40
board and box qualities 85
box manufacturers 30, 31, 32, 56, 85
    for washing powder 40
    price level 84
British market 101
brown boxes 30, 33, 34, 38, 85, 121,
brown kraftliner 37
business activities, coordination of 161,
    188
business administration 194
business connections 153, 155, 159
business context 24. 29
business development 35, 86
business embeddedness 127
business experience 68, 99
business firm 8, 9, 21–8
business interactions 166
business linkages 93
business network angle 1–11, 25, 72, 80,
    93–5, 99, 111, 131, 167
business network model 5–8, 133–6
business opportunities 60
business partners 6, 16, 23, 65, 174,
    177
business relationships 6, 9, 15–21, 28,
    78, 153
    interconnected 63
    long-term consequences 19
    of Danke 29–30, 42–3
    technological development, Danke 44

219